Trade Therapy

Trade Therapy
Deepening Cooperation to Strengthen Pandemic Defenses

World Bank and World Trade Organization

WORLD BANK GROUP   WORLD TRADE ORGANIZATION

ISBN (paper): 978-1-4648-1885-1
ISBN (electronic): 978-1-4648-1888-2
DOI: 10.1596/978-1-4648-1885-1

Cover and interior design: Melina Rose Yingling / World Bank

Library of Congress Control Number: 2022941749

Contents

Boxes

Figures

Tables

Preface

COVID-19 (coronavirus), the most severe pandemic in a century, tested the ability of the global system of open trade to deliver medical goods and services swiftly to the people who needed them most, anywhere in the world. In some respects, the trade system met the test; in others, it fell short. This report draws lessons from the pandemic experience and suggests concrete ways that trade can be leveraged to strengthen global health security and better prepare collectively for a future crisis.

Our research shows how open trade increases access to medical goods and services, allowing people in each economy to benefit from the innovation, skills, and advanced technology of others. During the COVID-19 pandemic, trade played a crucial role in ensuring the production and delivery of vaccines, therapeutics, diagnostics, and personal protective equipment. Trade in medical goods jumped by more than 13 percent, with products such as face masks increasing at 481 percent. Open trade spurred the development of life-saving vaccines. Governments fast-tracked vaccine approvals and provided financial support. Pharmaceutical companies built new supply chains, sourced mRNA and other key ingredients from foreign suppliers, and scaled up production to deliver more than 11.5 billion doses in less than two years.

But the pandemic also revealed weaknesses in the system of global trade. Many governments initially responded by imposing trade restrictions to hoard medical supplies. These actions, together with the concentration of production and trade among a small number of countries, meant that distribution of medical goods, particularly of vaccines, was highly uneven. More than two years after the pandemic struck, just 13 percent of people in low-income countries were fully vaccinated, compared with 74 percent in high-income countries, according to World Health Organization data. Also, divergent regulatory systems and sluggish border procedures hindered the global approval and deployment of vital medical goods, while incompatible qualification requirements—along with travel restrictions—restrained the movement of health care workers across borders.

How can trade be leveraged to improve global health security? One way is through multilateral trade cooperation. Mechanisms to improve transparency and coordination between countries that import and export medical goods can strengthen the role of trade in ensuring access to essential goods during a crisis. Regulatory cooperation can improve the resilience of supply chains and reduce the risks of illicit trade.

Trade agreements can support the increase of medical services' capacities to respond to an ever-increasing demand, promote new ways to deliver services (such as telehealth), and facilitate the international mobility of health professionals. Flexibilities in intellectual property regimes can encourage the sharing of technology and know-how needed to develop new therapeutics and vaccines.

Cooperation beyond trade agreements is also needed. Governments can set up procedures for joint purchases of medical goods during a crisis, adopt good practices in the establishment of national health regulations, and cooperate on international travel policies. Another step would be to work with the private sector to create a clearinghouse to support vaccine production, report bottlenecks, and exchange information on production capacity.

International organizations such as the World Bank Group and the World Trade Organization have a unique role to play by virtue of their global reach and convening power. They can ensure transparency and exchange of information, foster international standardization, bolster the capacity of national regulatory agencies, and encourage technology transfer.

COVID-19 has claimed more than 6 million lives. The rapid growth in trade in medical goods and services in recent decades shows that the global system of open trade is essential to health security. But we must also learn from experience to address weaknesses and ensure that trade works for everyone. Deepening cooperation is key—both to prepare the health care system for a future emergency and to craft responses that are fast, efficient, and fair.

Mari E. Pangestu
Managing Director
World Bank

Ngozi Okonjo-Iweala
Director-General
World Trade Organization

Acknowledgments

Trade Therapy: Deepening Cooperation to Strengthen Pandemic Defenses is a joint report by the World Bank and the World Trade Organization (WTO). Nadia Rocha and Michele Ruta from the World Bank and Marc Bacchetta and Joscelyn Magdeleine from the WTO are the coordinators of the report. The team members are grateful for the guidance and support of Mona Haddad (Global Director, Trade, Investment and Competitiveness) and Antonio Nucifora (Practice Manager, Trade and Regional Integration Unit) from the World Bank; and Anabel Gonzalez (WTO Deputy Director-General).

Many colleagues from the World Bank and the WTO contributed to this report: Rohini Acharya, Pamela Apaza Lanyi, Marc Bacchetta, Cosimo Beverelli, Antonia Carzaniga, Alex Chiang, Cristina Ileana Constantinescu, Seref Gokay Coskun, Carol Cravero, Barbara Carmelina D'Andrea, Edvinas Drevinskas, Alvaro Espitia, William Gain, Carlo Gamberale, Ian Gillson, Roger Kampf, Bassam Khazin, Roberta Lascari, Yan Liu, Joscelyn Magdeleine, Karen Maramatsu, Juan Marchetti, Darlan Marti, Andrea Mastromatteo, Maegan McCann, Devin McDaniels, Adelina Mendoza, Nora Neufeld, Simon Neumueller, Jesse Nicol, Thakur Parajuli, Josefita Pardo de Leon, Philippe Pelletier, Roberta Piermartini, Tristan Reed, Nadia Rocha, Martin Roy, Michele Ruta, Roy Santana, Shane Sela, Astghik Solomonyan, Irina Tarasenko, Jessyca Van Weelde, Thomas Verbeet, Elihu Wahid, Thomas Michael Woods, Dayong Yu, and Ruosi Zhang.

External contributions and background papers were provided by Chad Bown (Peterson Institute for International Economics), Rupa Chanda (UNESCAP), Allison Colbert (World Health Organization [WHO]), Peter Egger (University of Zurich), Simon Evenett (University of St.Gallen), Joseph Francois (World Trade Institute), and Bernard Hoekman (European University Institute). Giorgio Cometto, Ibadat Dhillon, and Agya Mahat from WHO contributed box 1.2 on health worker mobility.

The coordinators would like to thank the following colleagues for useful comments and guidance during various stages of preparation of the report: Paul Brenton, Xiaolin Chai, Mary Hallward-Driemeier, Matthias Helble, Markus Jelitto, Reto Malacrida, Graciela Miralles Murciego, Toomas Palu, Andreas Seiter, Antony Taubman.

Research assistance was provided by World Bank and WTO colleagues: Maria Alvarez de Cozar, Laura Baiker, Ravneek Bhullar, Berisford Codd, Sabreen Khashan, Nana Ramazashvili, Ester Rubio, and Cloé Torbay.

The publication of this report was led by Mary Fisk and Patricia Katayama (World Bank) and Anthony Martin (WTO). Mayya Revzina (World Bank) provided support during the publication process. The team is grateful to Chris Wellisz and Mary Anderson (World Bank) for their editorial services. The graphic concept, design, and layout were provided by Melina Rose-Yingling. Mohini Datt and Elizabeth Price (World Bank) offered guidance, services, and support on communication and dissemination.

Abbreviations

ACT-A	Access to COVID-19 Tools Accelerator
AMRH	African Medicines Regulatory Harmonization
APEC	Asia-Pacific Economic Cooperation
ASEAN	Association of Southeast Asian Nations
CDMO	contract development and manufacturing organization
CEPI	Coalition for Epidemic Preparedness Innovations
COVAX	COVID-19 Vaccines Global Access
COVID-19	coronavirus disease 2019
EAEU	Eurasian Economic Union
EU	European Union
FDI	foreign direct investment
GATS	General Agreement on Trade in Services (WTO)
GMP	good manufacturing practice
GPA	Government Procurement Agreement (WTO)
GTA	Global Trade Alert
G-20	Group of Twenty
GVC	global value chain
HS	Harmonized System
ICH	International Council for Harmonisation of Technical Requirements for Pharmaceuticals for Human Use
ICT	information and communication technology
IEC	International Electrotechnical Commission
IHR	*WHO International Health Regulations (2005)*
IMDRF	International Medical Device Regulators Forum
IP	intellectual property
IPR	intellectual property rights
ISO	International Organization for Standardization
ITA	Information Technology Agreement (WTO)
ITU	International Telecommunication Union
LMICs	low- and middle-income countries
MFN	most-favored-nation
MNC	multinational corporation

MPP	Medicine Patents Pool
MRA	mutual recognition agreement
NGO	nongovernmental organization
NQI	national quality infrastructure
NRA	national regulatory authority
OECD	Organisation for Economic Co-operation and Development
PIC/S	Pharmaceutical Inspection Co-operation Scheme
PPE	personal protective equipment
R&D	research and development
RTA	regional trade agreement
SAR	special administrative region
SPS	sanitary and phytosanitary
TBT	technical barriers to trade
TFA	Trade Facilitation Agreement (WTO)
TRIPS	Trade-Related Aspects of Intellectual Property Rights (WTO Agreement)
UHC	universal health coverage
UNICEF	United Nations Children's Fund
WHO	World Health Organization
WTO	World Trade Organization

Overview

INTRODUCTION

The COVID-19 pandemic has exposed the upsides and downsides of international trade in medical goods and services. Open trade can increase global access to medical services and goods (and to the critical inputs needed to manufacture them), improve quality, and reduce costs. Better global access to medical goods and services, in turn, contributes to global health security, which the World Health Organization (WHO) defines as "the activities required, both proactive and reactive, to minimize the danger and impact of acute public health events that endanger people's health across geographical regions and international boundaries."[1] But excessive concentration of production, restrictive trade policies, supply chain disruptions, and regulatory divergence can jeopardize the ability of public health systems to prepare for and respond to pandemics and other health crises—for instance, by limiting universal access to essential goods and services.

This report studies how to leverage trade to support global health security. It provides new data on the role of trade in medical goods and services and of medical value chains in the past decade; surveys the evolving policy landscape affecting trade in medical goods and services before and after the COVID-19 pandemic; and proposes an action plan to improve trade policies and deepen international cooperation to deal with future pandemics.

TRADE FLOWS IN MEDICAL GOODS AND SERVICES

Despite the contributions of these trade flows to global health security, the medical goods and services sectors also pose challenges and risks. Trade increases global access to medical services and goods (and to the critical inputs needed to manufacture them), improves quality, and reduces costs. Open trade allows countries across geographical regions and international boundaries to access these essential goods and services and promotes innovation through research and development (R&D) in both normal times and times of need. But several challenges are specific to the health care industry:

- For medical goods, economies of scale and high R&D and skill intensity lead to concentration in production that can be excessive and economically inefficient in emergencies.
- For both medical goods and services, complex and divergent regulation may fragment markets and impair an efficient supply response during an emergency.
- Access to medical goods and services may be unequal, and markets may neglect diseases specific to poorer countries.
- Finally, the risks of illicit trade have consequences for health security.

Trade in medical goods and services soared in the decade before the pandemic but remained highly concentrated despite the growing role of new players. Between 2010 and 2019, world trade in medical goods grew at an annual average rate of 4.7 percent (reaching US$1.3 trillion in 2019), compared with 2.8 percent growth for overall merchandise trade.[2] Trade in medical services showed a similar pattern, growing by an average 7 percent per year (to US$78.6 billion in 2019), compared with an average growth rate of 4 percent for overall services.[3]

The increasing roles of new players (such as China and India) notwithstanding, trade in medical goods and services remains highly concentrated, with high-income economies representing the bulk of exports and imports. Even for less sophisticated medical goods, such as personal protective equipment (PPE), concentration is high, with East Asian economies accounting for over 60 percent of world exports.[4] High-income economies are the largest importers of both medical goods and services. Low- and middle-income economies with poor domestic health systems substantially increased their imports of health services between 2010 and 2019, though the value of these imports remained low.

Since WHO declared a global pandemic in March 2020, trade in medical goods and services has had a mixed record, mostly because of unequal access across countries. International trade in medical goods was essential in the response to the pandemic, increasing by 13.2 percent in 2020, with critical COVID-19 products such as face masks registering a 481 percent *monthly* growth rate in April 2020.[5] Open trade, combined with government support, also spurred the innovation that led to rapid vaccine development. But supplies of these products were distributed unequally, with high-income areas initially having a larger share of imports. In contrast to the rapid trade growth in medical goods, trade in medical services fell by 9 percent in 2020, mainly because of travel and border restrictions.[6] This decline was partly offset by a surge in cross-border medical services (including telehealth), also mainly benefiting high-income countries.

Open trade in medical goods and services will remain key to ensuring global health security. Three trends suggest that health spending will increase as a share of gross domestic product: emergent infectious diseases, income convergence, and increasing life expectancy. Open trade will be essential to meeting the surge in global demand for medical goods and services, improving the efficiency and innovation of health systems and containing costs. Technological improvements and digitalization will make the delivery of medical products even more international, and increasingly complex global value chains will be crucial to innovation.

POLICIES AFFECTING TRADE IN MEDICAL GOODS AND SERVICES
The trade policy landscape before COVID-19

Although trade in medical goods and services is increasingly open, several impediments still limit the efficiency of these markets.

Tariff and regulatory gaps. Impediments to trade in medical goods have decreased but remain high in low- and middle-income economies. Trade restrictions imply higher prices for medical goods, which weigh on health care systems. These impediments take the form of tariffs—averaging 2.4 percent in high-income economies and more than double that rate in low- and middle-income economies[7]—or quantitative restrictions on medical goods, which typically consist of nonautomatic licensing requirements and full prohibitions on both imports and exports.

Trade facilitation bottlenecks and restrictions of trade in transport, logistics, and distribution services have further impeded trade in medical goods. Finally, divergent regulatory systems have hindered the global development, approval, and marketing of innovative vaccines, therapeutics, and diagnostics.

Trade restrictiveness in medical services. The medical services sector is gradually becoming more open to foreign competition, but major impediments remain. To ensure access to health care services and guarantee their quality, there is a need for a regulatory framework that efficiently uses existing resources and attracts new ones while controlling for risks associated with liberalization (for example, overall cost increases for the health financing system and health workforce shortages in sending countries).

It is in this context that a growing number of countries are liberalizing trade in medical services, albeit with significant restrictions remaining through quantitative and discriminatory measures. Furthermore, service suppliers' capacity to trade is affected by measures related to qualification requirements and procedures, technical standards, and licensing requirements. Although these domestic regulatory measures fulfill legitimate policy objectives, they may in certain cases unduly restrict trade in medical services.

Competition policies and government procurement. Government procurement and competition policies can make medicines, medical technologies, and services more accessible and affordable. Open, transparent, and competitive procurement procedures can save money for governments and citizens by providing access to the best products and services and the most cost-efficient suppliers globally. Competition law and policies have important roles to play in enhancing access to health technologies and fostering innovation.

Governments' trade policy responses to the COVID-19 pandemic

Since the start of the COVID-19 pandemic, governments have used a wide range of trade and trade-related policies to bolster domestic availability of critical medical goods and services. Some measures detracted from global health security—restrictions on exports of critical products being the leading example. Other measures have had positive effects on the countries implementing them and their trade partners, thus constituting a sort of public good.

Import and export controls. Governments imposed policies to influence cross-border shipments of medical goods during the pandemic. More than two-thirds of countries resorted to policy interventions to ensure domestic accessibility of medical goods. Both import reforms and export curbs surged in the first two quarters of 2020, reaching a total of 200 and 134, respectively, in May 2020 and stabilizing after that.[8] Less than 5 percent of border-related policy interventions remained in place for less than three months, casting doubt on their "temporary" nature.[9]

These policies disrupted trade flows and medical supply chains and increased consumer prices, with negative effects on global welfare. Analysis conducted for this report estimates that these measures were responsible for increases of up to 60 percent in the average trade costs of medical goods during the COVID-19 pandemic (Egger et al. 2022).

Regulatory easing. Governments also adopted emergency measures to facilitate trade, ease regulatory bottlenecks, and promote the diffusion of health technologies. Many countries expedited a transition from paper-based to electronic documents requested at the border to reduce the interaction between traders and border authorities. These changes increased trade efficiency. Countries also simplified trade procedures to facilitate the flow of critical supplies.

Many national regulatory authorities activated emergency use authorizations (EUAs) to fast-track the approval of key medical goods such as vaccines. Finally, to respond to concerns about vaccine equity, governments relaxed intellectual property (IP) rights, including through legislative amendments, easing of procedural requirements, and the use of policy options.

Easing telehealth and the movement of health professionals. Limitations on the movement of people had both negative and positive consequences for medical services trade. For example, patients were prevented from receiving treatment abroad, but governments implemented some liberalizing measures in areas such as telehealth services (whether supplied as cross-border services or through the establishment of commercial presence) or the movement of health professionals (by streamlining procedures for granting visa and work permits or easing the recognition of qualifications). Although many measures were initially taken temporarily as a response to the crisis, some were subsequently extended—particularly for telehealth services.

Government support measures. The use of subsidies, public procurement, and localization measures in the medical sector accelerated during the pandemic. Subsidies to medical goods firms were the most common measure, representing 88 percent of the total.[10] Governments provided financial grants, loan guarantees, and production subsidies, particularly for firms involved in discovering or producing vaccines and medicines that had significant positive spillovers to other countries.

DEEPENING COOPERATION ON MEDICAL GOODS AND SERVICES TRADE

This report offers an action plan that governments can implement to strengthen trade's contribution to global health security. The system of stable and predictable rules embedded in the World Trade Organization (WTO) Agreements and in regional trade agreements supported the expansion of trade before and during the pandemic, helped to boost capacity to scale up production of critical products, and offered a forum to cooperate and address evolving challenges. But the pandemic also uncovered certain gaps in international cooperation, including (a) a lack of information on the stocks and availability of critical inputs; (b) a lack of multilateral mechanisms to mobilize financing for development of vaccines and therapeutics; (c) weaknesses in systems to facilitate the rapid cross-border movement of certified medical products; and (d) lack of market access framework and necessary flexibilities to deal with health workforce shortages (mobility of health personnel and telehealth).

These gaps contributed to scarcity and inequitable access to essential medical goods and services. Some of these gaps can be addressed through existing trade cooperation mechanisms. Others call for new forms of cooperation between states, nonstate actors, and the private sector.

Cooperation through existing trade mechanisms

New commitments and disciplines in WTO and regional trade agreements can help countries better prepare for and respond to future pandemics in several ways:

- *An agreement to lower barriers to trade in medical goods and supporting services* would improve the efficiency of health care systems and increase preparedness. Empirical analysis produced for this report finds that lowering tariffs on medical products and reducing import costs for information and communication technology and business services in the health sector would increase income by more than US$6 billion annually, with more than half of that accruing to low- and middle-income countries.[11]
- *Commitments on import and export policy* could help avoid extreme market outcomes in a crisis. An agreement on trade and health could include commitments to limit the duration of restrictions on exports of critical goods during

a pandemic; improve trade policy transparency; ensure that trade is not interrupted for countries in need; and consult with other economies to assess the adverse impact of measures on partners.

- *Regulatory cooperation* can improve the resilience and functioning of supply chains and reduce the risks of illicit trade. Broadening and deepening this cooperation can help streamline regulatory frameworks, make them more coherent, and provide a playbook of regulatory flexibilities for smoother and faster approval of medical goods in the event of a pandemic. To this end, governments can pursue mutual recognition and equivalence regimes for critical medical goods and support the development of international standards.

- *A balanced global IP system,* including through the full implementation and use of flexibilities, will establish a solid basis for sharing technology and knowhow to jointly develop the capacity to respond to health crises and geographically diversify manufacturing capacity. In addition, other measures could encourage rights holders to (a) adopt open and humanitarian licensing models for pandemic-related technologies; (b) contribute to international technology sharing platforms, such as WHO's COVID-19 Technology Access Pool (C-TAP); and (c) include equitable access considerations in their R&D planning. Agreement among WTO members on an IP response to COVID-19 could serve as a blueprint in future emergencies.

- *Reduction of services trade barriers and improvement of regulatory systems* could expand access to medical services and enhance their quality in normal times while also bolstering pandemic preparedness. Initiatives on services trade could include
  - Adopting frameworks to narrow the gaps in national health systems through foreign investment in the medical services sector (for example, health establishments and telehealth firms);
  - Enhancing health workers' mobility according to identified needs (also taking into account, through dialogue, the needs of the countries of origin);
  - Recognizing foreign qualifications of medical-services suppliers; and
  - Cooperating to ensure cross-border liability of foreign-based medical services suppliers.

- *Rules in trade agreements on subsidies, public procurement, and competition* can form the basis for governments to react efficiently to health emergencies. The COVID-19 pandemic showed the need for (a) subsidies in helping to scale up capacity across medical supply chains, and (b) public procurement systems and competition authorities to work efficiently and in coordination. Much of this cooperation is bound to take place outside of trade agreements. Still, trade rules could envision ways to coordinate subsidies for crisis-related medical goods, develop joint purchasing tools to aggregate demand between countries in a crisis, and identify good practices for competition law in a pandemic.

Cooperation beyond trade agreements

Leveraging trade to strengthen pandemic defenses requires cooperation beyond trade agreements. The Multilateral Leaders Task Force on COVID-19 Vaccines, Therapeutics, and Diagnostics—set up by the International Monetary Fund (IMF), the World Bank, WHO, and the WTO—has called on the international community to step up its response to the current pandemic (WHO 2021). These efforts call for enhanced cooperation between states, nonstate actors, and international organizations.

Cooperation between states and nonstate actors. The first goal should be to create mechanisms to finance access to essential products such as vaccines in low-income countries and to expand supply and distribution capacity during a crisis and ensure that these facilities do not disappear when demand declines. This effort would include cooperation to build manufacturing facilities in low- and middle-income countries with a latent comparative advantage whose relatively small populations reduce the risk that the host-country governments will intervene to meet domestic needs and the impact of a potential intervention.

A second goal is to create mechanisms for sharing information on the operation of supply chains. A priority should be to establish a global clearinghouse to support production of critical medical products (ideally according to an internationally agreed-upon list; see chapter 4) and serve as a platform for companies to report bottlenecks, improve visibility on production capacity and distribution, and identify measures to respond to the pandemic.

Cooperation among international organizations. Efforts to strengthen collaboration should center on addressing the information and coordination gaps revealed by the pandemic, such as by

- Strengthening international standardization;
- Bolstering the capacity of national regulatory agencies;
- Developing good-practice policy frameworks for public procurement during crises; and
- Working with the private sector to encourage technology transfer and expand global emergency response capacity.

Multilateral organizations should continue cooperative efforts to provide transparency and achieve truly global health security. Building on the Multilateral Leaders Task Force, a jointly managed platform could ensure that information systems at the firm and supply chain levels are in place so data are available to all governments in an emergency.

NOTES

1. "Health Security: Overview" (n.d.), WHO website: https://www.who.int/health-topics/health -security#tab=tab_1.
2. Data on trade in medical goods are from the World Trade Organization (WTO) Integrated Database and the United Nations (UN) COMTRADE database.

3. Data on trade in medical services are from WTO estimates based on its Trade in Services Data by Mode of Supply (TISMOS) dataset.
4. Data on PPE trade volume, by region and country income group, are from the WTO Integrated Database and the UN COMTRADE database.
5. Data on medical goods trade during the pandemic are from the WTO Integrated Database and the UN COMTRADE database. Data on PPE export rates in 2020, including exports of face masks, are from Trade Data Monitor (http://tradedatamonitor.com).
6. Data on medical services trade during the pandemic are from WTO estimates based on its TISMOS dataset.
7. Data on most-favored-nation (MFN) applied tariffs on medical goods, by country income group, are from the WTO Integrated Database.
8. Data on liberalizing export reforms and import restrictions are from World Bank calculations using the Essential Goods Initiative (EGI) database. The EGI was launched in 2020 by the World Bank in cooperation with the St.Gallen Endowment for Prosperity through Trade and the European University Institute.
9. Data on the duration of active COVID-19 policy interventions affecting medical goods trade are from the Global Trade Alert database (https://www.globaltradealert.org/data_extraction).
10. Data on government support measures in the medical sector, including subsidies, are from the Global Trade Alert (GTA) database (https://www.globaltradealert.org/data_extraction).
11. For more about the empirical analysis of links between local health care costs, trade, and the potential benefits of tariff reductions in the health care sector, see chapter 2, box. 2.1.

REFERENCES

Egger, P., G. Masllorens, N. Rocha, and M. Ruta. 2022. "Estimating the Impact of Trade Policies on Trade Flows in Medical Goods." Unpublished manuscript, World Bank, Washington, DC.

WHO (World Health Organization). 2021. "From Vaccines to Vaccinations: Seventh Meeting of the Multilateral Leaders Task Force on COVID-19 Vaccines, Therapeutics and Diagnostics." News release, December 22.

Introduction

COVID-19 is a forerunner of more, and possibly worse, pandemics to come. Scientists have repeatedly warned that without greatly strengthened proactive strategies, global health threats will emerge more often, spread more rapidly, and take more lives. Together with the world's dwindling biodiversity and climate crisis, to which they are inextricably linked, infectious disease threats represent the primary international challenge of our times. Recognizing this new reality of a pandemic era is not fearmongering but rather prudent public policy and responsible politics. We must organize ourselves on a whole-of-society basis within nations and rethink how we collaborate internationally to mitigate its profound consequences for livelihoods, social cohesion, and global order.

Ngozi Okonjo-Iweala, Tharman Shanmugaratnam, and
Lawrence H. Summers, 2021

STRONGER TRADE SYSTEMS FOR BETTER GLOBAL HEALTH SECURITY

Trade in medical goods and services has been an essential weapon in the battle against the coronavirus (COVID-19) pandemic. During the first two years of the pandemic, suppliers stepped up global shipments of therapeutics, vaccines, diagnostic gear, and personal protective equipment. Barriers to the movement of goods, people, and technology, however, hampered that effort.

This experience shows that the world must be better prepared for the next pandemic that will inevitably arrive and that could be even more severe. Global public health security—which the World Health Organization (WHO) defines as "the activities required, both proactive and reactive, to minimize the danger and impact of acute public health events that endanger people's health across geographical regions and international boundaries"—must be improved.

The goals of this report are to identify the trade system weaknesses revealed by the COVID-19 pandemic and to propose concrete steps to address those weaknesses at the national level and through closer cooperation at the multilateral and regional levels. This study seeks to help policy makers leverage trade to bolster the world's pandemic defenses; it serves as a playbook that can be rolled out once an emergency starts.

This report deals specifically with such issues as trade and trade policy, including tariffs and quotas, cross-border investment, telehealth, international health worker mobility, and intellectual property rights. Clearly, trade is only one part of a broader global effort to prepare for and respond to the next pandemic—an effort that also involves health and development policy. Such issues have been addressed elsewhere and are discussed here only as they relate specifically to trade and trade policy.

ORGANIZATION OF THE REPORT

The report's contributions range from new data and analysis of medical goods and services trade—before and after the pandemic—to policy proposals on multiple levels, both within and beyond traditional trade support frameworks. It comprises four chapters:

- *Chapter 1, "Trade Flows in Medical Goods and Services,"* examines the main demand and supply characteristics of markets for medical goods and services. It also provides stylized facts on trends in international trade in those goods and services, including the functioning of medical supply chains before and during the pandemic.
- *Chapter 2, "Trade Policies in Medical Goods and Services,"* explores how trade policies and regulatory frameworks have affected international trade in medical goods and services—including critical inputs—under normal circumstances and during the COVID-19 pandemic.
- *Chapter 3, "Deepening Cooperation on Medical Goods and Services Trade,"* explores how improved international cooperation in trade and trade-related issues could contribute to global health security. Starting from the gaps in cooperation that emerged during the COVID-19 pandemic, the chapter outlines steps to ensure that rules in trade agreements and mechanisms of cooperation beyond trade support efforts to better respond to the next pandemic.
- *Chapter 4, "Leveraging Medical Goods and Services Trade for Future Pandemics: An Action Plan,"* summarizes the report's recommendations and presents a detailed menu of options for policy action and reform that can leverage various trade instruments and measures to improve crisis prevention, preparedness, and response.

REFERENCE

Okonjo-Iweala, N., T. Shanmugaratnam, and L. H. Summers. 2021. "We Don't Have to Fly Blind into the Next Pandemic." *Washington Post*, Opinion, September 16.

1 Trade Flows in Medical Goods and Services

ABOUT THIS CHAPTER

This chapter has two goals: (a) it looks at the main demand and supply characteristics of markets for medical goods and services and how they shape gains and risks from trade in these products; and (b) it provides stylized facts on trends in international trade in medical goods and services, including the functioning of medical supply chains, before and during the COVID-19 pandemic.

THE MEDICAL GOODS AND SERVICES TRADE: RELEVANCE, CHARACTERISTICS, AND WELFARE IMPLICATIONS

Definitions

Medical goods. Medical goods include all products used in the diagnosis, prevention, monitoring, treatment, and alleviation of disease and injury (table 1.1). These are pharmaceuticals (such as vitamins, over-the-counter pain relief, prescription cancer medication, and vaccines); medical equipment (such as magnetic resonance imaging apparatus and operating tables); orthopedic equipment (such as wheelchairs and spectacles); personal protective equipment (such as gloves and face masks); and other consumable medical supplies (such as oxygen and syringes).

   Medical services. Medical services (or health-related services) cover the provision of human health services, including

- *Hospital services:* inpatient services provided under the supervision of a medical doctor;
- *Services of health professionals:* medical and dental services (including services provided in outpatient clinics), services of midwives, nurses, physiotherapists, and paramedics; and

- *Other health-related services:* for example, ambulance services, residential care facilities, laboratories, and diagnostic imaging).[1]

As shown in table 1.2, trade in medical services can take place through the four modes of supply defined by the General Agreement on Trade in Services (GATS), a treaty of the World Trade Organization (WTO).[2]

Table 1.1 Medical goods covered in the report

Product category	Number of HS subheadings	Coverage
A – Pharmaceutical products	87	Products as defined by the WTO Pharma Agreement[a] (HS chapter 30, and headings 2936, 2937, 2939, 2941)
B – Medical equipment	40	Medical equipment and machines (majority in HS chapter 90) including magnetic resonance imaging apparatus, X-ray tubes, or operating tables
C – Orthopedic equipment	16	Orthopedic devices such as wheelchairs, spectacles, hearing aids, or artificial teeth
D – Personal protective equipment	20	Equipment and single-use items such as gloves and face masks (excluding protective garments because HS classifications largely overlap with products for nonmedical use)
E – Other medical supplies	34	Hospital and laboratory inputs and consumables, such as syringes

Note: A full list of HS items used in the definition is provided in an online appendix to the report. HS = Harmonized System (of nomenclature to classify traded products); WTO = World Trade Organization.

a. The WTO 1994 Agreement on Trade in Pharmaceutical Products (document L/7430), subsequently reviewed in 1996, 1998, 2007, and 2010.

Table 1.2 GATS modes of supply in trade of medical services

Mode of supply	Examples of medical services traded
Mode 1: Cross-border supply (service crosses border, with supplier and consumer remaining in their respective jurisdictions)	Cross-border telehealth services, telemedicine, teleradiology, telediagnosis
Mode 2: Consumption abroad (consumer crosses border)	Health travel, including specialized hospital and surgical care and alternative therapies accessed in other countries
Mode 3: Commercial presence abroad (establishment of the foreign supplier)	Setup and operation of foreign-owned hospitals, diagnostic facilities, clinics, or telemedicine companies
Mode 4: Presence of natural persons (supplier is abroad temporarily as either a self-employed person or an employee of a foreign service supplier)	Independent or self-employed health professionals; health professionals sent abroad by a medical facility, hospital, or health provider; or staff transferred to an affiliated health establishment abroad (including management in the health-related services sector). The persons concerned could cover physicians, nurses, midwives, paramedical personnel, technicians, and so on.

Source: Construction based on General Agreement on Trade in Services (GATS) of the World Trade Organization.

Characteristics

Medical goods and services have three defining characteristics: They are essential, have high research and development (R&D) intensity, and are heavily regulated. Combined, these features give the markets for medical goods and services unique economic properties.

Essentiality. Medical goods and services are essential in the sense that their consumption becomes a priority under certain circumstances. Among other things, this characteristic leads governments to use trade policy on these products differently than for other goods and services.

Specifically, shortages of medical goods and services can lead to major health consequences for populations. Just as an individual in a moment of personal health crisis would prioritize one's own health, nations do the same in an emergency. For instance (and as shown in chapter 2), at the onset of the COVID-19 pandemic, when demand for medical goods like personal protective equipment (PPE) and medical equipment exploded, many governments banned exports and lowered tariffs for medical goods but not for other products. When the COVID-19 vaccine became available, many vaccine-producing countries also restricted exports to prioritize their own populations.

Trade in medical services was affected by similar policies. For example, certain jurisdictions temporarily restricted health professionals from traveling overseas (as also discussed in chapter 2 regarding policies affecting trade during the pandemic). Activist trade policy in emergencies is well documented in markets for certain essential goods such as food. In times of high food prices, governments restrict exports and facilitate imports to ensure subsistence nutrition (Giordani, Rocha, and Ruta 2016).

High R&D intensity. Many medical products have a high R&D intensity—a firm's R&D expenditures divided by its sales—which generates economies of scale that are both external and internal to the firms or health establishments. Medical technology firms tend to cluster in the same locations to draw the same kinds of skilled workers, production inputs, and ideas as in the biotech clusters of Boston and the Upper Rhine "BioValley" spanning France, Germany, and Switzerland. Further scale economies are achieved when firms learn by doing, and costs decrease in firms that have been manufacturing more for longer. Though some goods, such as PPE and some generic pharmaceuticals, have lesser technological requirements and could be produced in more countries, production of these goods is also subject to these economies of scale.

Medical services trade, particularly medical travel, has also been spurred by policies encouraging the creation of health care hubs that supply services to foreign consumers on the basis of a country's specialization in certain services (resulting from medical research, innovation, and expertise developed over the years).

Such services include cancer, orthopedic, cardiovascular, dental, neurological, and cosmetic treatment.

Large economies of scale mean that countries with larger domestic markets are also major exporters (figure 1.1). A larger domestic market provides greater incentive to innovate and an opportunity to reduce costs. As a result, production of many medical products is concentrated in larger economies such as China, India, many European countries, and the United States.

A salient example of this so-called home market effect for medical goods is famotidine (known as Pepcid® in the United States), which is used to treat peptic ulcers and

Figure 1.1 The largest economies, not always high-income economies, are the largest exporters of medical goods and services, leading to concentration

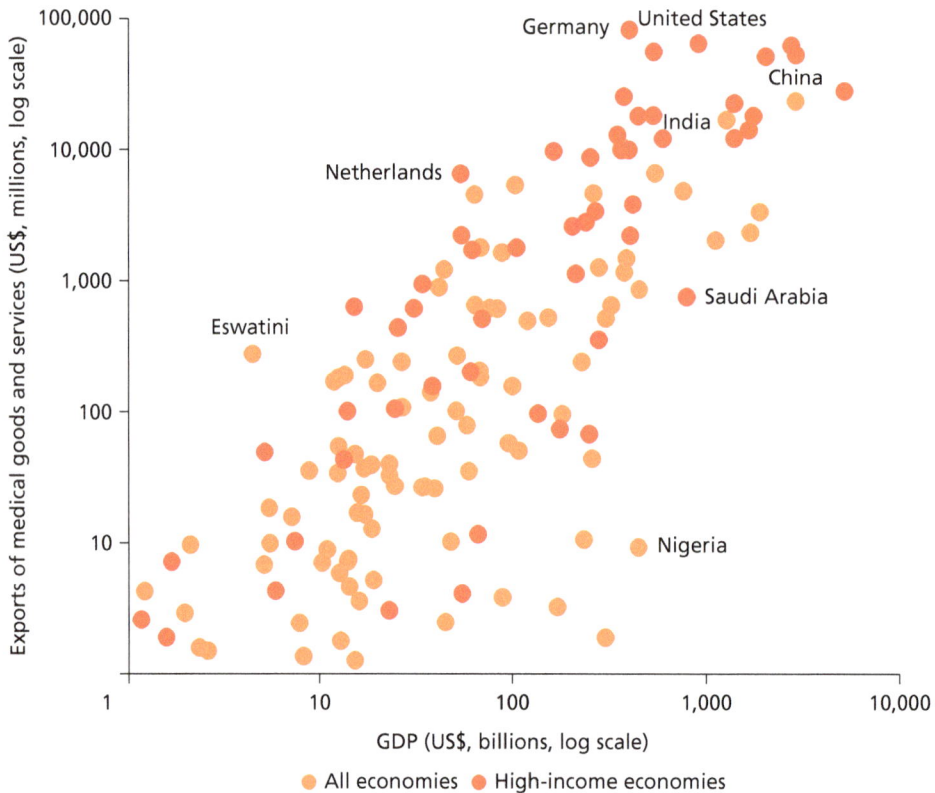

Sources: United Nations COMTRADE data; World Trade Organization's Trade in Services Data by Mode of Supply (TISMOS) dataset; World Development Indicators database.

Note: Data from 2019 are used to avoid capturing impacts of the COVID-19 pandemic on certain variables. Medical goods include pharmaceuticals, medical equipment, orthopedic equipment, personal protective equipment, and other consumable medical supplies. Medical services are those delivered through all General Agreement on Trade in Services (GATS) modes: (1) cross-border supply, (2) consumption abroad, (3) commercial presence, and (4) presence of natural persons. "High-income economies" are as classified by the World Bank in 2000, with gross national income (GNI) per capita of US$12,535.

was discovered in Japan. Japan is known for a high incidence of peptic ulcers, and individuals there are nearly twice as likely to die from digestive disorders as people in the rest of the world. Though Japan is, overall, a net importer of pharmaceuticals, it is a net exporter of drugs targeting peptic ulcers and related digestive diseases (Costinot et al. 2019). Domestic demand gave Japan an incentive for innovation, and local economies of scale allowed it to develop a cost advantage and capture the international market. For other goods, demand is determined more by the size of the population than by specific disease incidence. For example, China, the world's most populous country, accounts for about 50 percent of global PPE exports.

High regulation. Because of their impact on human health, medical goods and services tend to be more heavily regulated than other products, with foreign products facing additional barriers related to regulatory requirements. Medical products are subject to quality-related regulation (including competency standards for health professionals), which is essential to protect consumers but can also create barriers to entry. Most imported medical goods must be approved by a national regulatory authority before they can be used. Exporters of medical goods and services must apply for approval from the regulator, potentially giving an advantage to domestic suppliers that are familiar with the approval process. In addition, in most jurisdictions, the distribution of medical goods is also highly regulated with the sale of various products (especially medical drugs) having to be conducted through specialized establishments such as pharmacies.[3]

For medical services, recognition of qualifications is another key issue for exporters. As with medical goods, regulatory requirements may create barriers to entry and inefficiencies because the process must be repeated across multiple countries. In addition to quality-related regulations, medical goods are often subject to regulations aimed at protecting intellectual property rights (IPR) because of their high R&D intensity. As discussed in chapter 2, these regulations create additional trade-offs: designed to encourage innovation by providing monopoly rents, they allow patent holders to charge higher prices for drugs by limiting the diffusion of the innovation. In addition, patents may be used as collateral to finance the expansion of manufacturing capacity. IPR rules may also affect decisions on whether to launch drugs in a given country.

Welfare gains from trade

Openness to trade in medical goods and services brings potential welfare gains for a community in three broad categories: increased income, economic diversification, and domestic innovation.

Income gains. Examples where this trade has boosted income include Jordan (a center for in vitro fertilization that receives patients from all over the world) as well as US telehealth companies that provide services such as telediagnosis, surveillance, and consultation to Persian Gulf and Central American countries. Such income could be used to develop capacity to reach underserved populations in their home markets. Also, importing a product that can be produced more efficiently elsewhere frees up local resources that can be spent on other products. Although reliance on home production may provide reassurance that domestic capacity is available, it may be costly.

Economic diversification. A community that relies only on a single hospital can be health insecure in emergencies that strain local resources, such as a natural disaster that fills hospital beds. Similarly, relying on imports from a single low-cost supplier, or relying exclusively on domestic production, may reduce health security if the supplier faces an emergency and supplies are interrupted. Empirically, at a national level, openness to international trade can lower income volatility by reducing exposure to domestic shocks and allowing countries to diversify the sources of demand and supply (Caselli et al. 2020).

Innovation through R&D. In the pharmaceutical industry, market size has a clear positive effect on innovation (Acemoglu and Linn 2004). More generally, the global decline in tariffs in the 1990s can explain 7 percent of global innovation, as measured by the number of patents granted during that period (Coelli, Moxnes, and Ulltveit-Moe 2022). Increased competition from imports has an ambiguous effect on domestic innovation. On the one hand, it may reduce profits and hence the incentive to innovate; on the other, it may provide an incentive to patent new products to escape competition. Bloom, Draca, and Van Reenen (2016) find that increased competition from Chinese imports had a positive impact on the patenting activity of European firms, though Autor et al. (2020) find the opposite result for American manufacturing firms. Trade openness could also affect innovation by lowering the cost of inputs or improving their quality.

Risks associated with trade

Despite gains from trade, open markets in medical goods and services also expose societies to risks. Some of these risks are directly related to trade; others depend on the unique characteristics of medical goods and services and may in certain instances result from market failures.

Economic inefficiency. For medical goods, the concentration of production created by significant economies of scale can be excessive and economically inefficient in emergencies despite delivering lower costs in normal times. For instance, during the COVID-19 pandemic, export restrictions by economies that are large vaccine producers were a major cause of delay in vaccine deliveries to low- and middle-income countries. Smaller producers such as the Republic of Korea and South Africa had smaller domestic needs and exported most of the domestic production, albeit at high prices.[4] Yet smaller countries, because the sizes of their home markets limit economies of scale, often fail to achieve the cost advantage needed to succeed as exporters in normal times.

The judicious use of policies to develop diverse production capacities can therefore be justified from an economic efficiency perspective. Developing capacity in smaller countries has a double benefit, allowing them to meet domestic demand quickly, making them less likely to restrict exports during emergencies, and making any potential restrictive action less impactful because of volumes involved.

Insufficient R&D for neglected diseases. Another market failure concerns treatment of neglected diseases, which receive insufficient R&D effort considering the number of lives they affect. High-income countries account for about 80 percent of global health spending, compared with 17 percent from upper-middle-income countries, 2.8 percent from lower-middle-income countries, and 0.24 percent from low-income countries (WHO 2021a). As a result, global R&D efforts focus on diseases prevalent in wealthy countries (such as coronary heart disease) rather than those that primarily afflict poor-country populations (such as malaria and HIV/AIDS).

As with the concentration of production, government intervention can overcome this market failure. In 2007, as proposed by Kremer and Glennerster (2004), donors committed US$1.5 billion to a pilot advance market commitment (AMC) to help purchase pneumococcal vaccine for low-income countries. Three vaccines were developed and more than 150 million children immunized, saving an estimated 700,000 lives and demonstrating that vaccine developers will respond to government incentives (Kremer, Levin, and Snyder 2020).

Market fragmentation from regulatory divergence. Regulatory divergence may fragment markets for medical goods and services and impair an efficient supply response during an emergency. Part of the challenge is a lack of internationally recognized regulators in emerging markets. If a producer in an emerging market gains approval for a good from its national regulatory authority, this approval will not be recognized by other countries. Though some countries and the World Health Organization (WHO) recognize approvals by the European Medicines Agency or the US Food and Drug Administration, producers from emerging markets may not have experience with the approval processes of these agencies, which may not prioritize applications for approval of drugs that will be used primarily in other countries. If the regulatory authorities in large emerging markets like China and India are also internationally recognized as stringent regulatory authorities, their products will have access to much larger markets, and countries that export to these markets will also have access to larger markets.

Equity challenges. The gains from trade do not necessarily translate into more equitable and affordable access to medical services (Adams and Kinnon 1997; Bettcher, Yach, and Guidon 2000; Chanda 2001a, 2001b, 2002; UNCTAD 1997; Zarilli and Kinnon 1998). Medical services trade may result in a dual market structure, with a high-quality, expensive, more specialized segment catering to wealthy nationals and foreigners and a lower-quality, resource-constrained segment catering to lower- and middle-income people. Additionally, there are concerns that medical staff may be driven away from the resource-constrained segment. Resources may also be diverted to develop new services, such as telehealth, from basic health care facilities that have a bigger and more direct benefit for the poor.

Although these concerns are not necessarily driven by trade, they may be exacerbated by it. These negative effects and concerns are, however, dependent on the existing level of resources, the regulatory frameworks governing the health system, and the fiscal (tax and subsidy) policies that shape the effects on equity and access.

Health security risks. Especially in low- and middle-income countries, risks to health security are associated with *illicit* trade in medical goods. Because medical goods are both essential and highly regulated, they are prone to illicit trade. This may involve goods that are themselves illegal as well as those that may be legal but which, by virtue of how they are produced, distributed, or sold, are traded through illegal means. Illicit trade in medical products—and in particular the trafficking of substandard, unregistered, or falsified products—can have serious health, economic, and socioeconomic consequences.

Global estimates of illicit trade in the medical goods sector are scarce, remain sensitive to definition, and predate the current COVID-19 pandemic. In 2017, 1 in 10 medical products in low- and middle-income countries were falsified (WHO 2017a, 2017b). OECD and EUIPO (2019) report a value of global trade in counterfeit pharmaceuticals of up to US$4.4 billion in 2016, representing 0.84 percent of total worldwide pharmaceutical imports. Despite a general perception that, with COVID-19 vaccines and other commodities in high demand and short supply, criminal networks jumped in to fill the void with falsified health products of substandard quality, more and stronger evidence is needed to detect and quantify any trends in illicit trade of medical goods since the outbreak of the COVID-19 pandemic.

DRIVERS OF TRADE IN MEDICAL GOODS AND SERVICES
Drivers affecting trade in both medical goods and services

There are many macro-level drivers of trade in medical goods and services. On the demand side, demographic and economic development-related forces have increased demand for medical services and products. On the supply side, technological advancements, demographics, and policy changes are at play. Three trends suggest that health spending will increase as a share of gross domestic product (GDP) over time: emergent infectious diseases, income convergence, and increasing life expectancy.

Emergent infectious diseases. The twentieth century has seen an increasing rate of emergent infectious diseases—a trend attributed to human population density and environmental change (Daszak, Cunningham, and Hyatt 2001). Most emergent diseases are transmitted to humans from animals, mostly wildlife. A small but increasing share are drug resistant. Since 1600, the likelihood of a pandemic more severe than the 1918 influenza pandemic has roughly tripled (figure 1.2).

Figure 1.2   The yearly probability of a pandemic worse than the 1918 influenza pandemic has increased substantially since the 1600s

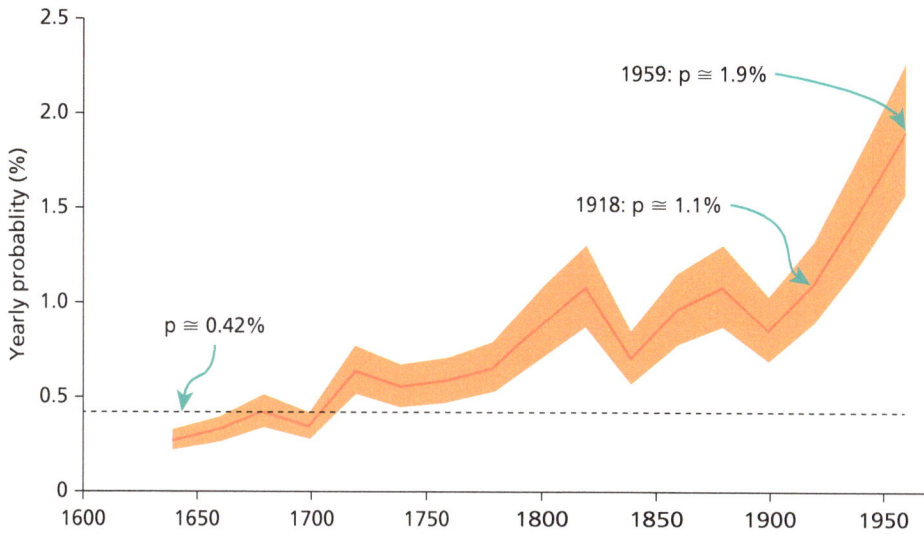

Source: Marani et al. 2021.

Note: The red line indicates the yearly probability (p) of an epidemic worse than the 1918 influenza, and the orange shaded area indicates a 95 percent confidence interval. The sample excludes epidemics since World War II and those that are still ongoing (for example, HIV/AIDS, malaria, and COVID-19) to ensure that the disease dynamics are unaffected by treatments or interventions and governed only by the properties of the pathogen and by transmission dynamics. The dotted line indicates the yearly probability under the naive assumption that it does not change over time.

The increasing frequency of new diseases and epidemics implies substantial costs, due to loss of life and livelihood, and increased demand for medical goods and services. As epidemics become more frequent, demand will become more volatile, but it will also grow more rapidly as governments, households, and private firms invest in prevention and mitigation. About 60 percent of health spending comes from government sources, with most of the rest from domestic private sources; only 0.21 percent comes from external aid (WHO 2021a).

Income convergence. Since the 1990s, income convergence has driven demand for health products. Average per capita income is growing faster in low- and middle-income economies than in high-income economies (Patel, Sandefur, and Subramanian 2021). Growth in GDP per capita and health spending per capita are tightly correlated (figure 1.3). This positive relationship, combined with income convergence across economies, implies that, in the long run, health spending will grow fastest in emerging markets and low- and middle-income economies, leading to a global surge in demand for health products.

Figure 1.3   Growth in GDP per capita is tightly correlated with growth in health spending, though slightly less so in high-income countries

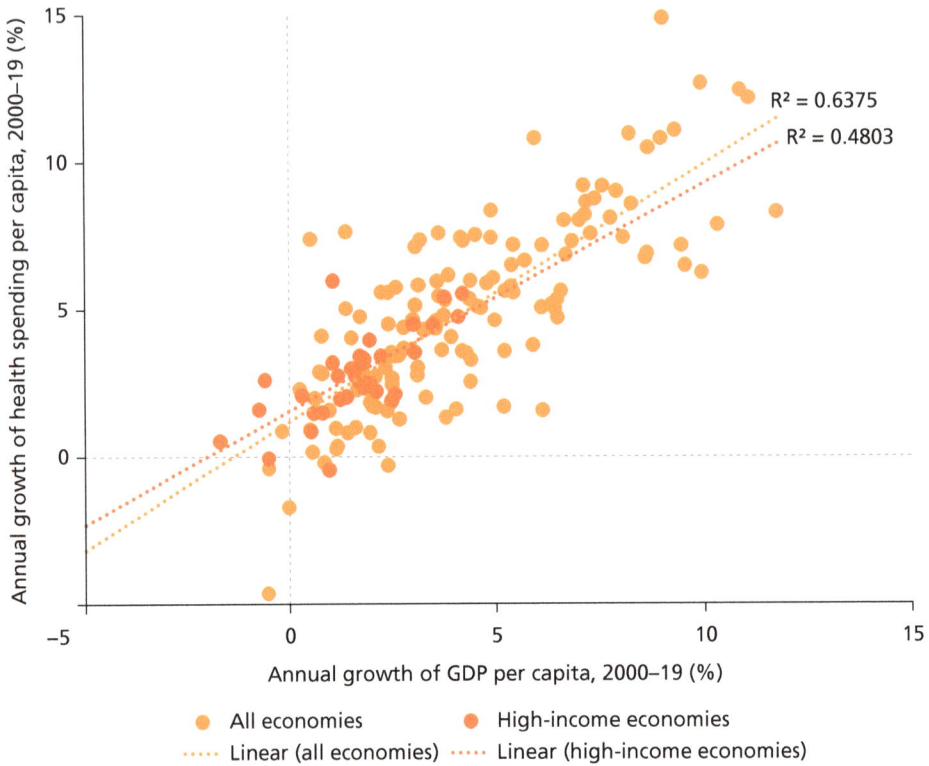

Sources: World Health Organization's Global Health Expenditure Database; World Bank data.

Note: "High-income economies" are as classified by the World Bank in 2000, with gross national income (GNI) per capita of US$9,265.

Improved life expectancy. Along with the income convergence across economies, increases in life expectancy are expected to increase health spending globally. In high-income economies, where a large part of the population is older than 65 (19 percent), health spending is higher (figure 1.4). Although the percentage of the population that is older than 65 is smaller in low- and middle-income countries (3 percent and 8 percent, respectively), it is expected to grow with the rise of life expectancy in almost every economy. Growing cohorts of seniors, who consume more health care goods and services than the young, will boost spending on health care globally (even beyond the effect of economic convergence alone).

In addition, technological innovation and policy reforms are expanding the supply of medical goods and services. These factors are particularly evident in services trade. The range of medical services tradable across borders has grown as advances in medical technology and information and communication technology

Figure 1.4   Across economies, population aging explains little of the growth in health spending per capita

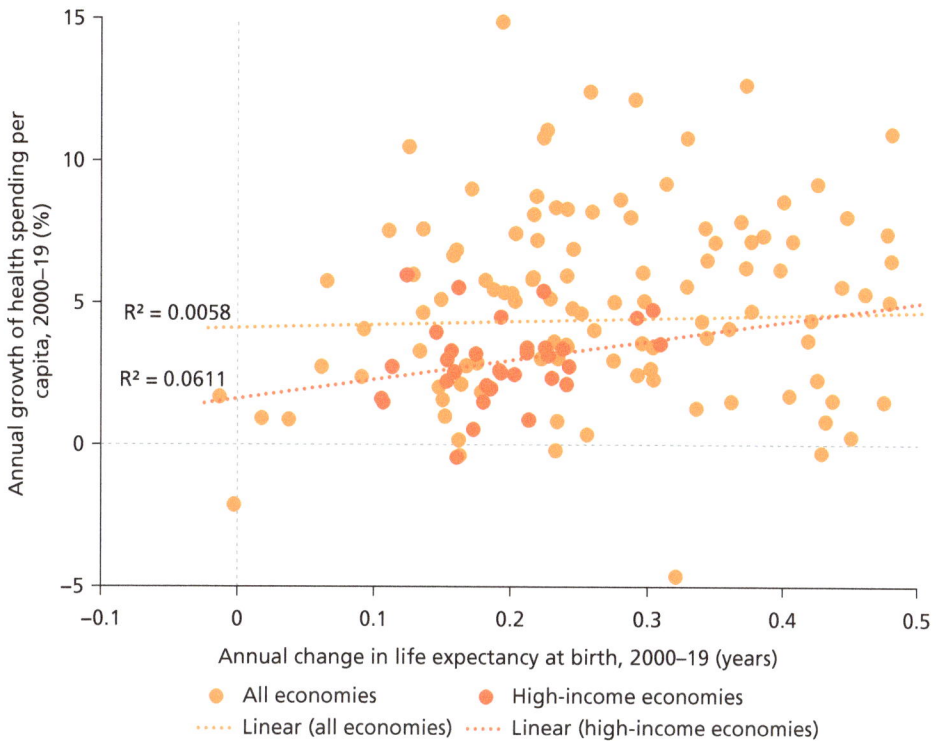

Sources: World Health Organization's Global Health Expenditure Database; United Nations World Population Prospects database (2019 revision).

Note: The relationship between change in life expectancy at birth and growth in health spending per capita is positive and statistically significant at 5 percent in high-income countries but not statistically different from zero in low- and middle-income economies. "High-income economies" are as classified by the World Bank in 2000, with gross national income (GNI) per capita of US$9,265.

(ICT) make it possible to outsource and fragment services into discrete tasks, such as consultations and diagnostics. The liberalization of related services, such as telecommunications and insurance, has also made it easier to deliver medical services across borders (box 1.1). As a result, health care providers and government policy makers are increasingly global in their outlook. In recent years, for example, health care hubs have been created, and regional trade and investment agreements increasingly cover medical services. Demographic differences across countries, coupled with the growing ease of travel, have created incentives for suppliers of health care services to tailor their offerings to individual markets and take advantage of price differentials through different modes of supply.

Box 1.1   Access to health care: The role of (trade in) health insurance services

Appropriately regulated (such as to ensure equity, protect consumers, and avoid cost escalation) and adapted to local needs and preferences, private health insurance—and potentially trade in health insurance services in that context—can play a positive role in improving access to health care in low- and middle-income countries.

Benefits of private health insurance

Two main benefits explain the potentially positive role of private health insurance: First, private health insurance may help households avoid large out-of-pocket spending on health services (the most common form of health financing in low- and middle-income countries). Second, when available to those who can afford it, private coverage allows the publicly financed health care system to focus on the most vulnerable groups (Sekhri and Savedoff 2005).

Although private health insurance is no panacea for universal health coverage (UHC), it may help to expand access to health care in various ways. Available research on UHC shows that, although the overall effect of private health insurance on UHC is ambiguous, compulsory private health insurance schemes are positively and significantly associated with specific health service coverage indicators (Wagstaff and Neelsen 2020).

Still, no two markets are the same, and depending on how national health care systems are organized, private health insurance may play a positive role. Private health insurance may be compulsory or voluntary. In the latter case, private insurance may play a *supplementary* role (allowing users to overcome the flaws of publicly financed systems, such as long waiting times); a *complementary* role (allowing users to fill the gaps in noncomprehensive publicly financed protection schemes); or a *substitutive* role (for users excluded from public schemes on grounds of age or income or who are allowed to choose between private and public coverage) (Thomson, Sagan, and Mossialos 2020).

Private health insurance plays an important role in health care financing in both high-income economies and low- and middle-income economies, and its role is not restricted to any particular region or level of development. Even in countries where UHC has been achieved, private health insurance (either voluntary or compulsory) continues to be significant. Figure B1.1.1 shows selected countries where private health insurance contributes at least 10 percent of current health expenditure.

Impact of regulation and policy on health insurance trade

Although trade in health insurance (in particular through commercial presence) is feasible in practice, restrictive regulation and policy, among other factors, may hinder uptake. As shown in figure B1.1.1, various low- and middle-income economies have a significant proportion of health care financed through insurance spending. Together with inadequate demand due to a population's risk aversion or misperception and the potentially high administrative costs involved (which may be higher than the risk premium that users are willing to pay), supply restrictions motivated by regulation may explain the small size of health insurance markets in many economies (Pauly et al. 2006).

Services trade policy may help widen the health insurance market and thus contribute—among many other factors—to expanding health insurance coverage. Adequately regulated (to ensure equity, protect consumers, and avoid cost escalation), foreign health insurance suppliers

(Continued)

Box 1.1   Access to health care: The role of (trade in) health insurance services (*Continued*)

may contribute to the uptake of private health insurance by bringing capital, technology, and know-how.

In that regard, India is a case in point. During 2020–21, general and health insurance companies have covered 514.7 million individuals under 23.7 million health insurance policies (66.6 percent of the individuals under government-sponsored health insurance schemes, 23.1 percent under group policies, and the remaining 10.3 percent under individual policies issued by general and health insurers). Out of the 21 private sector insurers and 7 stand-alone health insurers established in India, foreign investors participate in 16, with foreign equity participation ranging between 23 percent and 49 percent.[a]

Figure B1.1.1   Private health insurance schemes (sum of compulsory and voluntary) as a share of total health expenditure in selected countries, 2019

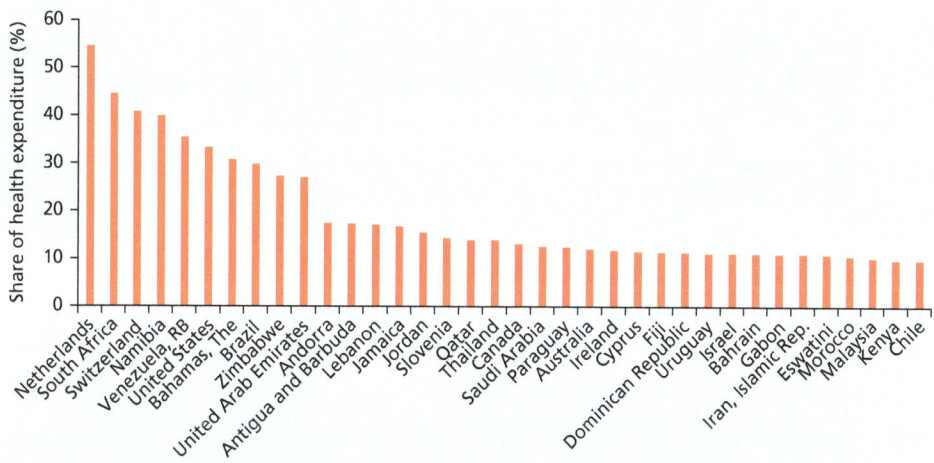

Source: World Health Organization (WHO) Global Health Expenditure Database.

Note: As quantified in the WHO Global Health Expenditure Database (GHED), health care spending is primarily financed through the following schemes: (a) government schemes and compulsory contributory health care financing schemes (including compulsory private insurance schemes [CPIS]); (b) voluntary health care payment schemes (including voluntary health insurance schemes [VHIS]); and (c) household out-of-pocket payments. The chart shows the sum of CPIS and VHIS as a percentage of total health care spending. (For more about the GHED methodology, see WHO 2021b.)

a. Forty-nine percent was the maximum allowable level of foreign equity until May 19, 2021, when the foreign investment limit in the insurance sector, to also benefit health insurers, was raised to 74 percent by the Insurance Amendment Act, 2021 (IRDAI 2021).

Mode-specific drivers of trade in medical services

As defined by GATS, international trade in medical services can take place through four modes of supply (summarized earlier in table 1.2): cross-border supply, consumption abroad, commercial presence, and the movement of individuals across borders.

Mode 1: Cross-border supply. Advancements in ICT have created greater possibilities for cross-border telehealth (particularly practitioner-to-practitioner services), health management, and the transfer and use of health data across countries. Telehealth is rapidly gaining acceptance—from regulators, health practitioners, and patients—and governments are increasingly focusing on national telehealth programs to expand health care capacity and fill shortages in certain specialized services. Social distancing measures during the COVID-19 pandemic have accelerated these trends.

However, the supply of telehealth services depends on sometimes uncertain internet connectivity and telecommunications quality. The lack of sound legal frameworks for telehealth, digital trade, and data protection may also constrain prospects for cross-border telehealth. For example, regulators must ensure that foreign service suppliers have the necessary qualifications and are insured against malpractice.

Mode 2: Consumption abroad. Consumption of medical services abroad is driven by greater demand, which is induced by potential increased insurance portability as well as the lower costs of treatment and the availability of specialized, high-quality health care services in destination countries. Patients may be driven abroad by shortcomings in their home markets, such as long waiting periods, lack of certain services, or the stigma attached to treatments such as assisted reproductive technologies and surrogacy. The greater affordability of international travel before COVID-19 was yet another factor. International accreditation of hospitals has also spurred growth of medical travel, and many countries (for example, Costa Rica, Jordan, Spain, and Thailand) are actively promoting themselves as medical travel hubs in specific segments. Geographic, linguistic, and cultural proximity and diaspora networks influence the pattern of this trade between certain countries (Helble 2011).

There are also constraints on the consumption abroad of medical services. These include the lack of compliance with conditions imposed by health insurers (such as supplier accreditation requirements or recognition of qualifications), cross-border liability insurance, particularly burdensome visa requirements, and limitations on cross-border payments.

Mode 3: Commercial presence. Trade in medical services based on commercial presence is driven by the willingness of health authorities to attract private foreign investment to complement or supplement public health services, combined with private investors' interest in investing in a country's health sector. There is also growing interest in investing in enterprises that develop applications and technology-based health solutions and delivery, including telehealth.

Establishing a commercial presence can be constrained by a lack of supporting physical and other infrastructure and the absence of an enabling environment. High costs of procuring medical equipment and technologies can also act as impediments. Finally, there may be concerns about creating a "brain drain" to locally established foreign facilities.

Mode 4: Presence of natural persons. Countries are seeking to attract health workers from abroad to fill domestic shortages. This form of trade is chiefly influenced by regulations concerning entry and presence as well as the qualification and recognition requirements in receiving countries. Although the number of individuals supplying medical services through temporary presence (as defined by GATS) represents a small proportion of health workers crossing borders (the latter generally seeking opportunities for employment or to establish themselves more permanently in a foreign jurisdiction),[5] the movement may be driven by pull and push factors that drive labor migration more generally.

Countries may impose limitations on the movement of health workers to other markets out of concern over the loss of human capital. Increasingly, global mobility of health care workers and related trade in medical services is affected by the importing country's adherence to international governance mechanisms, such as ethical recruitment codes and intergovernmental agreements including the Commonwealth Code of Practice (Commonwealth 2003) and WHO's Global Code of Practice on the International Recruitment of Health Personnel (WHO 2010), the latter being further discussed in box 1.2. These were established to prevent a brain drain from low- and middle-income countries and ensure adherence to certain principles and norms.

Box 1.2   WHO's Global Code of Practice on the International Recruitment of Health Personnel—and the blurred boundaries between trade in medical services and migration of health workers

Provision of health services by foreign-born or foreign-trained health workers has been characterized for decades by a recognition of the tension between (a) the right of health workers to pursue professional development opportunities and better working conditions abroad, and (b) the negative consequences that a substantial outflow of health workers from some countries could have on already stretched health systems (WHO 2006).

The long-standing difficulties facing many high-income countries in producing enough health workers to meet domestic needs, the large wage differential across countries of varying socioeconomic development, and the chronic underinvestment by countries at all development levels in education and jobs for the health workforce (WHO 2016) have conspired to determine a substantial level of dependence in many countries (particularly in high-income countries) on foreign-born and foreign-trained health workers (WHO 2020) along with a growing trend in international mobility of health personnel, which had risen by 60 percent in the decade preceding 2016 (Dumont and Lafortune 2017).

To facilitate collaboration and an ethical management of health personnel mobility, the World Health Organization in 2010 adopted a Global Code of Practice on the International Recruitment of Health Personnel (the "WHO Code"), whose provisions encompass (a) upholding the rights of internationally mobile health workers; (b) supporting countries' efforts to meet health system needs through production and employment of domestically trained health workers; and

(Continued)

Box 1.2   WHO's Global Code of Practice on the International Recruitment of Health Personnel—and the blurred boundaries between trade in medical services and migration of health workers (*Continued*)

(c) promoting data sharing and collaboration to ensure that mobility of health personnel translates into benefits for health workers and the health systems of countries involved (WHO 2010).

When countries decide to cover mobility of health personnel as part of trade agreements, sometimes the objectives are broad in scope (with health services being only one of several components and sectors) and limited in time (with provisions for health workers to return to the country of origin after completing their assignments or training periods). However, health workers may often have the opportunity to stay beyond the terms of the agreements, which can enhance concerns about exacerbating health workforce challenges in countries of origin. What may start as a short-term element in a broader trade conversation can, in the specific case of health workers, become part of a longer-term migration trend and no longer fall under trade in services.

In the context of trade relations and agreements between countries, the specific (intended and unintended) consequences on mobility of health personnel should be considered while striving to apply, as relevant, the provisions of the WHO Code. Among others, these provisions include the Ministry of Health's meaningful participation—together with other relevant authorities (such as trade, labor, and education)—in agreements involving health services, ensuring that benefits also accrue to the health sector and upholding the rights of health workers involved. In this context, services trade agreements and the WHO Code could be mutually reinforcing. For example, the application of health labor market analyses, in both sending and receiving economies, could further clarify the economic or labor market opportunities and further liberalize trade in services by better targeting demonstrated needs (Carzaniga et al. 2019).

The Indonesia-Japan Economic Partnership Agreement is an example of an agreement where the parties negotiated specific commitments and requirements related to temporary migration of Indonesian nurses and caregivers (Efendi et al. 2017). This was achieved through the participation of key Indonesian government institutions under the leadership of the Ministry of Trade, Ministry of Manpower and Transmigration, National Board for the Placement and Protection of Indonesian Overseas Workers, Ministry of Health, Ministry of Foreign Affairs, and Ministry of National Education. The agreement includes a technical assistance program and financial support through a multiyear Japan International Cooperation Agency (JICA) project designed to enhance nursing competency through in-person training.

The different modes of trade in medical services are interlinked and may be used in combination as complements or act as substitutes. These links can enhance medical services trade by facilitating sequential associations and complementing simultaneous ones (Chanda 2006). For example, there may be joint-venture-based foreign direct investment (FDI) in hospitals employing overseas personnel, which in turn helps attract foreign patients for specialized treatments and may result in supporting teleconsultation and telediagnosis services before and after treatment. On the other hand, restrictions on one mode of trade in services may lead to substitution through other modes. Factors such as technology, consumer preferences, the regulatory environment, infrastructure, human resources—all of which drive trade in medical services—also influence the links between modes of trade in health care services.

FUNCTIONING OF MEDICAL SUPPLY CHAINS

The health care global value chain and the role of multinational corporations

In the health care global value chain (GVC), resources, organizations, and institutions act together, primarily to improve, maintain, or restore patients' health (WHO 2012). It comprises both medical goods and services (figure 1.5). The medical goods segments mainly include pharmaceuticals, medical technology, and devices. Services are primarily provided by hospitals, clinics, health professionals, diagnostic laboratories, nursing homes, and integrated delivery networks. Health insurance, logistics, and distribution services also play important roles in the value chain.

The health care value chain features complex interactions among a diverse set of stakeholders. Each stakeholder—be it a health care establishment or a medical device

Figure 1.5   The health care global value chain

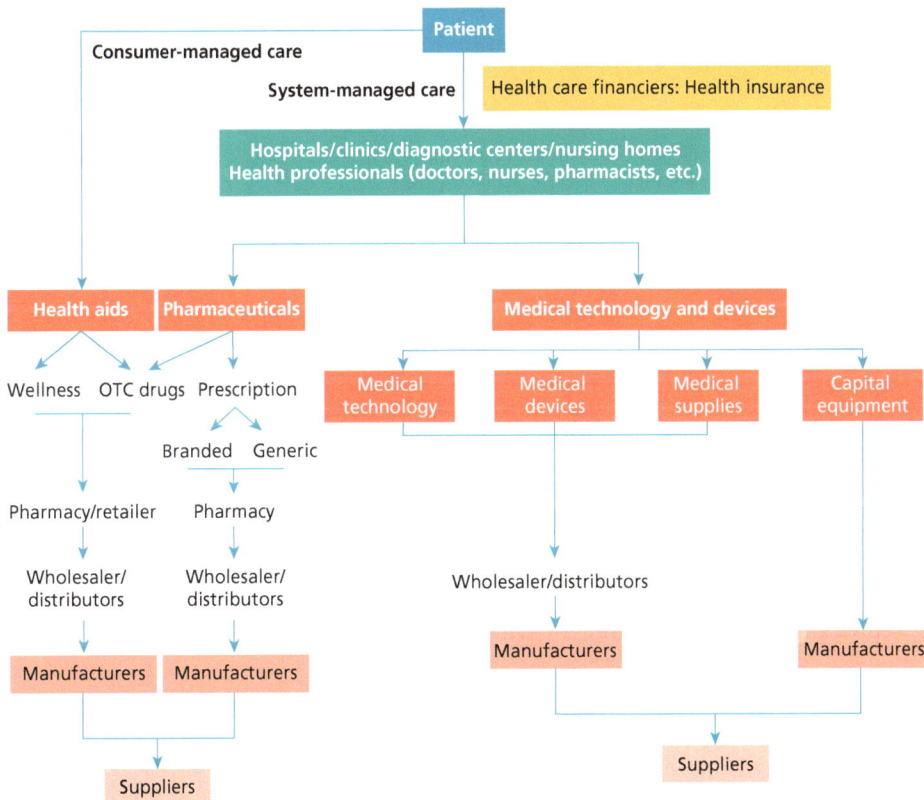

Sources: Adaptation based on OECD 2020 and Singh 2006. ©MIT Center for Transportation and Logistics. Further permission required for reuse. Republished with permission from MIT Center for Transportation & Logistics. Further permission required for reuse.

Note: OTC = over-the-counter.

company—has different concerns and is driven by often divergent objectives and prob-lems. The complexity and opacity of health care delivery is another critical factor. Uniquely to the health care industry, the consumer, or patient, has a limited say in the choice of a product or service. Instead, the multiplicity of regulations, the number of parties involved, and the high expertise required all mean that decision-making is widely dispersed. In addi-tion, products and services in the health care value chain are highly customized to perfectly match needs, making it almost impossible to plan their efficient supply on a large scale.

The supply of health care often starts with hospitals and clinics, where private sec-tor participation (measured as the share of private hospitals) varies considerably across countries—ranging from close to zero in Nordic countries to over 80 percent in Japan, the Netherlands, and the United States (OECD 2020). This variation is not linked to income level or stage of development: lower-middle-income countries like the Lao People's Democratic Republic, Myanmar, and Vietnam closely follow the Nordic coun-tries with less than 15 percent private sector participation, whereas Cambodia, India, and Indonesia fall at the other end of the spectrum with Japan and the United States. It is also important to note that medical services are often subject to stringent regulation and limited foreign capital participation.

The manufacturing and distribution of goods and technology is dominated by private firms, especially multinational corporations (MNCs), as discussed in box 1.3. Both the pharmaceutical and medical device segments are highly capital and innova-tion intensive and face a highly regulated environment requiring extensive data collec-tion and information exchange. Products often have high profit margins and are sold

---

Box 1.3   Recent FDI trends in medical goods and services

The health sector's share of global greenfield foreign direct investment (FDI) flows has been growing but remains small. Greenfield FDI in the sector has been volatile, fluctuating between US$10 billion and US$25 billion between 2003 and 2020 (figure B1.3.1). But its share in the total increased from 1.9 percent to 3.2 percent. Within the sector, the composition of greenfield FDI value has shifted from pharmaceuticals—by far the largest segment in 2003, with a 71 percent share—to biotechnology, whose share rose to 43 percent by 2020 (figure B1.3.1).

Almost all the greenfield FDI in the sector originates from high-income countries (mainly Germany, Switzerland, and the United States) and flows primarily to high-income countries as well (figure B1.3.2). Upper-middle-income countries also received a significant share while increasing their outward investments in high-income countries.

Typically for an innovation-driven industry, greenfield FDI in medical goods focuses on research and developmen (R&D). From 2003 through 2020, 20–30 percent of greenfield FDI in bio-technology, pharmaceuticals, and medical devices was invested in R&D activities (figure B1.3.3). The R&D intensity of greenfield FDI was about 10 times the level in the rest of the economy, which was 2.9 percent. Top multinational corporations in pharmaceuticals and medical devices usually spend 10–30 percent of their annual sales on R&D. Manufacturing remains the primary activity in medical goods, absorbing 60 percent of greenfield FDI.[a]

(Continued)

Box 1.3   Recent FDI trends in medical goods and services (*Continued*)

Figure B1.3.1   Greenfield FDI in the health sector, by segment, 2003–20

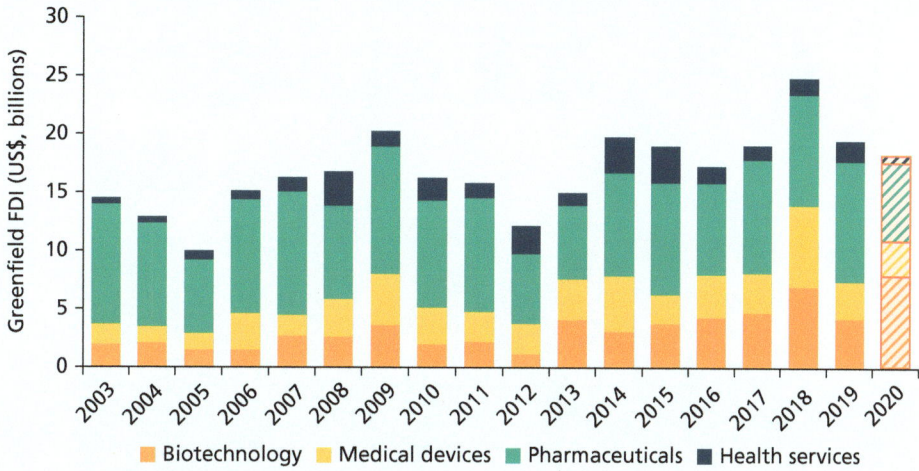

Source: Calculations based on fDi Markets database.

Note: FDI = foreign direct investment.

Figure B1.3.2   Greenfield FDI in the health sector, by income level of source and destination countries, 2003–20

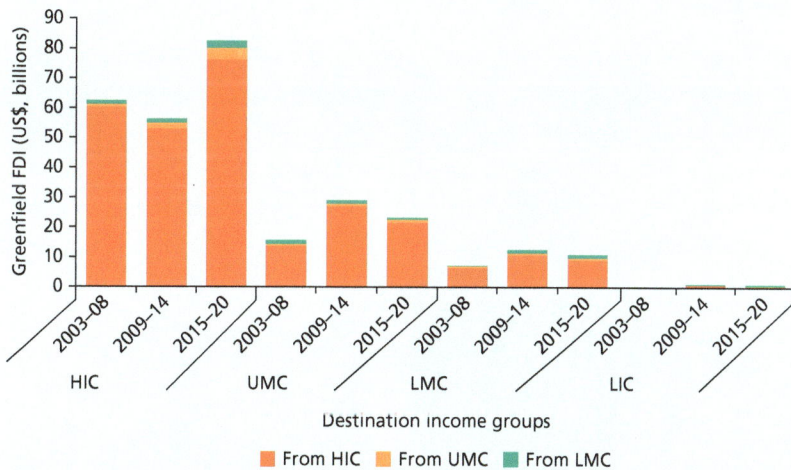

Source: Calculations based on fDi Markets database.

Note: FDI = foreign direct investment; HIC = high-income country; LIC = low-income country; LMC = lower-middle-income country; UMC = upper-middle-income country.

(Continued)

Box 1.3   Recent FDI trends in medical goods and services (*Continued*)

Figure B1.3.3   Composition of greenfield FDI in the health sector, by segment and business activity, 2003–20

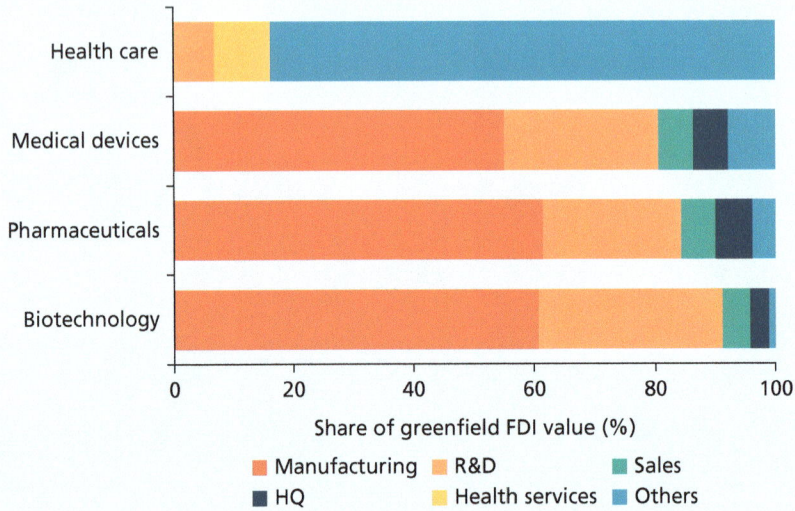

Source: World Bank calculations based on fDi Markets database.

Note: The figure reflects estimated values of announced greenfield foreign direct investment (FDI) projects from 2003 through 2020. HQ = headquarters; R&D = research and development.

Figure B1.3.4   Share of cross-border M&A projects in the health sector, by segment, 2015–20

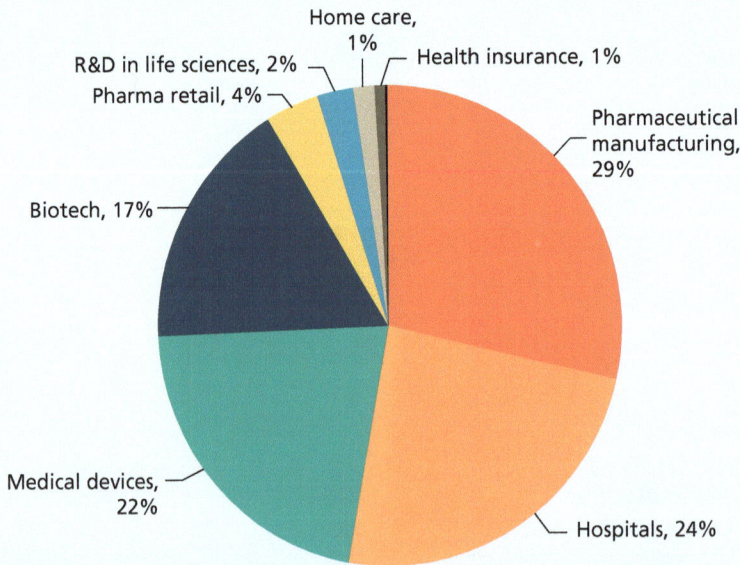

Source: World Bank calculations based on Refinitiv mergers and acquisitions (M&A) data.

Note: R&D = research and development.

(Continued)

| **Box 1.3** | **Recent FDI trends in medical goods and services (*Continued*)** |

Cross-border mergers and acquisitions (M&As) in the health sector are even more concentrated in high-income countries than greenfield FDI. Unlike greenfield FDI, nearly a quarter of cross-border M&A projects in the health sector target medical services. The number of cross-border M&A deals in the health sector hovered around 1,000 between 2015 and 2020.[b] Out of 5,300 total transactions, 4,000 involved companies headquartered in high-income countries acquiring each other. This is not surprising, since high-income countries have far more health care companies worth acquiring than low- and middle-income countries do. Most M&As are distributed among four segments: pharmaceuticals manufacturing (29 percent); hospitals and clinics (24 percent); medical device manufacturing (22 percent); and biotechnology (17 percent) (figure B1.3.4).

a. Data on greenfield FDI expenditures and R&D intensity are from World Bank calculations based on fDi Markets database.

b. Data on M&A transactions in the health sector are from World Bank calculations based on Refinitiv M&A data.

to professionals and institutional buyers. Lead firms try to entrench their positions by spending huge amounts on R&D and patenting, erecting high barriers to entry.

Leading pharmaceutical firms from a few high-income countries dominate brand-name drugs and new drug introductions, but MNCs from middle-income countries are increasingly competitive in the generic-drug market. Many major global pharmaceutical companies were founded more than a century ago in a few high-income economies. Whereas new introductions require massive capital investments, huge R&D efforts, a lengthy development process, and are highly unpredictable, mid-life-cycle products tend to have standard production processes, lower profit margins, and stable demand. Lead MNCs increasingly outsource production of these medicines to reduce costs, resulting in new opportunities for players from middle-income countries. For example, India has become a major provider of generic drugs globally; it was the third largest producer of pharmaceuticals by volume in 2019 and fulfilled approximately 50 percent of the global demand for vaccines (SRI 2021). Many pharmaceutical companies and contract manufacturers in Association of Southeast Asian Nations (ASEAN) countries have also internationalized and became MNCs themselves (ASEAN and UNCTAD 2019).

The medical technology and devices segment has even higher market concentration and stickier buyer-seller relationships than pharmaceuticals. Products are developed over a long period, allowing companies to benefit from time and technology accumulation. The life cycle of the product is also relatively long, and lead firms often establish long-term relationships with customers to offer training, maintenance, and aftercare services. Hospitals, doctors, and equipment manufacturers usually form a cooperative relationship. The device's stability and reliability are extremely important, and buyers are therefore less sensitive to prices. Once customers start to use a company's product, the switching cost is high, and the device cannot be easily replaced. Feedback from doctors and patients in turn enables manufacturers to improve the performance of their devices. These characteristics make the entry barrier extremely high in the medical device segment, so latecomers have trouble competing with established firms.

MNCs play a dominant role in health GVCs, though it varies significantly by segment. Globally, MNCs and their affiliates contributed 36 percent of output in 2016 (Qiang, Liu, and Steenbergen 2021), including about two-thirds of exports and more than half of imports. However, their share of medical goods and services varies hugely. In chemicals and pharmaceuticals, MNCs accounted for 87 percent of global value added and 83 percent of exports in 2016 (figure 1.6). MNCs account for such a large share in global value added because of highly localized regulations, prompting them to set up affiliates to produce for the domestic market. MNCs play a similarly outsize role in medical devices; the 10 biggest medical device MNCs accounted for approximately 40 percent of global sales in 2018 (Vara 2019).

In contrast, MNCs represented just 4 percent of global value added in health and social services—among the lowest MNC contribution in all industries. Heavy regulations on entry and the dominance of the public sector explain the limited role of MNCs in medical services.

Figure 1.6   MNCs' contribution to global value added and exports varies by industry

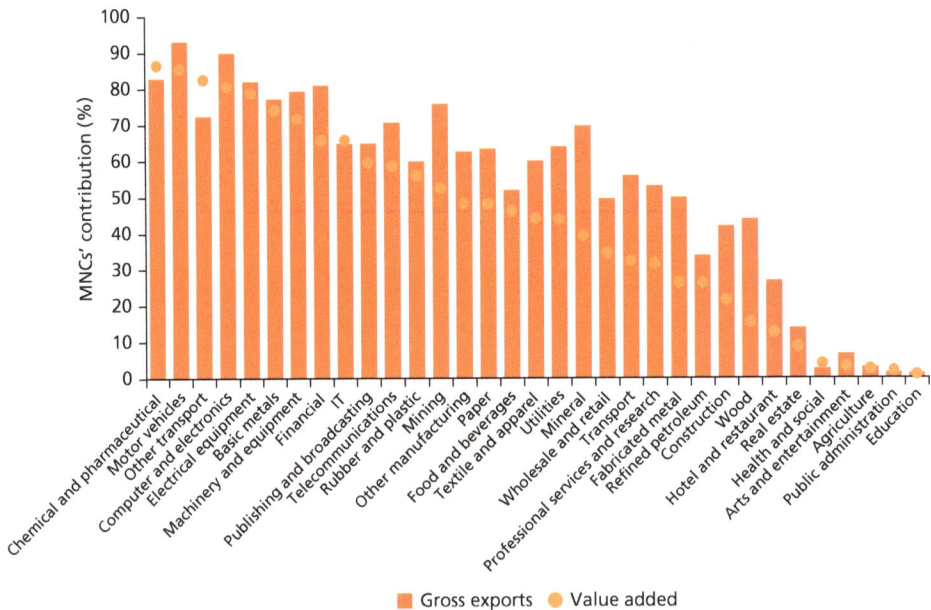

Source: Calculations based on the Organisation for Economic Co-operation and Development (OECD) Activity of Multinational Enterprises (AMNE) database (https://www.oecd.org/sti/ind/amne.htm).

Note: Data are from 2016. IT = information technology; MNCs = multinational corporations.

Services trade support of medical goods GVCs

Trade in services is fundamental for the existence and proper functioning of medical goods GVCs. Services enter at every stage of production, connecting participants in the chain and ensuring the transition between different production stages. The very existence of medical goods GVCs depends crucially on such services as R&D, product engineering, software development, sterilization, packaging, warehousing, transport, telecommunications (including the internet), financial services (including financing, payments, and insurance), distribution, and postsales services (such as training, consulting, maintenance, and repair).

Although all these services may be supplied purely domestically, trade is usually involved, and they are provided either on a cross-border basis (as in international transportation and payments), through the presence of foreign suppliers (as in insurance), or even through the movement of professionals (as in engineering, marketing, and contract negotiations).

Trade in logistics services. Logistics services, including trade in logistics services, play a critical role in the health care sector and are dominated by a limited number of actors. Logistics is not only part of the medical goods GVCs but is also at the core of the supply-chain management of health care institutions. The manufacturing of medical products tends to be geographically concentrated at the global level, but the goods are needed in and distributed to all countries. In addition, the concentrated mass manufacturing of medical goods depends on highly interdependent GVCs because inputs are usually sourced from numerous countries. As a result, the international supply of logistics services becomes essential not only for medical GVCs but also for medical services themselves. Medical devices and pharmaceuticals (including inputs) are associated with highly specific logistical needs, from packaging and transport to handling, storage, and final distribution, especially for temperature-sensitive products.

At the same time, logistics services are significantly affected by regulations related to the storage and distribution of medical products. Stringent regulatory requirements also imply high thresholds for market entry. In the global health logistics market, usually only integrated logistics operators are able to meet the rigorous regulatory requirements, which explains the market's high level of concentration.[6]

Trade in air transport services. Air transport is key to the international supply of medical goods, particularly those that are time-dependent. Trade in air transport services, comprising all international transport and domestic transport supplied by foreign-owned operators, is a crucial part of the logistics chain for medical goods. Air has significant advantages over other means of transport—offering the fastest routes, the possibility of serving geographically scattered airports, the ability to handle oversize cargo, and comprehensive cargo maintenance at airports. However, air transport is significantly more expensive than other means of transport.

Still, in instances when time trumps cost (such as with perishable and time-sensitive biologics, radioactive medications, or clinical trials), the speed of air freight merits

its higher price. For example, air transport has been the mode of choice during the COVID-19 pandemic for trade in medical goods in short supply and urgent need, such as PPE, ventilators, and vaccines. However, in the years before the pandemic, many drug companies switched to ocean shipping for less-time-dependent medical products, owing mostly to the relatively high cost of air freight, the development of temperature-controlled shipping containers, and the use of better monitoring and tracking equipment.

Trade in distribution services. Distribution services (wholesale and retail trade services) also play an essential role in the international supply of medical goods. In most jurisdictions, the distribution of medical goods is highly regulated, with the sale of various products (especially medical drugs) having to be conducted through specialized establishments such as pharmacies. These regulations have "health policy and safety" motivations but also have an impact on the efficiency of distribution and on cost.

Trade in insurance services. Insurance services help ensure the smooth functioning of medical GVCs. Supply-chain disruptions, which can bring production of goods and delivery of services to a halt, are among the most significant risks for businesses.[7] In such circumstances, companies participating in GVCs may incur significant financial losses if they are not adequately insured.

Supply-chain disruptions may arise from incidents affecting the policyholder (that is, the GVC's lead company) or its suppliers and may involve damage to machinery and other property (Swiss Re Institute 2020). Business interruption—whether resulting from regulatory actions (such as withdrawal of regulatory approval or license suspension) or from a company's own decision to suspend operations because of violations of good manufacturing practice (GMP) standards—may be particularly harmful for medical goods industries. Over recent years, the global insurance industry has developed specific nondamage business-interruption policies to insure medical goods companies against these risks (Swiss Re Institute 2020). Trade in insurance services through various modes often plays an important role in the supply of these policies.

PATTERNS IN MEDICAL GOODS AND SERVICES TRADE BEFORE THE PANDEMIC

Trade patterns in medical goods

Trade in medical goods grew faster than overall goods trade from 2010 to 2019, steadily increasing its share and showing more resilience. During the decade preceding the COVID-19 pandemic, trade in medical goods grew at an annual average rate of 4.7 percent, compared with 2.8 percent for overall merchandise trade, and its share of trade grew from 4.9 percent to 6.0 percent, reaching US$1.3 trillion (figure 1.7).

As discussed earlier in the section on medical supply chains, several factors contribute to this performance, including global income convergence, aging populations, technological innovation, and policy reforms. Trade in medical goods was more resilient than trade overall, reflecting the stability of demand for essential medical goods.

Figure 1.7 Global trade of medical goods has consistently increased

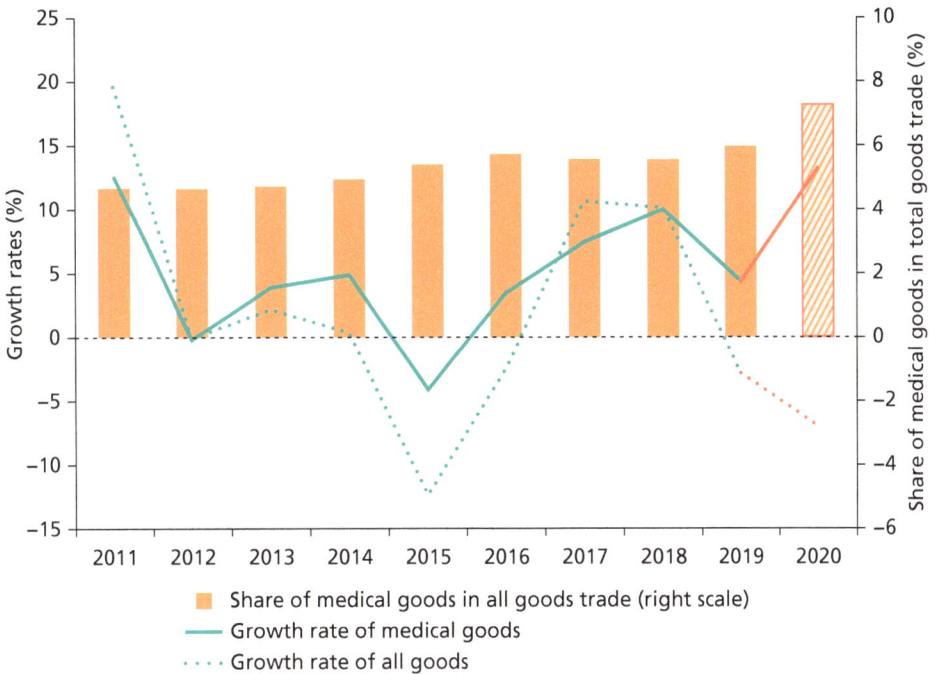

Sources: World Trade Organization Integrated Database; United Nations COMTRADE data.

Note: Teal lines and orange bars designate years preceding the COVID-19 pandemic, and the orange line and orange bar with lines, the first year of the pandemic (2020).

Patterns by product group. Pharmaceuticals dominate trade in medical goods. The share of pharmaceutical products exceeds the combined shares of the other four groups of medical goods—medical, orthopedic, PPE, and other equipment (figure 1.8). Pharmaceutical products consist of regular, recurrent, and consumable items (such as vitamins, drugs, and medicines), whereas the other categories, specifically medical and orthopedic equipment, include mostly durable goods (goods that are purchased infrequently). The share of pharmaceuticals among the product groups remained constant over the last 10 years.

Patterns by income group and region. Medical goods trade remains concentrated in high-income economies, but lower-income economies have steadily increased their share. From 2010 to 2019, an annual average of 11.4 percent of world medical goods exports came from upper-middle-income economies (figure 1.9, panel a), which increased their share from 9.9 percent in 2010 to 11.9 percent in 2019.[8] The low- and lower-middle-income groups barely participate in medical goods exports, representing an annual average over 2010-19 of 3.0 percent. However, lower-middle-income economies increased their share from 2.2 percent to 3.2 percent.

Figure 1.8   Pharmaceuticals dominate the medical goods sector, and the various product groups' shares in total medical goods trade have remained fairly constant

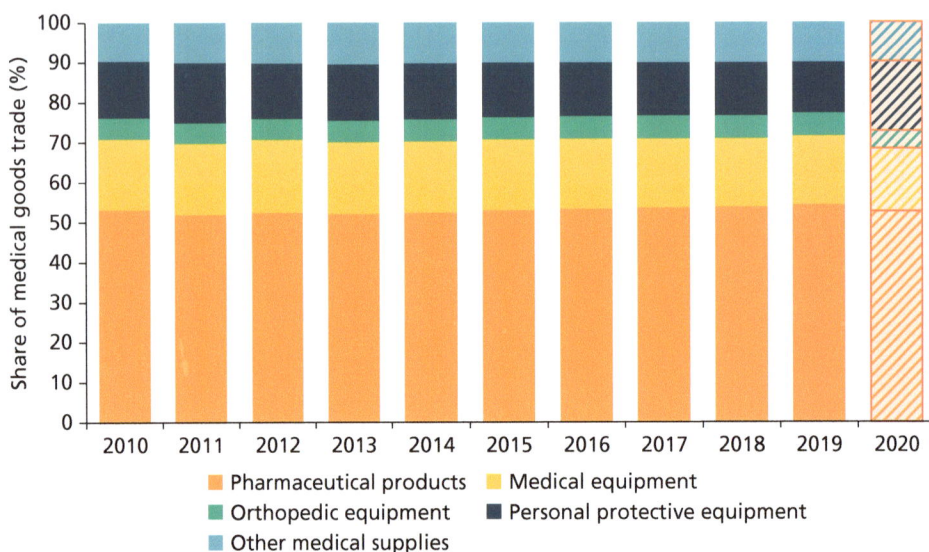

Sources: World Trade Organization Integrated Database; United Nations COMTRADE data.

Note: The bar for 2020 represents data during the first year of the COVID-19 pandemic.

Figure 1.9   Medical goods trade is highly concentrated in high-income economies

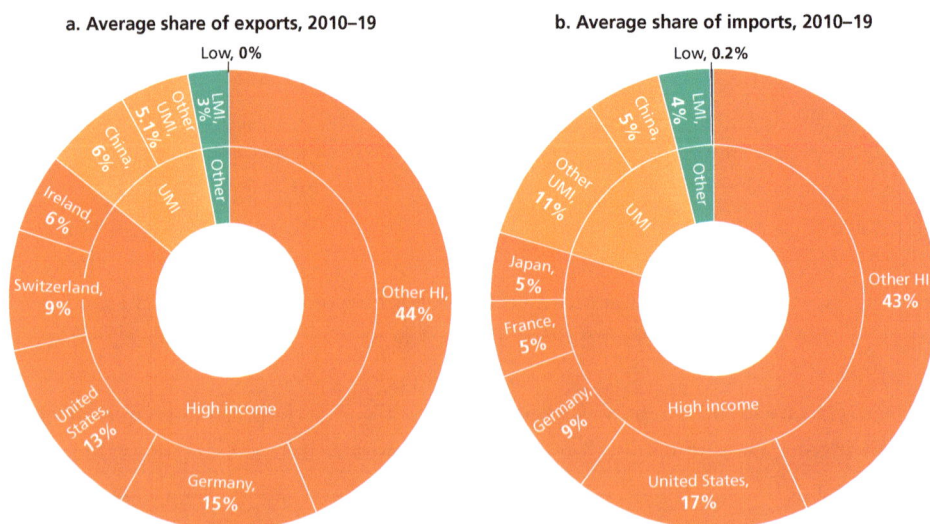

a. Average share of exports, 2010–19

b. Average share of imports, 2010–19

Sources: World Trade Organization Integrated Database; United Nations COMTRADE data.

Note: HI = high-income; LMI = lower-middle-income; UMI = upper-middle-income.

In the same period, the share of the high-income group in medical goods exports averaged 85.6 percent, falling from 87.8 percent in 2010 to 84.9 percent in 2019. Germany and the United States are the two leading exporters of medical goods. China is the largest exporter among non-high-income economies, with an average annual share of 6.3 percent from 2010 to 2019. In 2019, the European Union (EU), Switzerland, and the United Kingdom together accounted for approximately 60 percent of medical goods exports; China, India, Japan, and Singapore for 13.4 percent; and the United States for 12.6 percent.

Most of the main exporters of medical goods are also among the largest importers. However, middle-income economies averaged a higher share of imports than exports, and their share of imports grew steadily, reaching 20.9 percent in 2019. The share of imports for upper-middle-income economies averaged 16.3 percent (figure 1.9, panel b), increasing from 14.9 percent to 16.6 percent during the decade.

In the PPE category—the least technology-intensive product group—Asia accounts for 61 percent of exports. Malaysia has long dominated exports of rubber gloves, providing more than half of world supply. Eight Asian economies—China; Hong Kong SAR, China; Japan; Korea; Malaysia; Thailand; Vietnam; and the Separate Customs Territory Chinese Taipei[9]—are among the top 15 world suppliers of PPE and had a combined 58 percent share in 2020, an increase of 16 percentage points from the previous year. Other Asian economies accounted for an additional 3 percent, giving the continent a dominant share of 61 percent in 2020 (figure 1.10).

Figure 1.10   PPE trade increasingly originates in Asia

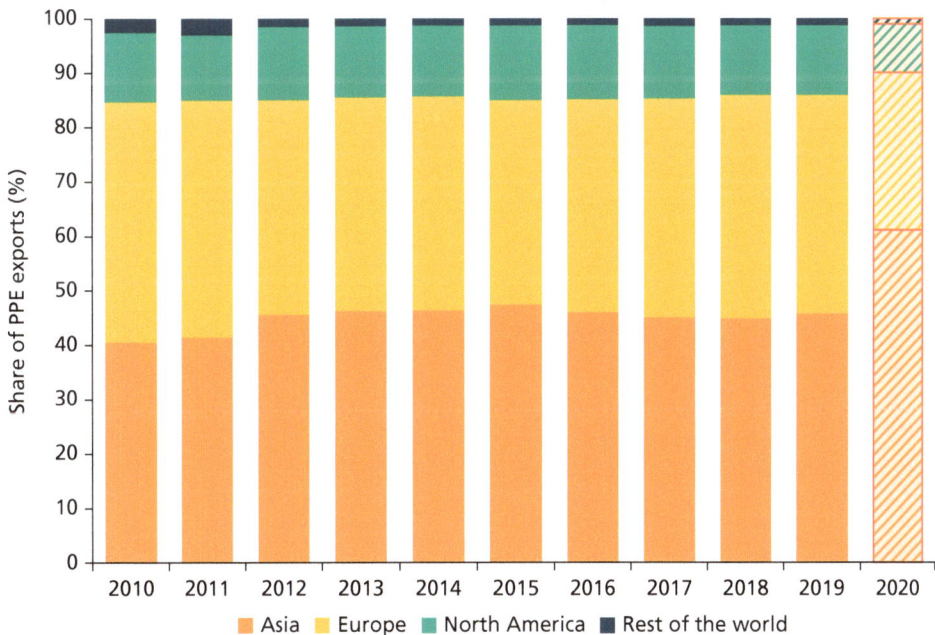

Sources: World Trade Organization (WTO) Integrated Database; United Nations COMTRADE data.

Note: "North America" follows the WTO definition, comprising Bermuda, Canada, Mexico, and the United States. PPE = personal protective equipment.

Trade patterns in medical services

Trade in medical services, from hospital to nursing services, has risen rapidly since 2010.[10] Trade through all four modes of supply was estimated at US$78.6 billion in 2019 (figure 1.11)—accounting for some 0.5 percent of global trade in services, up from 0.4 percent in 2010. It grew at an annual average of 7 percent since 2010, compared with 4 percent growth for other services, reflecting income convergence, demographic trends, and technological innovation (as discussed in the earlier section on drivers affecting trade in medical goods and services).

There is a positive relationship between income levels and participation in medical services trade. Low- and lower-middle-income economies together accounted for 1.2 percent of global exports of medical services in 2019, upper-middle-income economies for 14.0 percent, and high-income economies for 84.8 percent (figure 1.12).

Since 2010, medical services have been traded mainly by establishing a commercial presence in another country (GATS mode 3), but cross-border trade (mode 1) such as telehealth is gaining importance. In 2019, 74.4 percent of medical services were traded through affiliated hospitals and medical centers in other countries, and 16 percent were supplied to foreign patients during a stay abroad (mode 2).[11]

Increasingly, however, medical services may be supplied remotely as digitalization, fifth-generation (5G) technology, and robotics making distant diagnostics and

Figure 1.11   Trade in medical services hit US$78.6 billion in 2019

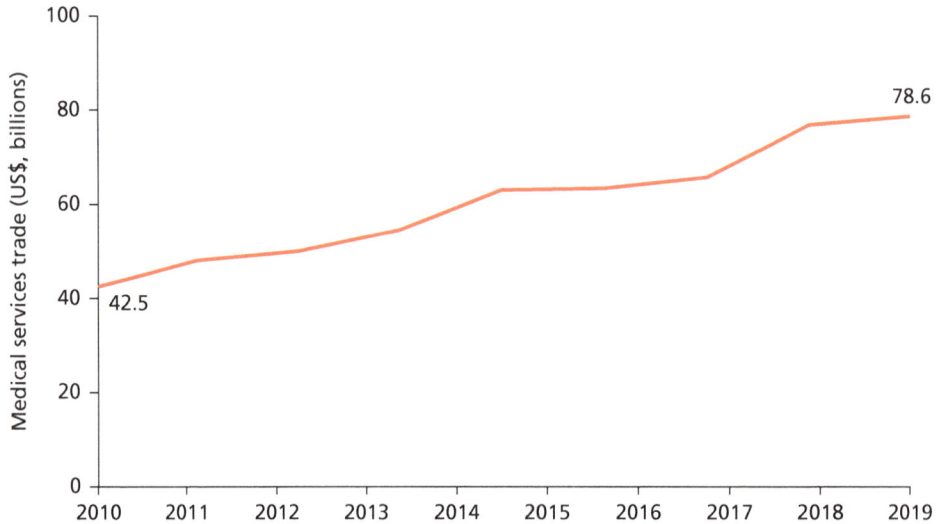

Source: World Trade Organization (WTO) estimates based on the WTO Trade in Services Data by Mode of Supply (TISMOS) dataset.

Note: Annual figures are the average of exports and imports. The data cover services delivered through all four modes of supply defined by the WTO's General Agreement on Trade in Services (GATS): (1) cross-border supply, (2) consumption abroad, (3) commercial presence, and (4) presence of natural persons.

Figure 1.12 High-income economies account for the bulk of trade in medical services

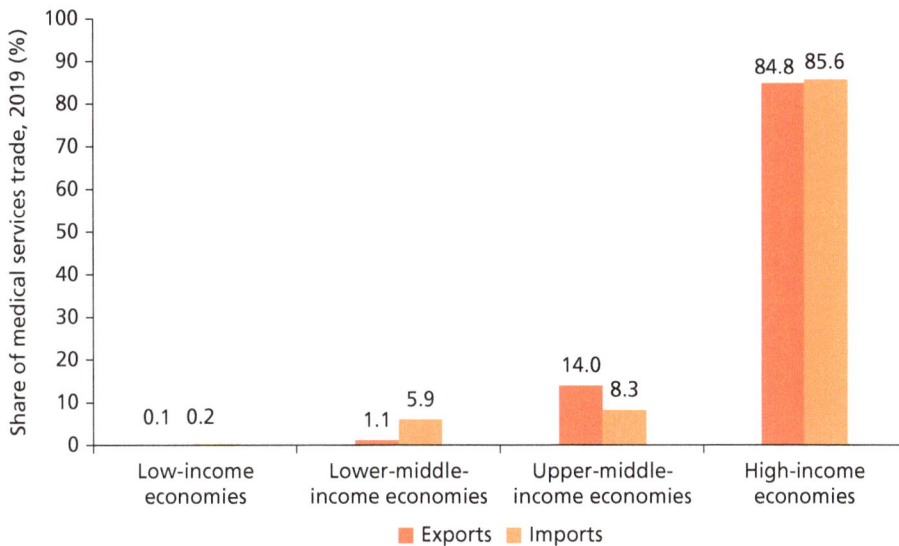

Source: World Trade Organization (WTO) estimates based on the WTO Trade in Services Data by Mode of Supply (TISMOS) dataset.

Note: Country income levels are defined by World Bank classifications. The data cover medical services delivered in 2019 through all four modes of supply defined by the WTO's General Agreement on Trade in Services (GATS): (1) cross-border supply, (2) consumption abroad, (3) commercial presence, and (4) presence of natural persons.

medical interventions possible in real time. In 2019, medical services traded across borders (mode 1) represented 5.6 percent of the total, while services supplied through the physical presence of health professionals abroad (mode 4) was lowest at 4 percent (including the temporary movement of self-employed practitioners or employees sent by institutions). The share of cross-border supply, which covers cross-border tele-health, has increased rapidly in countries such as the United States, where it rose from 3.3 percent in 2010 to 9.5 percent in 2019.

Patterns of exports

In 2019, the EU exported US$38 billion in medical services (including intra-EU exports), making it the world's top exporter with a 46 percent share (figure 1.13), up from 33.8 percent in 2010. The increase was mainly driven by supply through commercial presence, followed by medical travel. Within the EU, Germany was the main exporter, with 26 percent of the world market in 2019, followed by France and Spain. Other major exporters among high-income countries were (in this order) the United States, the United Kingdom, Australia, and Canada. Only three upper-middle-income countries (China, Cuba, and Turkey) were among the top 10 exporters.

Medical travel is important for many countries. Spain is the leading exporter on this basis, supplying medical services such as ophthalmology, dentistry, cosmetic

Figure 1.13   Medical services exports are concentrated in a few economies

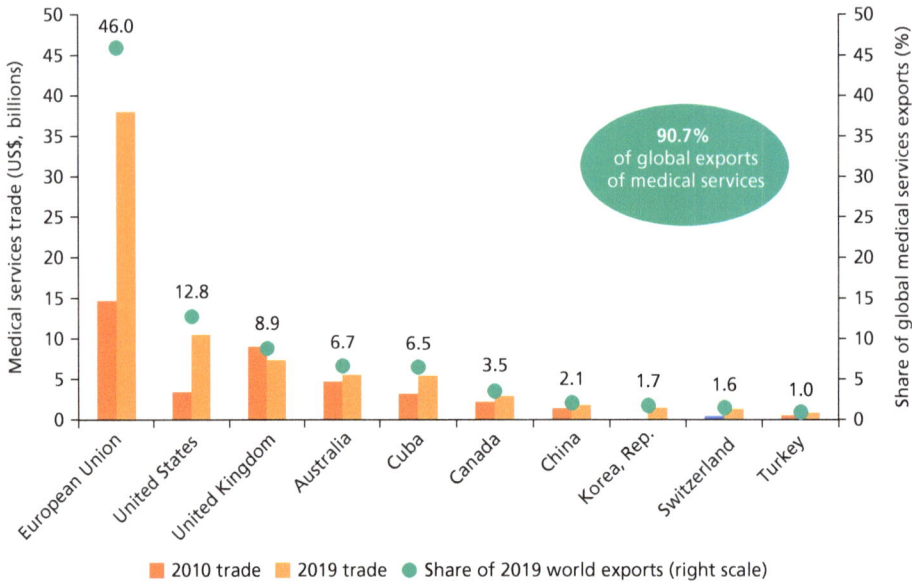

Source: World Trade Organization (WTO) estimates based on the WTO Trade in Services Data by Mode of Supply (TISMOS) dataset.

Note: The value of medical services trade (left axis) includes only exports. "European Union" includes intra-EU trade.

surgery, and fertility treatment. Its 9.2 percent share puts it ahead of China, with 7.8 percent, and the United States with 6.8 percent.[12] Among the countries specializing in medical travel, Costa Rica, Thailand, and Turkey provide over 95 percent of their medical services exports on-site to foreign patients. As discussed in the earlier section on mode-specific drivers of trade in medical services, medical travel has been favored by high-quality infrastructure, experienced health professionals, lower prices, and insurance companies that increasingly provide health coverage abroad.

Countries' respective specializations in services trade vary over time. For example, in 2019, medical travel (mode 2, consumption abroad) remained Singapore's largest mode of supplying medical services. However, the city-state's share of medical travel has dropped since 2010 as cross-border exports (mode 1) have grown, facilitated by digital technologies (figure 1.14, panel a).

Korea has recorded the most dynamic growth rate, with its medical services exports expanding by an average of 29 percent a year since 2010. The country is a respected medical destination, catering mainly to Asian patients, especially from China, but it also attracts patients from the United States and the Russian Federation. Medical centers treating foreign patients provide interpretation and multilingual consultation services and are required to carry insurance for possible adverse events.[13] In recent years, the value of medical services supplied through a commercial presence (mode 3)

Figure 1.14   Different Asian exporters of medical services trade differently

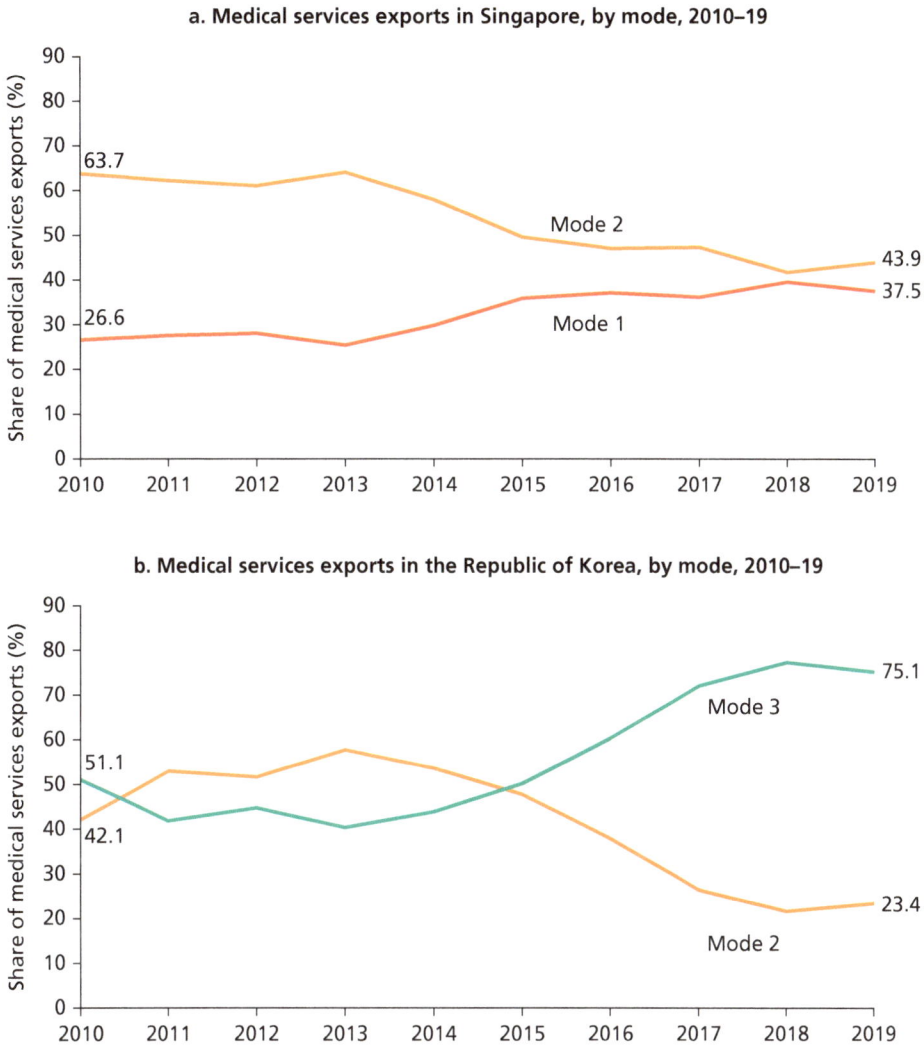

a. Medical services exports in Singapore, by mode, 2010–19

b. Medical services exports in the Republic of Korea, by mode, 2010–19

Source: World Trade Organization (WTO) estimates based on the WTO Trade in Services Data by Mode of Supply (TISMOS) dataset.

Note: Modes refer to the WTO General Agreement on Trade in Services (GATS) modes of service delivery: (1) cross-border supply, (2) consumption abroad, (3) commercial presence, and (4) presence of natural persons.

has overtaken that of services to foreign patients in-country (mode 2) as medical institutions have expanded abroad, establishing hospitals and diagnostic and fertility centers (figure 1.14, panel b).

Patterns of imports

Imports of medical services are also concentrated. The top 10 importers accounted for 87.5 percent of global imports of medical services in 2019 (figure 1.15).

Figure 1.15   Medical services imports are concentrated in a few economies

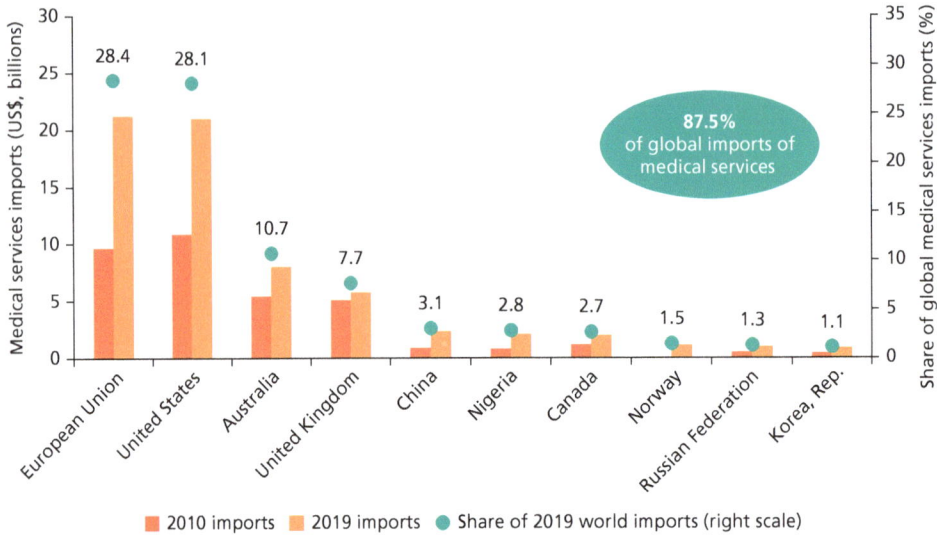

Source: World Trade Organization (WTO) estimates based on the WTO Trade in Services Data by Mode of Supply (TISMOS) dataset.

Note: The value of medical services trade (left axis) includes only imports. "European Union" includes intra-EU trade.

The EU ranked first with US$21.2 billion, more than double the value imported in 2010, giving it a share of 28.4 percent. It imported medical services largely through commercial presence (80.8 percent).[14] With imports worth US$21.0 billion in 2019, the United States ranked second, and it was a net importer of medical services. Medical services supplied to US residents through commercial presence have been growing, totaling US$19.8 billion in 2019. The share of US medical services imports from cross-border supply has also risen, from 0.4 percent in 2010 to 2.1 percent in 2019.

Nigeria is also a major importer of medical services and ranks first in Africa. Some 98 percent of its medical services imports are consumed abroad. Given the gaps in the supply of medical services locally, a growing number of Nigerians have traveled to China, India, Saudi Arabia, the United Arab Emirates, the United Kingdom, the United States, and other countries for cancer treatment, transplants, heart surgeries, and neurosurgeries. Travel for routine checkups and childbirths has also increased (Ogunrinde 2021). Nigeria's imports of medical services have risen by an annual average of 11 percent since 2010. At US$2.1 billion in 2019, Nigeria's payments for medical treatment overseas almost matched China's.

Destinations for Chinese citizens include other Asian countries such as Korea, Singapore, and Thailand, as well as the United States. Imports through consumption abroad accounted for almost one-third of China's total.

DEVELOPMENTS IN MEDICAL GOODS AND SERVICES TRADE DURING THE PANDEMIC

Trade flows of medical goods

International trade in medical goods has been essential in the response to the COVID-19 pandemic. With the global economy almost at a standstill as a result of quarantines, border closures, lockdowns, and other measures imposed to stop the contagion, total goods trade declined in 2020 (see figure 1.7), but medical goods trade increased by 13.2 percent, jumping to 7.3 percent of total goods trade.

Early on, soaring demand for PPE

Early in the pandemic, when there was no known treatment for COVID-19, stopping the spread of the contagion was the recommended best course of action. Thus, demand for PPE fueled the tremendous increase in medical goods trade, and the product group registered at least 50 percent annual growth in 2020. PPE also crowded out the other product groups, increasing its share by more than 4 percentage points, while shares for the other groups decreased or stagnated (figure 1.8).

China's exports of medical products in the first pandemic year, 2020, soared by 93 percent, lifting the country from fourth place among top exporters in 2019 to second place in 2020, when the country exported 11.7 percent of the world's medical goods (figure 1.16).[15] Germany remained the top exporter, while the United States and

Figure 1.16   The growth rate of China's medical goods exports in 2020 dwarfed those of the other top five suppliers

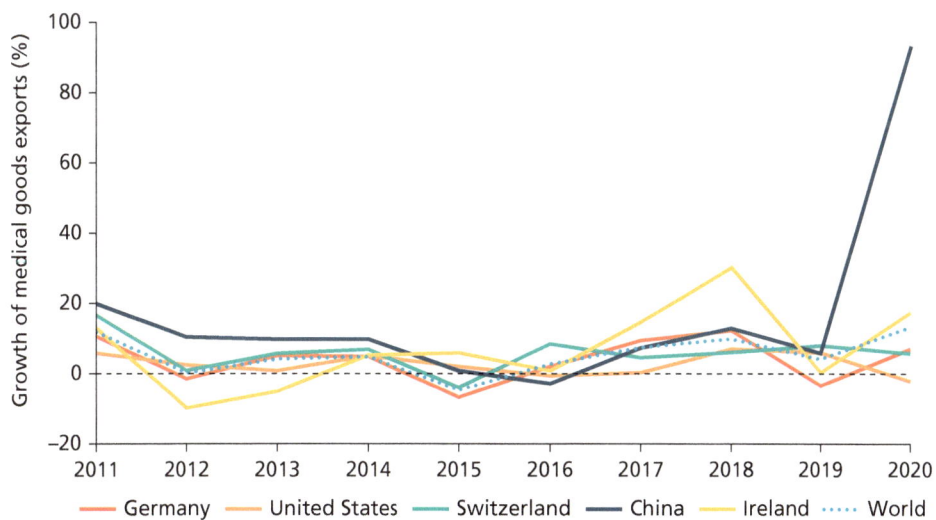

Sources: World Trade Organization (WTO) Integrated Database; United Nations COMTRADE data.

Switzerland were both pushed one level lower, to third and fourth place, respectively. Exports increased in 2020 for all the major suppliers except the United States, which showed a 2.2 percent contraction. Beyond the meteoric surge of Chinese exports during the early stages of the pandemic, several other Asian economies—including Malaysia, Chinese Taipei, Thailand, and Vietnam—largely fed the growing global demand for less sophisticated products like PPE.

Exports of face masks, disinfectants, and rubber gloves all registered triple-digit growth early in the pandemic but have since stabilized. Many governments mandated the use of face masks and recommended regular handwashing to stem the spread of coronavirus, boosting demand for PPE. Exports of textile face masks jumped by 481 percent in 2020, while exports of disinfectants and of rubber gloves rose by 199 percent and 113 percent, respectively. Monthly export growth rates for face masks and disinfectants peaked in April 2020, when WHO reported 1 million COVID-19 cases worldwide (figure 1.17).

Supply shortages also pushed up prices, accounting for part of the surge in the value of exports in 2020, especially for face masks. Shortages were exacerbated by trade-policy interventions (discussed further in chapter 2). Early 2021 data indicate a tapering off of global exports because of increased domestic production and a decrease in prices.[16]

Vaccines: Fast development, unequal distribution

New technology accelerated the development of vaccines in a small group of countries that accounted for the lion's share of exports. Supplies were not equally distributed, with high-income areas initially having a larger share of imports. With new technology, the development of vaccines against COVID-19 was relatively fast, and production accelerated. Companies offered different types of vaccines, and in less than a year, these vaccines were being exported globally (as discussed in the earlier section on the health care GVC). From nearly zero in 2020, more than 650 million doses were exported in December 2021 alone and 4.4 billion in all of 2021 (out of a total of 11.7 billion doses, both exports and domestic supply).

The biggest exporters were China, the EU, and the United States, which together accounted for around 87 percent of the total (figure 1.18, panel a). India, Russia, and South Africa started to export more vaccines by the end of 2021, though their shares were much smaller.

The world relied on imports from a limited number of producing countries. The evolution of imports by different income groups is varied. Imports of high-income and upper-middle-income countries increased rapidly and plateaued by July 2021 (figure 1.8, panel b). Low- and lower-middle-income countries started receiving larger volumes of imports only in the second half of the year.

Trade in vaccine ingredients started to increase in 2020, driven by key ingredients such as messenger ribonucleic acid (mRNA). Most of this trade included a small group of producing countries. The manufacture of COVID-19 vaccines requires active substances such as mRNA, inactive ingredients, consumables, packaging, and equipment. According to data from China Customs, Eurostat, and the U.S. Census Bureau, trade in such inputs increased by 15 percent relative to prepandemic levels as early as July 2020, with the gap since then varying from 20 percent to more than 60 percent. As of December 2021, the three economies' combined exports of inputs were 38 percent higher than in December 2019, and imports of inputs were 66 percent higher.

Figure 1.17 Exports of PPE soared early in the COVID-19 pandemic

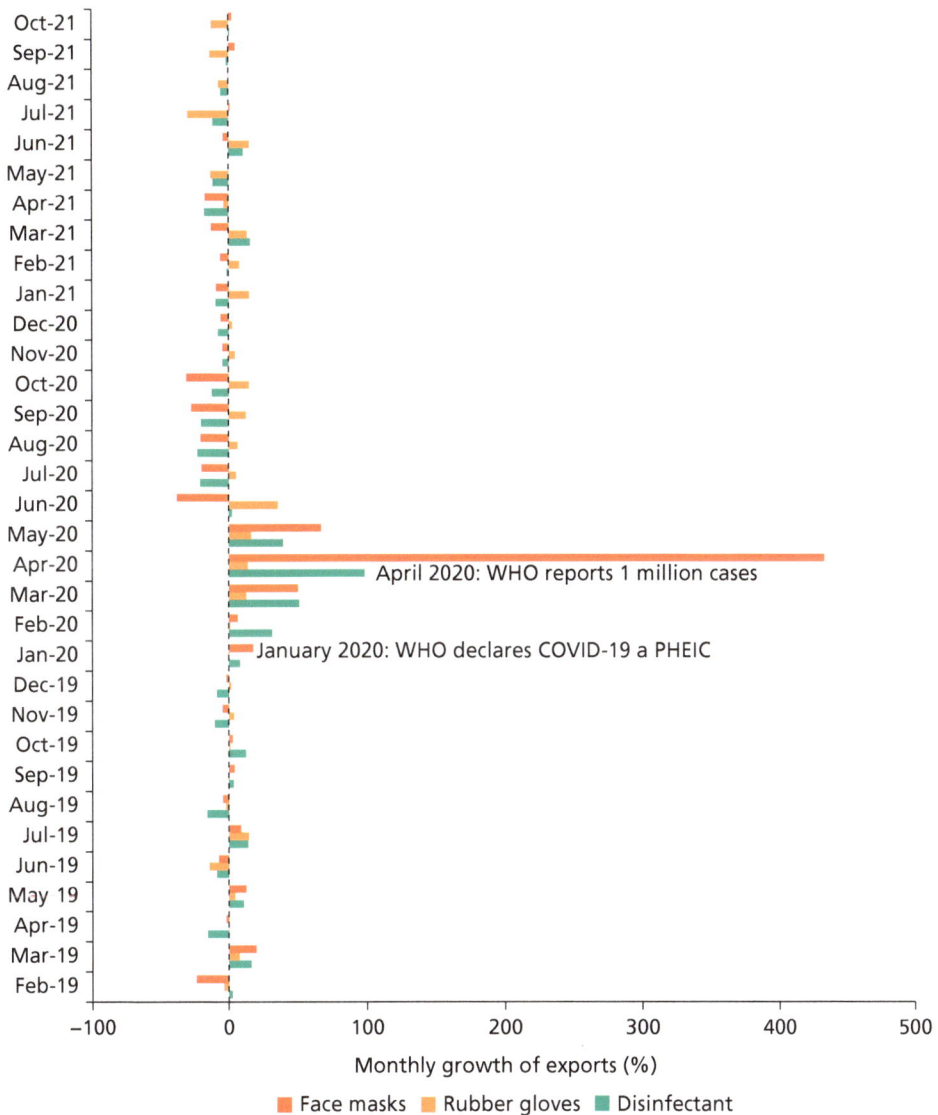

April 2020: WHO reports 1 million cases

January 2020: WHO declares COVID-19 a PHEIC

Monthly growth of exports (%)

■ Face masks ■ Rubber gloves ■ Disinfectant

Source: Trade Data Monitor (http://tradedatamonitor.com).

Note: PHEIC = public health emergency of international concern; WHO = World Health Organization.

Figure 1.18   Trade in COVID-19 vaccines grew at an accelerated pace, but distribution was unequal

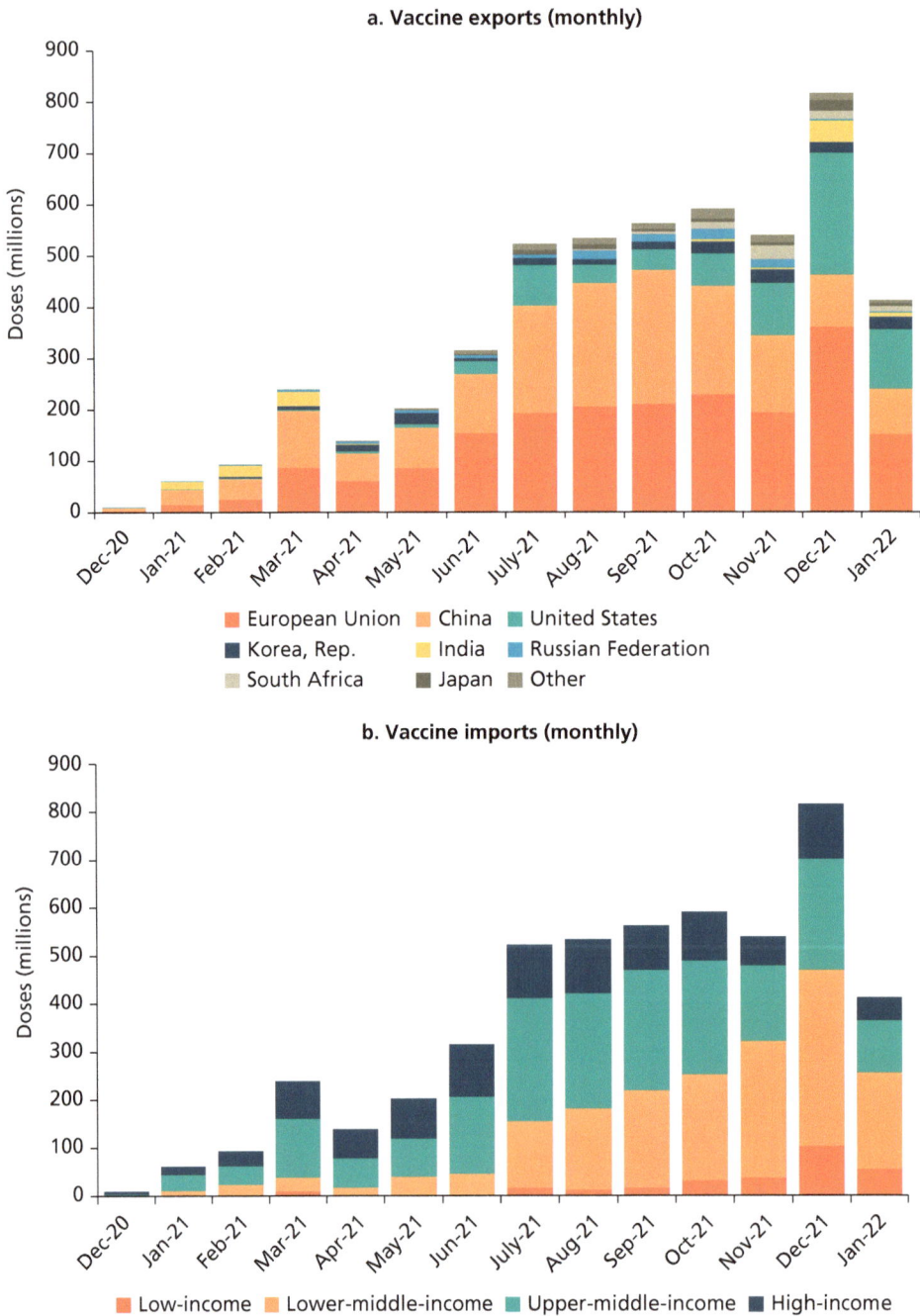

a. Vaccine exports (monthly)

b. Vaccine imports (monthly)

Source: Data from the World Trade Organization and International Monetary Fund's COVID-19 Vaccine Trade Tracker (accessed April 2022), https://www.wto.org/spanish/tratop_s/covid19_s/vaccine_trade_tracker_s .htm.

A closer look at the data highlights that key inputs such as mRNA were the main drivers of import growth. Vaccine ingredients were mainly traded among a few countries, especially those involved in vaccine manufacturing. Up to 70 percent of the key vaccine inputs that China, the EU, and the United States imported in 2021 came from top vaccine producers (Evenett et al. 2021).

Trade flows of medical services

In 2020, global trade in medical services fell by 9 percent, hindered significantly by pandemic-related travel restrictions, border closures, and decreased movement of health care workers across borders. Trade through the cross-border movement of patients (mode 2) and health care workers (mode 4) dropped by 58 percent and 39 percent, respectively (figure 1.19, panel a). As a result, trade in medical services decreased by 9 percent, to US$71.6 billion.

In contrast, cross-border supply (mode 1) of medical services (including telehealth) soared in 2020. The pandemic and its associated lockdown measures accelerated the provision of medical services remotely (a trend that started in the past decade) and the rise of digital health services. Services using audiovisual tools (in particular, practitioner-to-practitioner services) and digital platforms connecting health professionals and patients boomed. World cross-border trade in medical services rose by 14 percent to US$4.8 billion (figure 1.19, panel b).

Figure 1.19   In 2020, medical services traded through modes 2 and 4 fell sharply while mode 1 surged

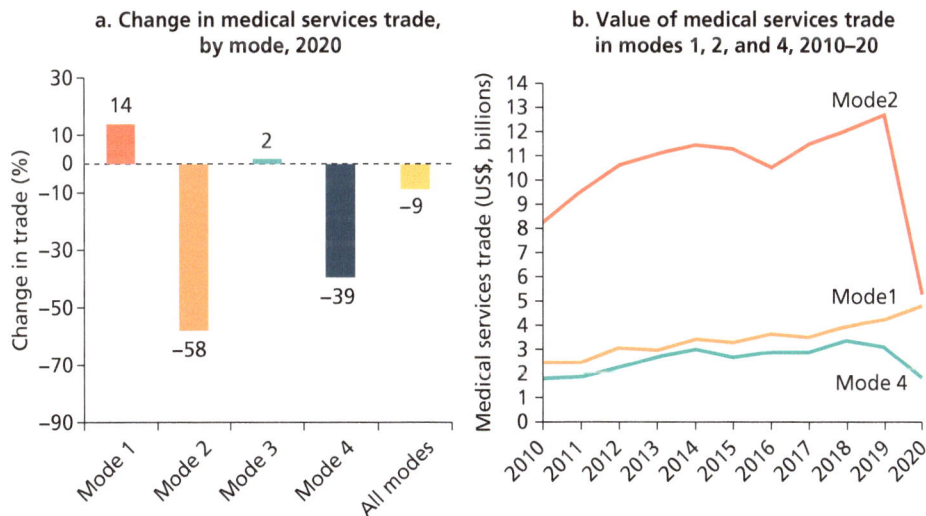

Source: World Trade Organization (WTO) estimates based on the WTO Trade in Services Data by Mode of Supply (TISMOS) dataset.

Note: The modes of services trade refer to the WTO General Agreement on Trade in Services (GATS) modes of delivery: (1) cross-border supply, (2) consumption abroad, (3) commercial presence, and (4) presence of natural persons. Mode 3 is excluded from panel b to enable visualization of the trends for the three other modes of supply.

In high-income economies, which benefited from superior information technology and better-trained health care staff, exports expanded by 23 percent.

Medical services supplied through commercial presence (mode 3) remained resilient globally, increasing by 2 percent to US$59.5 billion. Large exporters such as the EU and the United States saw only modest declines because the bulk of supply was provided through commercial presence in other countries. Because nonurgent medical interventions and checkups in hospitals were postponed in many countries, foreign-owned hospitals and diagnostic facilities also treated COVID-19 patients, carried out tests, and addressed the health emergency. In 2020, total trade in medical services recorded a relatively small contraction of 6 percent in high-income economies, where commercial presence accounted for 84 percent of trade in 2019.[17]

The pandemic disproportionately affected countries relying on the cross-border movement of people (mode 4) to export medical services, hurting their economies. In 2020, low- and middle-income economies' exports of medical services dropped by 37 percent (figure 1.20, panel a). Before the pandemic, some 48 percent of their medical services exports were supplied through medical travel and 31 percent through the movement of health care professionals (figure 1.20, panel b). But in 2020, exports

Figure 1.20 Low- and middle-income economies saw sharp declines in health services trade in 2020

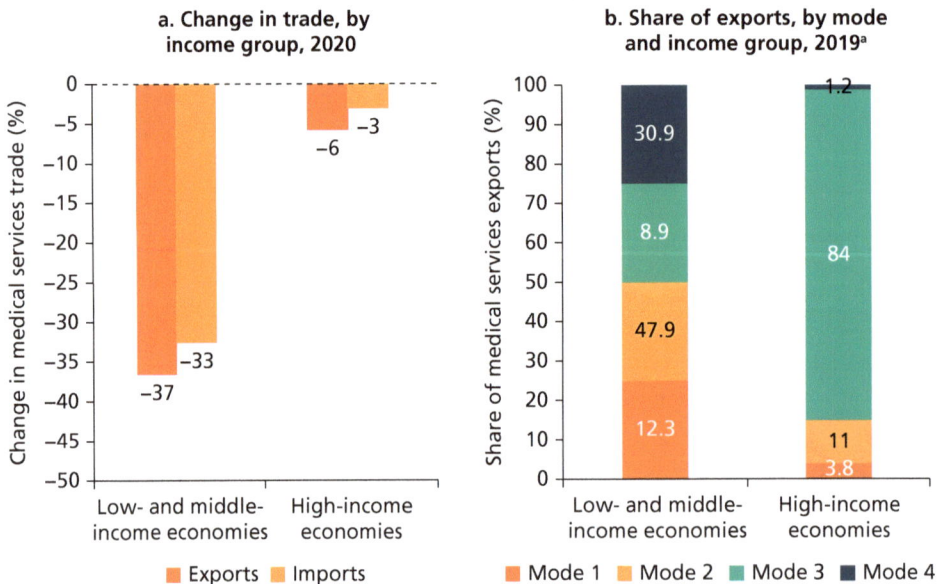

Source: World Trade Organization (WTO) estimates based on the WTO Trade in Services Data by Mode of Supply (TISMOS) dataset.

Note: Country income groups are according to World Bank classifications.

a. The health service delivery modes refer to WTO General Agreement on Trade in Services (GATS) modes: (1) cross-border supply, (2) consumption abroad, (3) commercial presence, and (4) presence of natural persons.

Figure 1.21   Medical services exports through mode 2 dropped in 2020

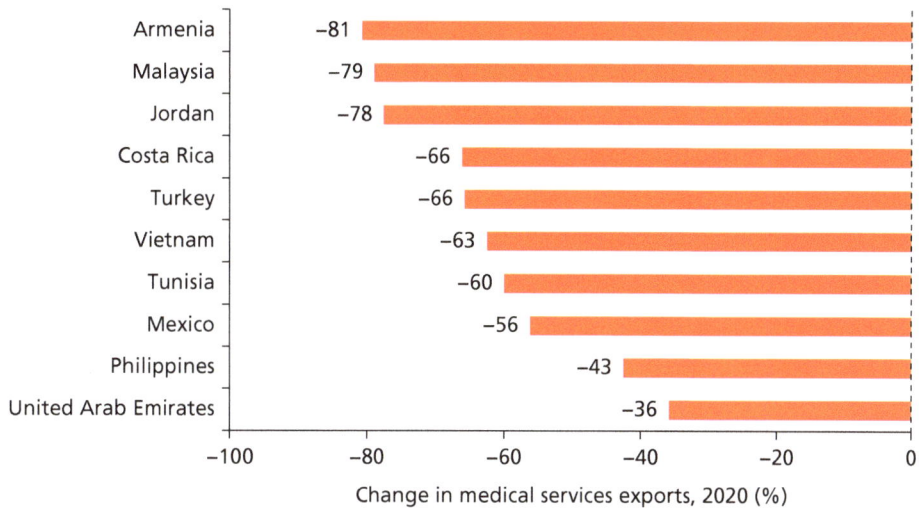

Change in medical services exports, 2020 (%)

Source: World Trade Organization (WTO) estimates based on the WTO Trade in Services Data by Mode of Supply (TISMOS) dataset.

Note: Within the WTO General Agreement on Trade in Services (GATS), mode 2 service delivery is consumption abroad such as consumers' travel to obtain medical services.

through health travel declined by 57 percent and exports through cross-border movement of health professionals by 28 percent. For low- and middle-income economies, the pandemic caused a loss of US$4.6 billion in revenue from exports of medical services in 2020.[18]

The pandemic exacerbated inequality, disproportionately affecting economies relying on revenue from medical travel and also affecting people in poorer countries seeking treatment abroad. In Turkey, medical services exports contracted by 66 percent in 2020, and exports fell on average by 45 percent in countries other than the 10 leading exporters. Health travel export revenues were down by 81 percent in Armenia and close to 80 percent in Malaysia and Jordan (figure 1.21).

Preliminary estimates suggest that in the first half of 2021, global health-related travel exports were still 53 percent below their prepandemic levels in 2019.[19] Travel restrictions also affected countries where outbound medical travel is important because of a lack of domestic infrastructure and staff; for example, Nigeria saw a 60 percent drop in imports of medical services in 2020.[20]

Emergence of the COVID-19 vaccine supply chain

The emergence of the COVID-19 vaccine supply chain illustrates both the potential and the limitations of trade in the response to pandemics. It was an amazing accomplishment to invent, get through clinical trials, and manufacture 11.5 billion doses of COVID-19 vaccines in less than two years. But still, doses did not arrive quickly enough. Accelerating their arrival by one, two, or three months could have saved an estimated hundreds of thousands of lives and trillions of dollars of economic activity (Athey et al. 2022).

Also, the distribution of COVID-19 vaccines was skewed toward the regions where doses were manufactured (as noted earlier), which is why many have called for efforts to diversify vaccine manufacturing capacity globally to better prepare for future health emergencies. Furthermore, the scale of production was too small. The lack of sharing meant that less than 10 percent of the population in poor countries were inoculated by the end of 2021. New demand for boosters along with waste of unused and expired doses pushed the overall need for capacity far above 11.5 billion doses.

Getting a new vaccine from beginning to end requires investment in sizable sunk costs (figure 1.22). These include the scientific research to invent the vaccine; the clinical trials to develop and check that it is effective and safe; the creation of a dedicated

Figure 1.22   The vaccine value chains

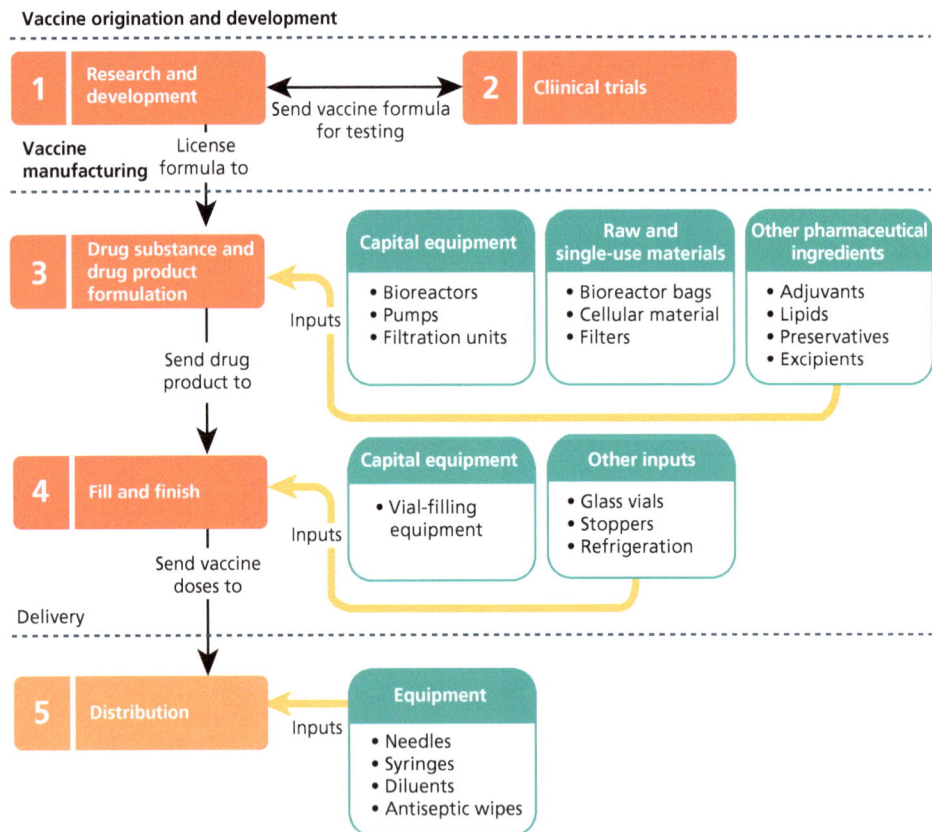

Source: Bown and Bollyky 2022. ©John Wiley and Sons. Reproduced with permission from John Wiley and Sons; further permission required for reuse.

Note: Stages and inputs depicted illustrate the general vaccine production process and are not comprehensive.

manufacturing facility with specialized equipment needed to produce the vaccine's drug substance; and a separate manufacturing facility to formulate the drug substance into drug product for fill and finish, assembly-line style, into hundreds of thousands of tiny vials for distribution (Bown 2022).

During the pandemic, a new COVID-19 vaccine value chain was created. Prepandemic, the world manufactured roughly 1.5 billion doses of vaccines annually. With the onset of COVID-19, the global pharmaceutical industry was tasked with reallocating production facilities, establishing new supply chains, and creating new input streams to suddenly manufacture roughly 11 billion doses of new vaccines. Even once COVID-19 vaccines had been invented and successfully passed clinical trials, the effort required a tremendous increase in dedicated production lines as well as inputs into a sophisticated and highly regulated manufacturing process.

The supply chains announced as forming over this period had some of these key characteristics:[21]

- *None of the supply chains was in place before 2020,* and they almost all relied heavily on contract development and manufacturing organizations (CDMOs). Although some partnerships formed for COVID-19 vaccine production had prior commercial relationships before COVID-19, many were new, including between firms that might otherwise be rivals for other pharmaceutical products.

- *Production of every vaccine was fragmented across multiple facilities and jurisdictions.* Most of the vaccine candidates set up parallel manufacturing supply chains across different geographies. Each had at least a US-based and Europe-based supply chain for drug product formulation and fill and finish, for example, with some setting up *additional* parallel supply chains in Africa, Asia, and South America.

- *Although every vaccine candidate brought in partners for additional production facilities, the matching of innovators and producers proved challenging.* Companies complained about the shortage of facilities and firms with the technological know-how to partner for the new mRNA vaccines, including for fill and finish. In some instances, the shortage of plants caused CDMOs to break prepandemic contracts with other pharmaceutical companies to create the emergency space needed, especially for fill and finish.

- *Certain critical inputs, sometimes feeding in through mini supply chains, faced shortages.* These inputs were especially needed for manufacturing and distribution. For example, all vaccines required specialized inputs—such as bioreactors and other capital equipment in addition to single-use items or consumables (for example, bioreactor bags and filters)—that would require a continual stream of input providers feeding into drug substance and product formulation. As production was scaled up, shortages of such inputs emerged; by early 2021, virtually all of the vaccine sponsors were reporting an insufficient quantity of inputs, indicating that this was holding up their ability to meet production and delivery targets. Indeed, in such a highly regulated and complex production process, missing one input could have a devastating impact on output. Some of the vaccines also required specialized inputs that may not have been previously manufactured at the volumes needed for commercial scale, let alone pandemic scale. Companies had to bring in a suite of contractors to supply the lipid nanoparticles needed for the mRNA vaccines, for example.

- *All of the vaccines also needed relatively homogenous ancillary inputs.* Examples include vials and glass stoppers for packaging as well as syringes and needles for administering vaccines. Because of cold-chain requirements, refrigeration was also needed to transport mRNA vaccines from the plant to the places where they would be administered.

NOTES

1. Although not covered in this definition, "other" services are those that complement and facilitate access to medical goods and services. They include health insurance services; wholesale and retail sale of various pharmaceuticals as well as medical and surgical goods and devices (including pharmacies, which are key in the final distribution of testing devices and other products to the population); health education; claims processing or medical transcription services; research and development (R&D) medical sciences; maintenance and repair services for medical equipment; and technical testing and analysis services.

2. For more about trade in services by modes of supply, see Chanda (2017) and WTO (1998, 2017, n.d.).

3. These regulations have "health policy and safety" motivations but also have an impact on the efficiency of distribution and on cost.

4. For data on vaccine supply and the vaccine exports of Korea, South Africa, and other vaccine-producing countries, see the COVID-19 Vaccine Trade Tracker, built on the work of the WTO and the International Monetary Fund: https://www.wto.org/spanish/tratop_s/covid19_s/vaccine_trade_tracker_s.htm.

5. Mode 4 covers individuals who are either service suppliers (such as independent professionals) or are employed by a foreign service supplier, and it does not include job seekers.

6. Major health logistics operators at the global level are the world's top end-to-end logistics services providers such as DHL, FedEx, UPS, Kuehne + Nagel, CEVA, and the like.

7. Business interruption (including supply chain disruption) has figured as the top business risk identified by 2,650 risk managers in 89 countries and reported in the Allianz Risk Barometer since its launch in 2011 (AGCS 2022).

8. Data on export and import shares of medical goods, by country income group, are from the World Trade Organization's Integrated Database and United Nations COMTRADE data.

9. "Chinese Taipei"—defined by the WTO as the "Separate Customs Territory of Taiwan, Penghu, Kinmen and Matsu"—is used in this report to refer to a jurisdiction admitted to WTO membership since January 1, 2002. See https://www.wto.org/english/thewto_e/countries_e/chinese_taipei_e.htm.

10. Estimates on trade in health services by mode of supply are produced using the WTO Trade in Services Data by Mode of Supply (TISMOS) methodology (2019, based on the recommendations of UN DESA 2012), further improved in 2021. A new TISMOS dataset is forthcoming. For more information, see WTO, "Statistics on Trade in Commercial Services" (web page): https://www.wto.org/english/res_e/statis_e/tradeserv_stat_e.htm.

11. Data on the shares of medical services, by GATS mode of supply, are from WTO estimates based on the Trade in Services Data by Mode of Supply (TISMOS) dataset.

12. Data on the various economies' shares of medical services exports through medical travel and other modes of supply are from WTO estimates based on the Trade in Services Data by Mode of Supply (TISMOS) dataset.

13. For more about Korea's standards for international patient services, see "Global Cooperation," Ministry of Health and Welfare website: https://www.mohw.go.kr/eng/pl/pl0104.jsp?PAR_MENU _ID=1003&MENU_ID=100327.

14. Data on the various economies' shares of medical services imports, by mode of supply, are from WTO estimates based on the Trade in Services Data by Mode of Supply (TISMOS) dataset.

15. Medical goods export data are from the WTO Integrated Database and United Nations COMTRADE data.

16. For example, in the first quarter of 2020. Japan tripled its volume of production by operating 24 hours a day and subsidizing companies to start new manufacturing lines ("Current Status of Production and Supply of Face Masks, Antiseptics and Toilet Paper" (web page), Ministry of Economy, Trade and Industry [last updated May 19, 2020], https://www.meti.go.jp/english /covid-19/mask.html).

17. Medical services trade data are from WTO estimates based on the Trade in Services Data by Mode of Supply (TISMOS) dataset.

18. Medical services revenue data from WTO estimates based on the Trade in Services Data by Mode of Supply (TISMOS) dataset.

19. Health-related travel export data from WTO estimates based on the Trade in Services Data by Mode of Supply (TISMOS) dataset.

20. According to WHO data, in 2011–19, there were on average only 4 doctors and 15 nursing or midwifery personnel per 10,000 people in Nigeria, compared with 43 and 87, respectively, in the EU. WTO calculations for the EU are from WHO 2021c.

21. The COVID-19 vaccine supply chain characteristics are based on Bown and Bollyky (2022), which describes the details behind the manufacturing supply chains for four different vaccine candidates: Pfizer-BioNTech, Moderna, AstraZeneca, and Johnson & Johnson.

REFERENCES

Acemoglu, D., and J. Linn. 2004. "Market Size in Innovation: Theory and Evidence from the Pharmaceutical Industry." *Quarterly Journal of Economics* 119 (3): 1049–90.

Adams, O., and C. Kinnon. 1997. "Measuring Trade Liberalization against Public Health Objectives: The Case of Health Services." Technical Briefing Note, Task Force on Health Economics, World Health Organization, Geneva.

AGCS (Allianz Global Corporate & Security SE). 2022. "Allianz Risk Barometer 2022." Annual corporate risk survey report, AGCS, Munich.

ASEAN and UNCTAD (Association of Southeast Asian Nations and United Nations Conference on Trade and Development). 2019. *ASEAN Investment Report 2019 – FDI in Services: Focus on Health Care*. Jakarta: ASEAN Secretariat.

Athey, S., J. C. Castillo, E. Chaudhuri, M. Kremer, A. S. Gomes, and C. M. Snyder. 2022. "Expanding Capacity for Vaccines against Covid-19 and Future Pandemics: A Review of Economic Issues." Working paper, Dartmouth College, Hanover, NH.

Autor, D., D. Dorn, G. H. Hanson, G. Pisano, and P. Shu. 2020. "Foreign Competition and Domestic Innovation: Evidence from US Patents." *American Economic Review: Insights* 2 (3): 357–74.

Bettcher D. W., D. Yach, and G. E. Guidon. 2000. "Global Trade and Health: Key Linkages and Future Challenges." *Bulletin of the World Health Association* 78 (4): 521–34.

Bloom, N., M. Draca, and J. Van Reenen. 2016. "Trade Induced Technical Change? The Impact of Chinese Imports on Innovation, IT and Productivity." *Review of Economic Studies* 83 (1): 87–117.

Bown, C. P. 2022. "Why the WTO Is Critical for Vaccine Supply Chain Resilience during a Pandemic." Unpublished manuscript, Peterson Institute for International Economics, Washington, DC.

Bown, C. P., and T. J. Bollyky. 2022. "How COVID-19 Vaccine Supply Chains Emerged in the Midst of a Pandemic." *The World Economy* 45 (2): 468–522.

Carzaniga, A., I. Dhillon, J. Magdeleine, and L. Xu. 2019. "International Health Worker Mobility & Trade in Services." World Health Organization and World Trade Organization (WTO) Joint Staff Working Paper No. ERSD-2019-13, WTO, Geneva.

Caselli, F., M. Koren, M. Lisicky, and S. Tenreyro. 2020. "Diversification through Trade." *Quarterly Journal of Economics* 135 (1): 449–502.

Chanda, R. 2001a. "Trade in Health Services." Working paper for the Commission on Macroeconomics and Health, Paper No. WG 4: 5, World Health Organization, Geneva.

Chanda, R. 2001b. "Trade in Health Services." Working Paper No. 70, Indian Council for Research on International Economic Relations, New Delhi.

Chanda, R. 2002. "Trade in Health Services." *Bulletin of the World Health Organization* 80 (2): 158–63.

Chanda, R. 2006. "Inter-Modal Linkages in Services Trade." Trade Policy Working Paper No. 30, Organisation for Economic Co-operation and Development, Paris.

Chanda, R. 2017. "Trade in Health Services and Sustainable Development." In *Win-Win: How International Trade Can Help Meet the SDGs*, edited by M. Helble, B. Shepherd, and G. Wan, 400–36. Tokyo: Asian Development Bank Institute.

Coelli, F., A. Moxnes, and K. H. Ulltveit-Moe. 2022. "Better, Faster, Stronger: Global Innovation and Trade Liberalization." *Review of Economics and Statistics* 104 (2): 205–16.

Commonwealth. 2003. "Commonwealth Code of Practice for the International Recruitment of Health Workers." Adopted at the Meeting of Commonwealth Health Ministers in Geneva, May 23. https://www.aspeninstitute.org/wp-content/uploads/files/content/images/%7B7BDD970B-53AE-441D-81DB-1B64C37E992A%7D_CommonwealthCodeofPractice.pdf.

Costinot, A., D. Donaldson, M. Kyle, and H. Williams. 2019. "The More We Die, the More We Sell? A Simple Test of the Home-Market Effect." *Quarterly Journal of Economics* 134 (2): 843–94.

Daszak, P., A. A. Cunningham, and A. D. Hyatt. 2001. "Anthropogenic Environmental Change and the Emergence of Infectious Diseases In Wildlife." *Acta Tropica* 78 (2): 103–16.

Dumont, J. C., and G. Lafortune. 2017. "International Migration of Doctors and Nurses to OECD Countries." In *Health Employment and Economic Growth: An Evidence Base*, edited by J. Buchan, I. Dhillon, and J. Campbell, 81–118. Geneva: World Health Organization.

Efendi, F., T. K. Mackey, M. C. Huang, and C. M. Chen. 2017. "IJEPA: Gray Area for Health Policy and International Nurse Migration." *Nursing Ethics* 24 (3): 313–28. doi:10.1177/0969733015602052.

Evenett, S. J., B. Hoekman, N. Rocha, and M. Ruta. 2021. "The Covid-19 Vaccine Production Club: Will Value Chains Temper Nationalism?" Policy Research Working Paper 9565, World Bank, Washington, DC.

Giordani, P. E., N. Rocha, and M. Ruta. 2016. "Food Prices and the Multiplier Effect of Trade Policy." *Journal of International Economics* 101: 102–22.

Helble, M. 2011. "The Movement of Patients across Borders: Challenges and Opportunities for Public Health." *Bulletin of the World Health Organization* 89 (1): 68–72. doi:10.2471/BLT.10.076612.

IRDAI (Insurance Regulatory and Development Authority of India). 2021. "IRDAI Annual Report 2020–21." IRDAI, Hyderabad, India.

Kremer, M., and R. Glennerster. 2004. *Strong Medicine: Creating Incentives for Pharmaceutical Research on Neglected Diseases.* Princeton, NJ: Princeton University Press.

Kremer, M., J. Levin, and C. M. Snyder. 2020. "Advance Market Commitments: Insights from Theory and Experience." *AEA Papers and Proceedings* 110: 269–73.

Marani, M., G. G. Katul, W. K. Pan, and A. J. Parolari. 2021. "Intensity and Frequency of Extreme Novel Epidemics." *PNAS* 118 (35): e2105482118.

OECD (Organization for Economic Co-operation and Development). 2020. "Can FDI Improve the Resilience of Health Systems?" Policy note for OECD Roundtable on Investment and Sustainable Development, Paris, September 30–October 1.

OECD and EUIPO (Organisation for Economic Co-operation and Development and European Union Intellectual Property Office). 2019. *Trends in Trade in Counterfeit and Pirated Goods*. Paris: OECD Publishing; Alicante, Spain: EUIPO.

Ogunrinde, A. 2021. "Helping Nigeria Overcome the Medical Tourism Malady." *TheCable*, May 14. https://www.thecable.ng/helping-nigeria-overcome-the-medical-tourism-malady.

Patel, D., J. Sandefur, and A. Subramanian. 2021. "The New Era of Unconditional Convergence." *Journal of Development Economics* 152: 102687.

Pauly, M., P. Zweifel, R. Scheffler, A. Preker, and M. Bassett. 2006. "Private Health Insurance In Developing Countries." *Health Affairs* 25 (2): 369–79.

Qiang, C. Z., Y. Liu, and V. Steenbergen. 2021. *An Investment Perspective on Global Value Chains*. Washington, DC: World Bank.

Sekhri, N., and W. Savedoff. 2005. "Private Health Insurance: Implications for Developing Countries." *Bulletin of the World Health Organization* 83: 127–34.

Singh, M. 2006. "Transforming the Global Health Care Supply Chain." Introductory report for the MIT Center for Transport and Logistics, Cambridge, MA.

SRI (Smart Research Insights). 2021. "Global Pharmaceutical Market Competitive Landscape 2021." Market research report, SRI, New Delhi.

Swiss Re Institute. 2020. "De-risking Global Supply Chains: Rebalancing to Strengthen Resilience." *Sigma* No. 6/2020, Swiss Re Institute, Zurich.

Thomson, S., A. Sagan, and E. Mossialos. 2020. "Why Private Health Insurance?" In *Private Health Insurance – History, Politics and Performance*, edited by S. Thomson, A. Sagan, and E. Mossialos, 1–40. Cambridge: Cambridge University Press.

UNCTAD (United Nations Conference on Trade and Development). 1997. "International Trade in Health Services: Difficulties and Opportunities for Developing Countries." Background Note TD/B /COM.1/EM.1/2, UNCTAD Secretariat, UNCTAD Geneva.

UN DESA (United Nations Department of Economic and Social Affairs). 2012. *Manual on Statistics of International Trade in Services 2010*. New York: United Nations.

Vara, V. 2019. "The Top Ten Medical Device Companies by Market Share in 2018." Analysis, Medical Device Network, March 7 (updated March 16, 2022), https://www.medicaldevice-network.com /features/top-medical-device-companies/.

Wagstaff, A., and S. Neelsen. 2020. "A Comprehensive Assessment of Universal Health Coverage in 111 Countries: A Retrospective Observational Study." *The Lancet Global Health* 8: e39–49.

WHO (World Health Organization). 2006. *World Health Report 2006: Working Together for Health*. Geneva: WHO.

WHO (World Health Organization). 2010. "WHO Global Code of Practice on the International Recruitment of Health Personnel." Adopted at the 63rd World Health Assembly (WHA63.16), Geneva, May 17–21.

WHO (World Health Organization). 2012. *Toolkit for Assessing Health-System Capacity for Crisis Management. Part 1: User Manual*. Copenhagen: WHO Regional Office for Europe.

WHO (World Health Organization). 2016. *Global Strategy on Human Resources for Health – Workforce 2030*. Geneva: WHO.

WHO (World Health Organization). 2017a. *A Study on the Public Health and Socioeconomic Impact of Substandard and Falsified Medical Products*. Geneva: WHO.

WHO (World Health Organization). 2017b. *WHO Global Surveillance and Monitoring System for Substandard and Falsified Medical Products*. Geneva: WHO.

WHO (World Health Organization). 2020. *State of the World's Nursing 2020: Investing in Education, Jobs and Leadership*. Geneva: WHO.

WHO (World Health Organization). 2021a. *Global Expenditure on Health: Public Spending on the Rise?* Geneva: WHO.

WHO (World Health Organization). 2021b. "Methodology for the Update of the Global Health Expenditure Database, 2000–2019." Technical note, Version December 2021, WHO, Geneva.

WHO (World Health Organization). 2021c. *World Health Statistics 2021: Monitoring Health for the SDGs*. Geneva: WHO.

WTO (World Trade Organization). 1998. "Health and Social Services." Council for Trade in Services, Background Note by the Secretariat, September 18, WTO, Geneva.

WTO (World Trade Organization). 2017. "Annex 1B – General Agreement on Trade in Services." In *The WTO Agreements, The Marrakesh Agreement Establishing the World Trade Organization and Its Annexes*. 2nd ed., 357–95. Cambridge: Cambridge University Press.

WTO (World Trade Organization). n.d. "The General Agreement on Trade in Services (GATS): Objectives, Coverage and Disciplines" (web page), WTO, Geneva (accessed April 2022), https://www.wto.org/english/tratop_e/serv_e/gatsqa_e.htm.

Zarilli, S., and C. Kinnon, eds. 1998. *International Trade in Health Services: A Development Perspective*. Geneva: United Nations Conference on Trade and Development and World Health Organization.

2 Trade Policies in Medical Goods and Services

POLICIES AFFECTING MEDICAL GOODS AND SERVICES TRADE UNDER NORMAL CONDITIONS

Medical goods trade

Governments adopt a wide range of policy measures that may affect trade in medical goods and services. Some may have a direct impact on trade, such as tariffs, prohibitions, and import and export licenses. Others affect trade indirectly—such as trade facilitation measures; services trade policies (for example, transport, logistics, insurance); regulatory frameworks; and intellectual property rights, which can foster innovation and access to health technologies—along with facilitation of technology partnerships, transfer of technology through production chains, and knowledge spillovers.

Import and export policies

Tariffs. Tariffs on medical goods are relatively low on average but vary considerably by country and product. For some lower-income countries, tariffs may serve mostly to collect revenue. Elsewhere, the level of tariffs likely reflects government efforts to find a balance between the interests of consumers and producers of medical goods. Low tariffs favor consumers by keeping prices down, whereas higher tariffs can be used to support and develop domestic industry.

The average applied most-favored-nation (MFN) tariff on medical goods is 5 percent, compared with an average of 8 percent for manufactured goods as a whole. Applied MFN tariffs of high-income economies average 2.4 percent—less than half the average of low- and middle-income economies (figure 2.1).[1] Pharmaceutical products have the lowest MFN applied tariffs, followed by medical equipment, orthopedic equipment, and other medical supplies. Personal protective equipment

(PPE) faces the highest duties (twice the average for all medical goods) among the economies of all income groups. The average tariff on textile face masks, for example, is 13.5 percent.

Reducing the restrictions imposed on the imports of medical goods and on the inputs necessary for their production would boost income gains. Empirical analysis produced for this report (box 2.1) suggests that full tariff liberalization on

Figure 2.1 High-income economies have consistently lower tariffs across all medical product groups

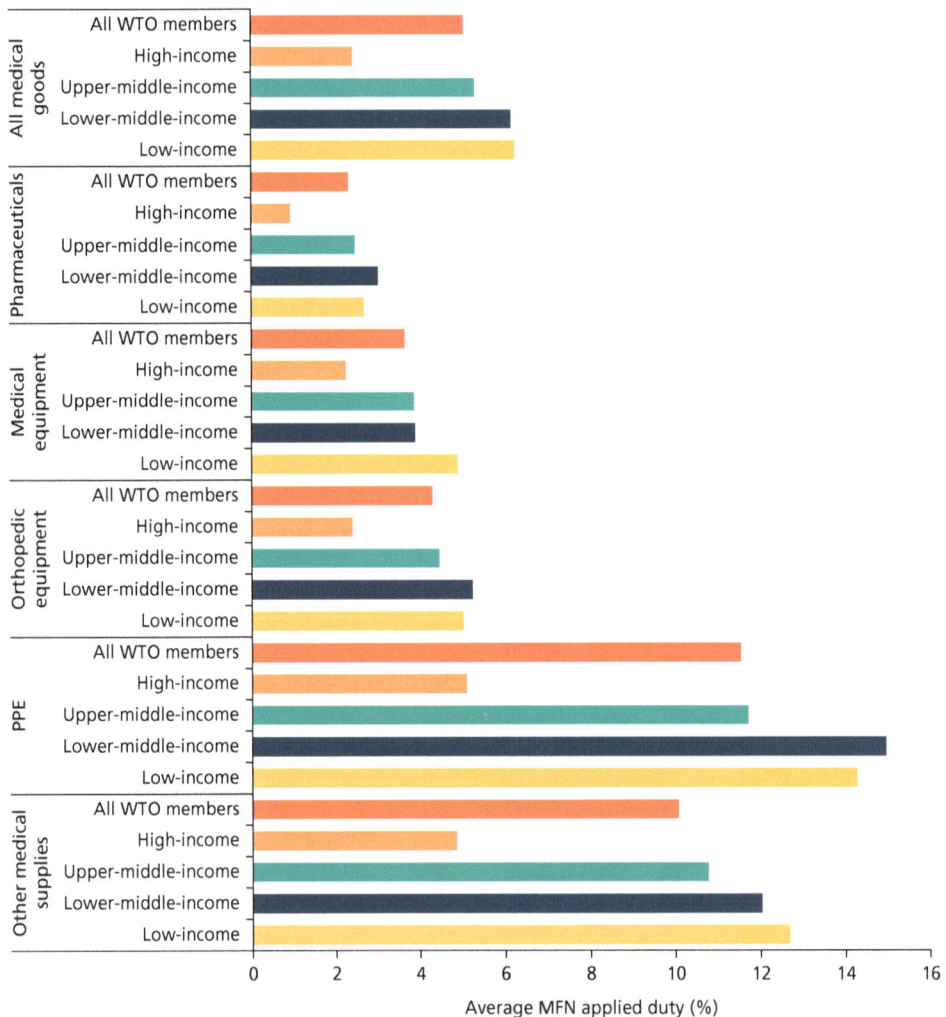

Source: World Trade Organization Integrated Database.

Note: Country income categories are according to World Bank classifications. MFN = most-favored-nation; PPE = personal protective equipment; WTO = World Trade Organization.

pharmaceutical products, inputs (chemicals), and equipment and machinery used in health care would lead to long-term income gains of US$4.75 billion annually. This gain would increase to US$6.18 billion once a reduction of import costs for information and communication technology (ICT) and business services in the health sector is also considered. Most of the total gains would go to middle-income countries where trade restrictions are higher, thus helping to improve health security in these countries.

Box 2.1   General equilibrium analysis of trade and health care costs

This box examines the links between local health care costs and the global economy. Specifically, it investigates the potential benefits of tariff reductions targeting products important to health care costs (such as pharmaceuticals) on national income gains.

Over the past 15 years, the foreign value-added[a] share of health care costs has risen from 7.73 percent in 2004 to 9.77 percent in 2019 (table B2.1.1). This rise has been driven, to a large extent, by rising shares in high-income countries and, to a lesser extent, by a rise in low-income countries. For middle-income countries, which are the global suppliers in the sector, the shares of foreign value added have fallen but still remain well above the global average share.

Table B2.1.1   Foreign value-added share of local health care costs, 2004–19

Percent

Income group or region	2004	2007	2011	2014	2017	2019
Income group						
High income	6.79	7.83	8.53	8.90	8.88	8.84
Middle income	13.57	12.30	12.25	12.83	11.71	11.87
Low income	20.42	21.23	18.91	20.09	21.14	21.18
World	7.73	8.70	9.48	9.97	9.73	9.77
Region						
Asia and Pacific	8.86	10.21	9.79	11.54	10.39	10.40
Europe	8.63	9.51	10.65	11.10	11.60	11.69
Middle East and Africa	16.39	16.11	15.54	15.95	15.94	15.81
Americas	5.79	6.59	7.41	7.24	7.17	7.17

Source: Multi-Region Input-Output (MRIO) calculations based on the Global Trade Analysis Project (GTAP) database v11p2 (pre-release, with some updates).

Note: Country income categories are according to World Bank classifications. "Americas" comprises North, Central, and South America and the Caribbean.

(Continued)

Box 2.1   General equilibrium analysis of trade and health care costs *(Continued)*

Further analysis of these 2019 data[b] suggests that the value-added costs of providing health care (costs of the health sector staff and physical infrastructure) range from 47.4 percent of total costs in low-income countries to 60.6 percent of total costs in high-income countries. Roughly half of the remaining health care costs come from (a) purchases of basic pharmaceutical products, and (b) the combination of information and communication technology (ICT) and business services. The two sectors of pharmaceuticals and ICT are therefore an obvious target for trade cost reductions.

Focusing on the pharmaceutical sector, intermediate pharmaceutical products accounted for 27.4 percent of gross input costs, while intermediate chemicals accounted for another 8.5 percent (excluding value-added costs). Together, these two categories accounted for roughly 36 percent of gross input costs for pharmaceutical production. An examination of the direct contribution of trade costs to health costs suggests that roughly US$153 billion was spent in 2019 on imports of basic pharmaceuticals for final consumption (including drugs used by the health care sector).

To assess the potential benefits of tariff reductions targeting products important to health care costs, we consider a scenario (a hypothetical set of tariff cuts) involving full elimination of tariffs in the following categories (table B2.1.2): pharmaceutical products (column a), equipment and machinery used in health care (column b), and chemicals used by the pharmaceutical sector (column c). We also simulate the impact of a trade cost reduction equivalent to 5 percent of import costs for ICT and business services in the health care sector (column d). This reduction is very conservative and reflects the reality that any trade cost reductions in services have proved problematic in practice. Table B2.1.2 presents the general equilibrium results for the long run (where capital and labor are mobile and investment adjusts to policy changes).[c]

The long-run income gains globally (available for health care expenditures or, alternatively, for other final expenditures) are US$6.18 billion annually. Most of this goes to middle-income countries (US$3.07 billion annually), over half of which is driven by elimination of pharmaceutical tariffs. Geographically, most gains accrue to Europe and Asia.

As for reductions of health care costs, low- and middle-income countries experience the highest decreases in health costs, with average reductions of 0.11 percent and 0.15 percent, respectively. Among the regions, the highest reductions in health costs will take place in Middle East and Africa (0.12 percent reduction) and Asia and Pacific (0.08 percent reduction).

(Continued)

Box 2.1   General equilibrium analysis of trade and health care costs *(Continued)*

Table B2.1.2   Simulation results: Long-run annual income gains from tariff cuts in the health care sector, by income group and region

US$, millions (2019 benchmark)

Income group or region	Total	Pharma tariffs eliminated (a)	Equipment, machinery tariffs eliminated (b)	Chemical tariffs (for pharma sector) eliminated (c)	Business, ICT trade costs reduced[a] (d)
Income group					
High income	2,862.8	1,513.0	177.1	207.8	964.9
Middle income	3,070.5	1,765.0	344.4	532.1	429.0
Low income	244.8	176.2	22.7	8.7	37.2
World	6,178.1	3,454.3	544.2	748.6	1,431.1
Region					
Asia and Pacific	2,147.0	1,277.8	206.8	379.9	282.6
Europe	2,756.1	1,796.5	109.1	92.6	757.9
Middle East and Africa	751.4	274.4	173.1	154.3	149.6
Americas	523.6	105.5	55.3	121.8	241.0

Source: Results from simulations with CGE model estimates using a version of the GTAP model modified to include sector specific duty rebates and imported input cost reductions. See text and background note.

Note: Country income categories are according to World Bank classifications. "Americas" comprises North, Central, and South America and the Caribbean. CGE = computable general equilibrium; ICT = information and communication technology.

a. Trade costs are reduced equivalent to 5 percent of import costs for information and communication technology and business services in the health care sector.

a. "Foreign value added" refers to the value added in foreign countries that contributes to final expenditures at home on health care. This may involve foreign production of drugs that are then imported (direct contribution) or imported chemicals that feed into local production of drugs (indirect contribution) that are then sold to local households.

b. These findings are based on multiregion input-output (MRIO) calculations using the Global Trade Analysis Project (GTAP) database v11p2 (pre-release, with some updates).

c. See the background note for a technical discussion of the methodology involved for the computable general equilibrium (CGE) modeling. The modeling is based on the Global Trade Analysis Project (GTAP) database (version 11p2), pre-release with some updating. We work here with a version of the GTAP modeling framework that includes scope for the rebate of import duties paid for goods used by directly the health care and pharmaceutical sectors, as well as reductions in trade costs for services used directly by the health care sector.

Restrictions and prohibitions. Quantitative restrictions on imports and exports of medical goods include nonautomatic licensing requirements, outright prohibitions, and qualified prohibitions. Quantitative restrictions can take many forms, but in the case of medical goods they typically consist of nonautomatic licensing requirements (50 percent of all notified measures) and full prohibitions (19 percent), followed by other types of restrictions, such as prohibitions except under specific conditions (31 percent).[2]

World Trade Organization (WTO) member economies use these measures to ensure that medical goods meet specific safety, quality, and efficacy standards and do not pose any risk to human, animal, and plant life or health. In 2018–19, prohibitions and restrictions on both exports and imports most heavily affected pharmaceutical products, PPE, and other medical supplies such as syringes, needles, disinfectants, and oxygen (figure 2.2). Import and export licensing procedures vary significantly by economy.

Figure 2.2 WTO-notified quantitative restrictions, by type and member income group, 2018–19

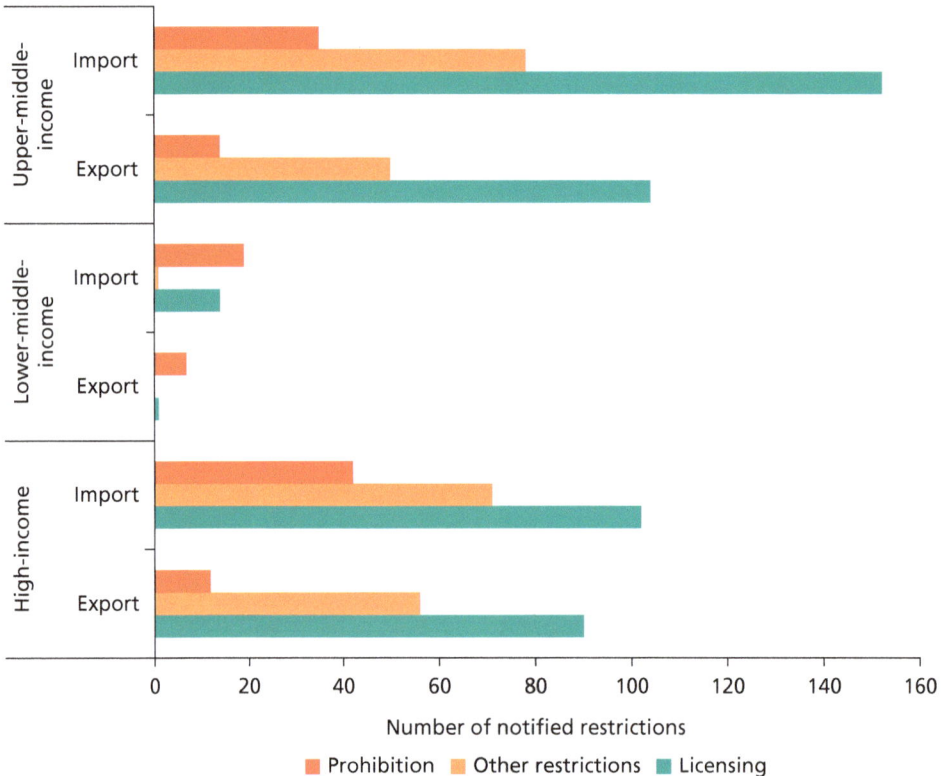

Source: World Trade Organization (WTO) Quantitative Restrictions Database.

Note: Only about 50 percent of WTO members submit quantitative restrictions notifications, with many least developed countries and other low- and middle-income members missing. For more information, see the Quantitative Restrictions Database: https://qr.wto.org/en#/home. The income categories of WTO member economies are according to World Bank classifications.

Trade facilitation measures

Trade facilitation measures have significant benefits for trade in medical goods. They aim to create a more transparent and predictable trading environment that accelerates release and clearance procedures. This is especially important for medical goods because, as discussed in chapter 1, they are essential and their production is concentrated in a small number of larger economies, so trade can generate significant gains. Trade facilitation is particularly relevant for the small subset of goods, such as vaccines, that rapidly decay and need special storage. In times of crisis like a pandemic, trade facilitation is vital.

Releases and clearances at the border. Some facilitation measures are particularly important for products that must cross borders rapidly and reliably, such as PPE, medical supplies, and pharmaceuticals. For instance, it is crucial to facilitate the release and clearance processes at the border by allowing certain procedures to take place before or after the good has reached the border (for instance, through provisions on prearrival processing or postclearance audit). Similarly, payment of duties, taxes, and charges collected by customs through electronic means can speed the movement of medical goods across borders.

Reduced data and inspection requirements. Trade can also be accelerated by granting facilitation measures—as appropriate—such as low documentary and data requirements or a low rate of physical inspections and examinations to operators who meet specified criteria such as a good compliance record. Additional benefits can be reaped by implementing measures on expedited shipments. These measures reward importers who meet criteria such as submission before the shipment's arrival of the information necessary for accelerated clearance and release.

Other measures. Other trade facilitation measures important for medical goods include

- Allowing the release of perishable goods by customs or other authorities before final determination of applicable duties, taxes, fees, and charges;
- Simplifying import and export fees and charges as well as related formalities;
- Allowing goods to be brought into a customs territory conditionally relieved from payment of import duties and taxes (a particularly helpful measure during a health crisis);
- Creating a "single window portal," which allows traders to submit all required documentation and data requirements through a sole entry point, avoiding the need for multiple inputs to multiple authorities and agencies;
- Improving cooperation between border agencies within and between countries (for example, through alignment of procedures and formalities, harmonized working hours, shared facilities, joint controls, and border controls); and
- Enabling the free transit of goods before they reach their final destination (especially important for landlocked lower-middle-income countries [LMICs]).

WTO Trade Facilitation Agreement. The WTO's Trade Facilitation Agreement (TFA) must be fully implemented to reap all its benefits. High-income countries were required to implement all the TFA's provisions by 2017. But the TFA allows low- and middle-income members and least developed members to decide when they are prepared to implement its disciplines and to identify measures that require international capacity-building assistance to implement. As a result, implementation has been gradual, and the rates of implementation vary by income group (figure 2.3).

Services trade policies affecting medical goods trade

Restrictions on logistics, transport, and distribution services hinder trade in medical goods. These sectors, particularly health logistics, face various impediments that not only adversely affect trade in medical goods but also prevent health services from being

Figure 2.3   Progress on implementation commitments under the WTO Trade Facilitation Agreement

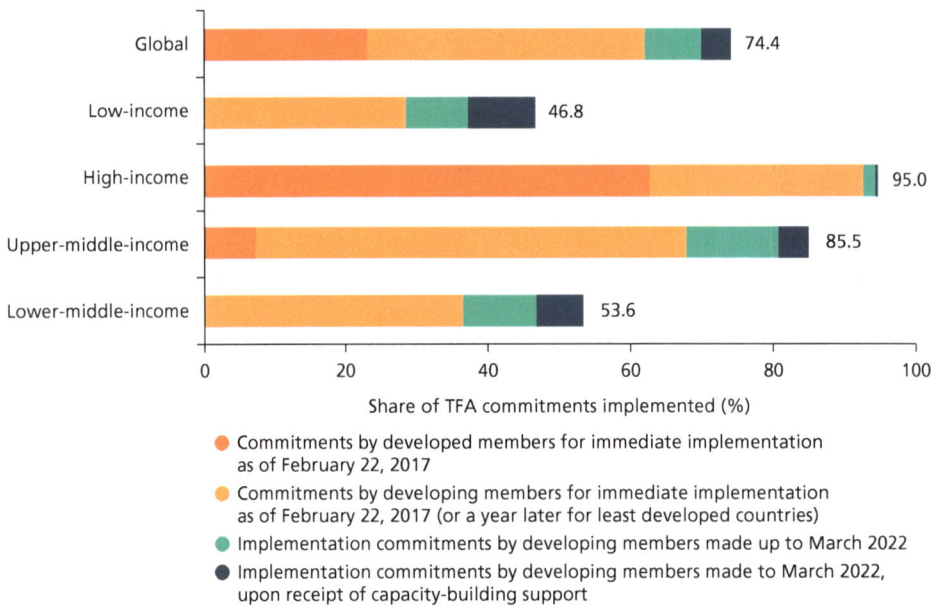

Source: World Trade Organization (WTO) Trade Facilitation Agreement Database (TFAD), http://www.tfadatabase.org.

Note: The bars show the share of Trade Facilitation Agreement (TFA) commitments that WTO members agreed to implement (using data as of March 2022). For example, globally (top bar), 74.4 percent of commitments that WTO Members have agreed to implement—23.3 percent by the WTO's "developed" members by the February 22, 2017, deadline; 39.0 percent by "developing" members by the same date (or a year later for least developed countries); 7.8 percent by developing members up to March 2022; and 4.3 percent by developing members agreed upon receipt of capacity-building support up to March 22. "Developed" members in the chart cover Australia, Austria, Belgium, Bulgaria, Canada, Croatia, Cyprus, Czech Republic, Denmark, Estonia, Finland, France, Germany, Greece, Hungary, Iceland, Ireland, Italy, Japan, Latvia, Liechtenstein, Lithuania, Luxembourg, Malta, the Netherlands, New Zealand, Norway, Poland, Portugal, Romania, Slovak Republic, Slovenia, Spain, Sweden, Switzerland, the United Kingdom, and the United States. Country income categories are according to World Bank classifications.

provided more efficiently and at lower cost. Such impediments include restrictions on the supply of (health) logistics by foreign service suppliers, and many are linked to restrictions in the transport sector, arbitrary or burdensome licensing requirements, lack of regulatory transparency, and burdensome border and customs procedures. Air transport services, which are key for the medical goods value chain (such as for time-dependent goods), face highly restrictive policies.[3]

Differences in national regulations also negatively affect the efficiency and costs of trade in health logistics services. As logistics services grow in scope and complexity and become highly dependent on digital technologies, restrictions on cross-border data flows may also impede trade in these services. Similarly, restrictions on the cross-border delivery and supply through commercial presence of wholesale and retailing services of medical goods, such as limits on the number of suppliers or foreign equity restrictions, can limit competition and negatively affect the cost and performance of these distribution services, in turn reducing the affordability and availability of the medical products.

Open trade policies in insurance services may provide a supportive framework for medical goods trade. However, the uptake of supply chain interruption (SCI) insurance has been hindered by several restrictions. As explained in chapter 1 (on services that support global value chains in medical goods), SCI insurance products have been gradually introduced over the past few decades, with some insurers providing coverage to pharmaceutical and medical device companies. SCI insurance is common in Europe and North America (where large companies with complex worldwide operating structures buy policies), but it has been slow to gain traction in other regions. Impediments include limited capacity by the local insurance industry, high premiums, and burdensome risk-data requirements. The introduction of these innovative insurance solutions is further hindered by broader restrictions on foreign non-life insurers and on cross-border operations of large reinsurers that specialize in this niche market.

Regulatory frameworks

National regulatory authorities (NRAs) are responsible for ensuring the safety, quality, and efficacy of medical goods that enter their markets. They exercise a range of regulatory functions throughout the life cycle of medical goods—oversight of clinical trials; product marketing authorization and registration; licensing (for example, of products and manufactures); inspection (for example, of manufacturing facilities); testing; post-marketing surveillance; and vigilance activities. Manufacturers must obtain marketing authorization from NRAs to produce or import regulated medical goods, which includes providing evidence that the product meets safety, efficacy, and quality requirements. These functions are vital for protecting public health.

Harmonization of medical goods regulation between countries and regions is limited, hindering global development, approval, and marketing of innovative vaccines, therapeutics, and diagnostics. Procedures and requirements for medical goods frequently diverge between NRAs, increasing costs and time to market as well as creating barriers to international trade (Ball, Roth, and Parry 2016; Saxon 2017; WTO 2021). In practice, this means that developers and manufacturers must navigate multiple regulatory systems to register the same drug or medical device in different countries.

Given that production of medical goods is global, involving inputs and components from many different countries (as detailed in the chapter 1 section on global value chains), this regulatory divergence can hinder the smooth functioning of supply chains and create barriers for access to medical goods by driving up costs. Divergence arises throughout the regulatory life cycle, at the level of clinical trials; in product registration dossiers and timelines; in quality, efficacy, or safety requirements; or in processes for managing postapproval changes (Beierle et al. 2022; Saxon 2017; WTO 2021). As a result, regulators and manufacturers often duplicate efforts and use resources inefficiently (Ball, Roth, and Parry 2016).

Intellectual property rights

IPR benefits and impacts. The importance of intellectual property rights (IPR) in providing incentives for the development and dissemination of new medicines has been well documented in the literature. In addition to their importance in securing return on investment, several empirical studies further support their importance in fostering pharmaceutical innovation and accelerating the availability of innovative medicines (Dai and Watal 2021). For example, Qian (2007) evaluates the effect of patent protection on pharmaceutical innovation in countries that established pharmaceutical patent laws and finds that national patent protection accelerates innovation in countries with higher levels of development. Using variation in patent examiner leniency, Gaulé (2018) finds that US biotech start-ups that obtain a patent are considerably more likely to succeed in either going public or being acquired for more than twice the amount raised from venture capitalists.

The exclusive protection provided by IPR influences access to the pharmaceutical market. Patent owners can (and typically do) set prices considerably above marginal cost. The pricing of pharmaceutical products may prevent some patients from accessing life-saving drugs, which explains why extending IPR protection for pharmaceuticals in LMICs has been controversial. That said, given the territorial nature of IPR, there is no single effect of IPR protection and enforcement on health technology innovation and dissemination across all countries. Alongside supply-side incentives, differences in indigenous absorptive capacity and human capital also explain LMICs' divergent experiences in effective knowledge transfer (Branstetter and Maskus 2022).

Support and facilitation of R&D. The intellectual property (IP) system has several features that may support and facilitate health technology research and development (R&D) and access, including certain exclusions from patentable subject matter. Although international IP standards may substantially influence innovation systems (for example, in requiring pharmaceutical inventions to be patentable), the choices made at the regional and national levels within the international legal framework are key. National or regional IP systems have flexibilities regarding the definition of patentability criteria. These flexibilities, in addition to potentially influencing the R&D of new medicines, may also affect the further development and repurposing of existing medicines, including through incremental innovation, new medical indication claims, and limitations on "evergreening" (whereby drug manufacturers seek to extend a monopoly by modifying an existing drug and seeking new patents).

For example, according to the High Court of Delhi in 2015, Section 3(d) of India's Patents Amendment Act 2005 encourages incremental innovation in pharmaceuticals.[4] However, measures to limit secondary pharmaceutical patents in certain LMICs, such as Brazil and India, have limited impact because such patents are granted at the same rate as primary pharmaceutical patents (Sampat and Shadlen 2017). The same study also finds, however, that in Argentina—an upper-middle-income country that also has such measures—grant rates for secondary patents were lower than those for primary patents.

Research exceptions enable researchers to examine the patented inventions and to research improvements without infringing the patent. Under regulatory review exceptions, a patented invention can be used, without the consent of the patent holder, to develop information to obtain regulatory marketing approval. Although there is limited empirical evidence of the effect of these commonly implemented exceptions,[5] a 2016 study commissioned by the European Union (EU) suggests that broadening this exception to cover any medicines and marketing authorizations in any country could save between €23 million and €34.3 million per year (WIPO 2018).

Available policy measures include compulsory licenses and government-use authorizations, which may have an impact on government spending related to pharmaceuticals. Compulsory licensing allows the exploitation of a patented technology during the patent term without the consent of the patent holder but with the authorization of competent national authorities. This authorization may be given to a third party or, in the case of a government-use authorization, to a government agency or to a third party authorized to act on the government's behalf. Although particular attention has been paid to compulsory licensing for pharmaceuticals, it applies to patents in any field, including other health technologies.

Patents and market access. The existence of a patent may also affect whether drugs are launched in a country in the first place. Launching a drug may involve fixed costs to obtain regulatory approval as well as for marketing and distribution and thus be sensitive to the drug's profitability. Stronger patent protection accelerates drug launches (Cockburn, Lanjouw, and Schankerman 2016; Dai and Watal 2021; Kyle and Qian 2014). Taken together, the evidence suggests that the effect of patents on access may depend on market size, defined in terms of the number of patients affected in a country. In larger markets, the pricing effect would dominate, and patents would restrict access; in smaller markets, the product-launch effect might prevail, and patents might enhance access.

Other elements of IPR such as trade secrets and clinical trial data, as well as IP enforcement generally, also affect health technology development and trade. The protection of trade secrets and clinical trial data may influence pharmaceutical R&D, the time to market of generic pharmaceuticals, and pharmaceutical prices.[6]

Finally, strategies to manage IP at the institutional or project level (whether within the private, public, or philanthropic sector) have a bearing on health-product development and dissemination. These strategies include practical choices, such as whether to file for a patent, whether to license, and under which conditions (Taubman 2010). The United Nations–backed Medicines Patent Pool (MPP), for example, negotiates transparent, nonexclusive licenses with patent-holding pharmaceutical companies, enabling the MPP to grant sublicenses to manufacturers in LMICs to make and sell low-cost generic versions in certain territories. Some MPP agreements also provide for technology transfer.

Research institutions and funders—including the University of California, Berkeley (Mimura 2010) and the University of Manchester (2020)[7]—have implemented socially responsible licensing (SRL)-type policies. SRL policies generally provide that licensing agreements on IP must include contractual requirements ensuring that the end product is accessible in resource-poor settings. For example, this may include a requirement not to assert the patent rights in LMICs or to supply the product at the cost of production.

Medical services trade

Main types of trade barriers

The health services market is opening up to foreign competition. A growing number of countries are liberalizing trade in medical services, which provides more options for an efficient health care system and expands choice, improves service quality, and lowers prices. For example, commercial presence of foreign medical services suppliers "can contribute to upgrading health care infrastructure, create jobs, encourage the transfer of know-how and medical expertise to local providers and practitioners, and provide a broader array of specialized medical services than those available locally" (Sauvé et al. 2015, 85), hence contributing to health security.

Certain economies have developed increasingly friendly environments for this type of trade (Chanda 2001), as further discussed in box 2.2.[8] However, policy makers also need to evaluate and mitigate the risks of liberalizing the sector, such as creating a two-tiered system benefiting the wealthier (including foreign patients) in the context of mode 3 (commercial presence) or creating issues associated with ensuring service quality and patient safety through other modes of supply (Chanda 2017).[9]

Trade in medical services remains significantly restricted. Barriers to trade in services are more complex than for trade in goods because they are exclusively regulatory in nature (WTO 2019). They include market access restrictions (mainly in the

> **Box 2.2   Development of export-oriented medical services in selected countries**
>
> **India**
>
> Health care providers from India such as doctors, nurses, and technicians go to Australia, Canada, the Middle East, the United Kingdom, and the United States, mainly on short-term assignments to provide health care services. These assignments supply countries that have shortages of health care professionals while allowing Indian health care providers to upgrade their skills abroad.
>
> Conversely, foreign patients from high-income countries (such as the United Kingdom and the United States) as well as lower-income countries (such as Bangladesh, Nepal, and Sri Lanka) also come to India in search of less costly, high-quality treatments, namely surgery and specialized health services. Neighboring countries including those in Central Asia also benefit from India's exports of telehealth services.
>
> **Thailand**
>
> Thailand has developed a large medical tourism sector geared toward foreign patients. To mitigate internal brain drain, doctors and nurses receive public funding of their education. In return, they are required to serve three years in the public system (including in rural areas) before working in private hospitals.
>
> Policies to keep these doctors in the public health sector while also maintaining the quality of the sector have also been implemented. These included increasing the salaries of physicians, nurses, and dentists in all community hospitals.
>
> **Tunisia**
>
> Tunisia has used its geographic proximity to both Africa and Europe to attract foreign patients. Incentives to upgrade the health care system include tax exemption for medical equipment and devices; exemption of value added tax for treatments of foreign patients; a 50 percent tax cut on investments in medical institutions and infrastructure; partnerships with foreign companies; development of medical cities; and investment zones to attract foreign medical companies.
>
> **European Union**
>
> The EU's eHealth Action Plan 2012–2020 provides several guidelines on supporting patients' rights in cross-border health care services by focusing on supporting research, development, and innovation; promoting international cooperation; and achieving wider interoperability of telehealth services.
>
> *Source:* Gillson and Muramatsu 2020.

form of quantitative measures as well as specified legal forms authorized for firms) and discriminatory measures disadvantaging foreign services and services suppliers. For medical services, the restrictions can be partly explained by the fact that authorities set policy objectives to ensure health care access and quality, and consequently the need to use existing resources efficiently and attract new resources—all while controlling the overall cost of the health care financing system. Data collected by the WTO and World Bank illustrate the many significant barriers to trade in medical services—including, among others, foreign equity limits, nationality requirements, foreign exchange limitations, and restrictions on advertising (figure 2.4).[10]

Figure 2.4   Trade in medical services faces many trade barriers

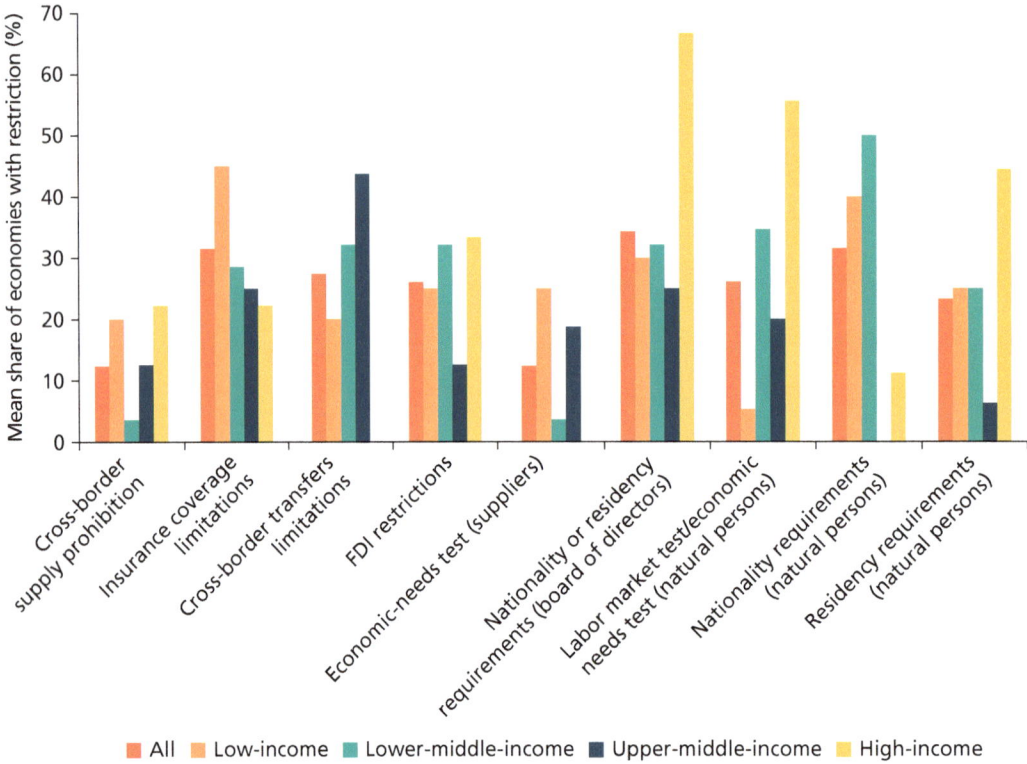

Source: World Trade Organization and World Bank, Services Trade Policy Database, http://i-tip.wto.org/services/.

Note: The study, using 2022 data, covers 73 economies encompassing all income levels (9 high-income economies, 16 upper-middle-income, 28 lower-middle-income, and 20 low-income, as defined in World Bank classifications). Measures on foreign direct investment (FDI), economic-needs tests on suppliers, and nationality or residency restrictions on boards of directors refer to activities of private health establishments. Measures referring to natural persons cover medical doctors, dentists, nurses, midwives, and paramedic personnel. For some economies included in this study, data are being collected and are not yet publicly available.

Barriers to seeking care abroad and cross-border services. The nonportability of health insurance across borders may restrict trade in medical services. Trade in medical services often occurs when patients go to another country for treatment (mode 2, or consumption abroad). However, in many jurisdictions, health expenditure is covered through state-funded health insurance systems, where only domestic expenditures can be recouped except in exceptional circumstances—for example, when specialist care is not available domestically. National health systems increasingly encourage patients to seek medical care abroad to lower costs or reduce demand pressure. However, in many cases, the portability of public health insurance coverage is not assured (as shown in figure 2.4), posing a major impediment to trade through the movement of patients (mode 2) as well as to cross-border telehealth services. This is particularly striking in low- and lower-middle-income groups, where this is not assured for 45 percent and

29 percent of the economies, respectively. Cross-border payment limitations also represent an important barrier for low- and middle-income economies.

Telehealth—in particular, cross-border supply of health services (mode 1)—is either heavily restricted or not well regulated, with unintended restrictive effects.[11] In some cases, regulation of electronic delivery of medical services is not well developed. In many others, electronic delivery is covered by health legislation that was not developed for that purpose, resulting in restrictive practices, particularly for cross-border supply. For example, nationality or residency requirements for health professionals may render cross-border supply impossible for many services. In 12 percent of the countries covered by available data, cross-border supply is identified as not possible. Even when it is allowed, it is difficult to identify what is permitted. Cross-border health services are also affected by restrictions on cross-border data flows and data localization requirements.

Barriers to foreign investment. Many barriers to the supply of medical services through commercial presence (mode 3) are horizontal, meaning they apply across sectors. For example, the medical services sector is often constrained by broad limitations on foreign investment. Many of the surveyed countries restrict foreign direct investment (FDI) (mainly with ceilings on foreign equity ownership), but the few restrictions specific to the medical sector are mainly in low- and lower-middle-income countries.

However, health is increasingly included among sectors where foreign investment is screened for national security considerations, particularly in high-income economies, which may consequently prevent foreign suppliers from entering their markets.[12] Other restrictions concern economic-needs tests (particularly in low-income countries), limitations on the membership of boards of directors, staffing restrictions, or other horizontal policies affecting FDI, such as limits on the acquisition of land by foreigners and discriminatory taxes or subsidies.

Barriers to mobility of health workers. Many types of barriers hinder the mobility of health professionals (mode 4). The temporary entry of foreign professionals to provide services is often subject to quantitative limits. In the countries covered by the survey, entry is often allowed based on horizontal "labor market tests" (prevalent in high-income countries) that aim to determine that no local resources are available. Such tests are often discretionary, based on opaque criteria.

Other regulations pertain to registration or licensing and include discriminatory requirements or procedures that can constitute trade barriers, such as nationality requirements. Available data show that this is the case in a third of countries in the sample, mainly in the low- and lower-middle-income groups.

Domestic regulation and recognition of qualifications

Regulatory requirements. Medical services suppliers face regulatory requirements to practice. To meet public policy objectives, the sector is subject to significant regulatory interventions (not considered "trade barriers" as described in the previous section).

For example, medical services may only be provided by "accredited professionals" or institutions, which implies a legal requirement to meet minimum requirements and qualifications and obtain authorization before they can provide services. The rationale behind regulatory requirements in the health sector relates in particular to the safety of patients and the effectiveness of care. At the same time, regulations applicable to medical services suppliers can lack transparency or predictability, or they may be applied arbitrarily, which can particularly affect foreign suppliers. Furthermore, regulations vary considerably across countries, which may hinder the mobility of medical services suppliers.

Transparent, predictable, and effective regulation is an important complement to medical services liberalization. The goal is to improve efficiency without compromising quality or other public policy objectives. Numerous countries have implemented regulatory reforms based on the good regulatory practices promoted by international agencies; such practices also apply to trade in medical services (Baiker, Bertola, and Jelitto 2021). Important measures refer to policy transparency and facilitative administrative procedures.

Available information confirms that some good regulatory practices have already been implemented in the national legislation of countries covered in this study, particularly regarding transparency (figure 2.5). For example, more than two-thirds of countries make publicly available (a) information on the licensing of health professionals and establishments, (b) monitoring of compliance with requirements, and (c) the allocation method mandated or described in the law or policy. However, many jurisdictions have yet to address several domestic regulatory issues, such as setting deadlines to accept or reject applications, submitting applications electronically, or telling unsuccessful applicants why they were rejected.

Recognition of qualifications. The recognition of qualifications earned abroad—a key issue for foreign medical services suppliers—requires a mechanism to verify the qualifications and competence gained by the applicant in a foreign country. Recognition can be achieved through harmonization or equivalence. Equivalence is the most common method and requires identifying possible gaps between foreign and domestic qualification requirements and appropriate compensatory measures (for example, additional courses or taking an exam).

Foreign qualifications for medical services are generally recognized in the surveyed economies. However, 20 percent of them lack laws or regulations to establish a process for recognizing degrees earned by health professionals abroad; the share is higher for low- and lower-middle-income economies. Of countries in the survey, 25 percent require foreign medical doctors to pass an exam, and 14 percent require them to obtain additional domestic education (figure 2.6, panel a). In 33 percent of countries, nurses, midwives, and other paramedical personnel must pass an exam (figure 2.6, panel b). The share is 56 percent in high-income economies. And 12 percent of countries require nurses and midwives to get additional domestic education.

Figure 2.5   Implementation of good governance practices in the medical services sector

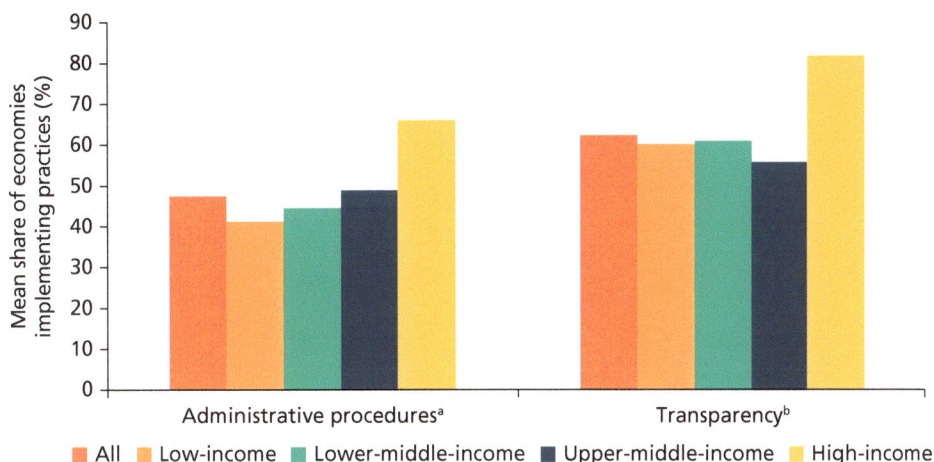

Source: World Trade Organization and World Bank, Services Trade Policy Database, https://i-tip.wto.org/services.

Note: The study, using 2022 data, covers 73 economies encompassing all income levels (9 high-income economies, 16 upper-middle-income, 28 lower-middle-income, and 20 low-income, as defined in World Bank classifications). For some of the countries included in this study, data are being collected and are not yet publicly available.

a. The selected administrative procedures include an allocation method mandated or described in law or policy; a single window for submission of applications; the possibility of submitting applications electronically; acceptance of authenticated copies; decisions made within a certain period of time; and informing unsuccessful applicants of reasons for rejection.

b. The selected transparency measures include making licensing information publicly available (criteria, procedures, monitoring, fees, contact information, time frame); establishing a single online portal; making prior notice and comments open on proposed regulatory changes; and considering comments received on proposed new legislation.

Health data transfer. The ability to move data is essential to the cross-border supply of telehealth services, but health data are also highly sensitive. The ability to digitally supply medical services internationally, particularly business-to-business, is crucially dependent on the ability of service providers to move relevant data across borders (Global Data Alliance 2020). At the same time, because personal health data are understandably sensitive, many governments have enacted stringent regulatory frameworks to ensure that the privacy of the data holders and the security of their data are safeguarded.

Regulations often limit the ability to move or process health and medical data abroad, either subjecting data transfer to conditions (such as to conform with certain benchmarks or to secure prior government approval) or prohibiting it altogether.[13] Although such measures seek to guarantee a high level of protection of personal medical information, they may hinder remote trade in health services and the associated benefits.

Figure 2.6   Recognition of foreign qualifications in the medical services sector

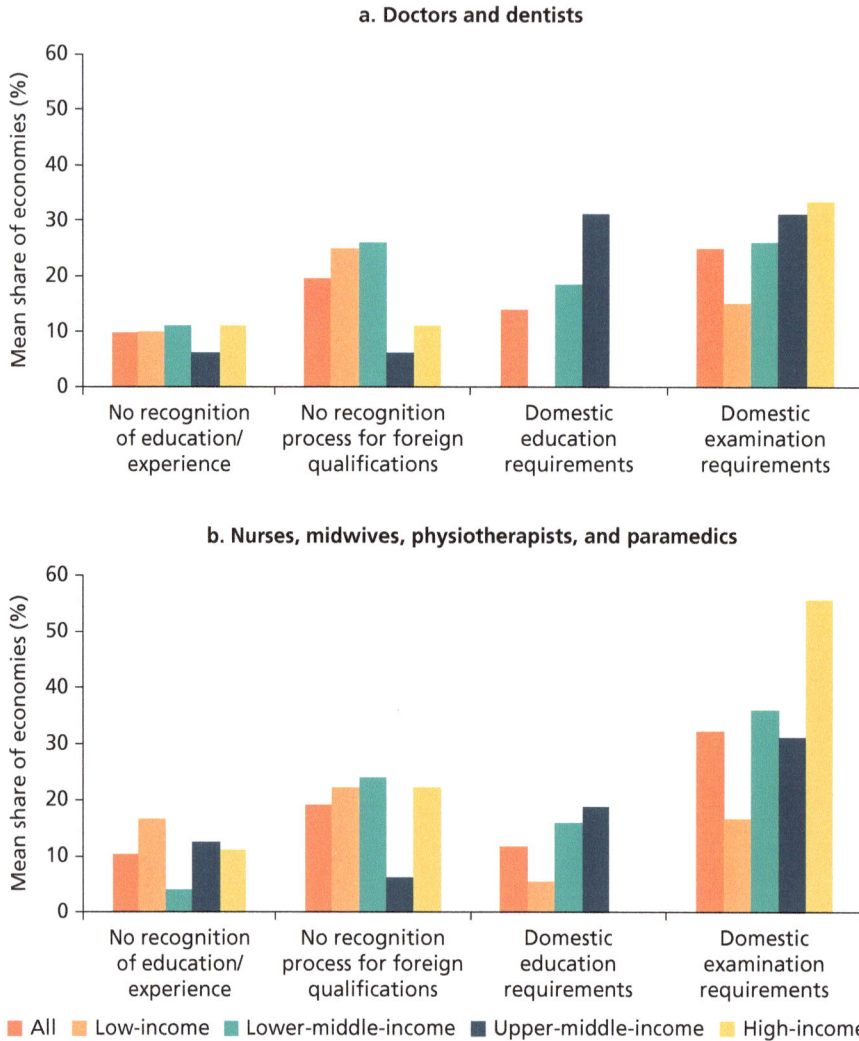

a. Doctors and dentists

b. Nurses, midwives, physiotherapists, and paramedics

■ All   ■ Low-income   ■ Lower-middle-income   ■ Upper-middle-income   ■ High-income

Source: World Trade Organization and World Bank, Services Trade Policy Database, https://i-tip.wto.org/services.

Note: The study, using 2022 data, includes 73 economies encompassing all income levels (9 high-income economies, 16 upper-middle-income, 28 lower-middle-income, and 20 low-income, as defined in World Bank classifications). For some of the countries included in this study, data are being collected and are not yet publicly available.

Policies affecting trade in both medical goods and services

Subsidies and local content requirements

Direct support to commercial operators figures prominently among the measures governments use to influence the provision of medical goods and services. Data collected by the Global Trade Alert (GTA) project show year-by-year the total number of subsidy, public procurement, and localization measures (however, note that this does not

Figure 2.7 Government support measures for the medical goods sector predated the pandemic

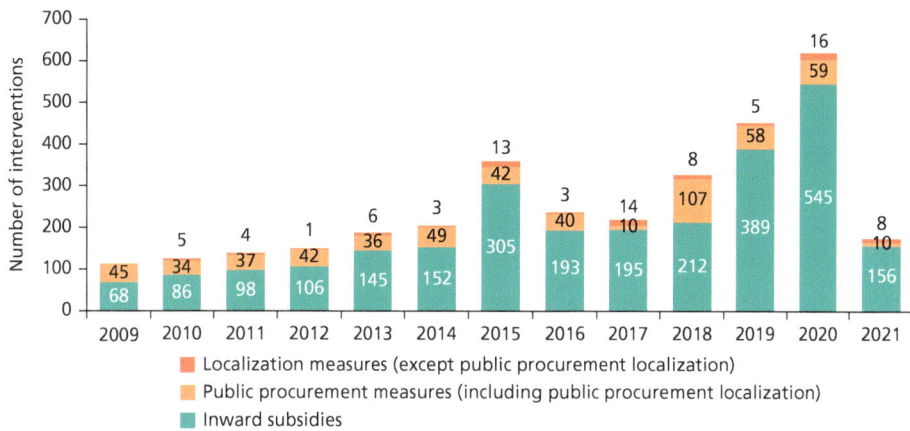

Source: Global Trade Alert (GTA) database, https://www.globaltradealert.org/data_extraction.

Note: The government support measures represent a total of 156 economies (across all income groups) tracked by GTA data between 2009 and 2021.

provide information on the impact of measures) found to favor local firms in the medical goods sector (figure 2.7). A total of 3,305 instances of such government support measures have been recorded in a total of 156 economies from 2009 through 2021, all of which have been implemented. Of that total, 2,650 are subsidies to commercial medical goods operators. In addition, 569 changes to public procurement regulations or laws favor local suppliers of medical goods. As figure 2.7 also shows, the number of government support measures was rising in the years before the COVID-19 pandemic. Then more than 600 instances of government support measures using these three policy instruments were recorded in 2020.

The number of subsidies awarded to producers of medical goods has been on the rise since the 2008–09 Global Financial Crisis. The three-year moving average rises from 84 for the years 2009–11 to 265 in the three years before the pandemic (2017–19) and rises further to 350 (for the years 2020–21). To put this fourfold increase in perspective, consider the following: over the same period (2009–21), the total number of subsidies in all sectors recorded each year in the GTA database rose by just under 150 percent. The faster growth in recorded subsidies to the medical sector is not a pandemic-era phenomenon; annual subsidy awards rose by 71 percent across all sectors of the economy before the pandemic, whereas they more than tripled in the medical sector.

Government procurement

The introduction of competitive and transparent government procurement procedures holds the potential to contribute substantially to improving the accessibility and affordability of medical goods and services, thus helping to establish more efficient and cost-effective health delivery systems. According to data from different studies, the prices of medical goods procured for public health systems through competitive and transparent tenders are lower than the prices of medical goods sold in the private sector (WHO, WIPO, and WTO 2020a). For example, competitive government procurement of HIV/AIDS, tuberculosis, and malaria drugs showed a reduction of originator and generic prices by 42 percent and 35 percent, respectively, compared with retail pharmacy prices (Danzon, Mulcahy, and Towse 2015).

When Guatemala introduced more competitive and transparent government procurement procedures (for example, by eliminating technical specifications that favor a particular tender), the costs of medical goods fell by 43 percent (Grosso and Moïsé 2003). Bangladesh, Colombia, Nicaragua, and Pakistan reaped similar savings. Conversely, a government procurement approach that limits transparency and competition (such as the use of limited tendering) can increase the prices and reduce the quality of medical goods and services. Nepal's use of limited tendering to buy medicines in hospital pharmacies proved to be less than optimal as well as costly (Shrestha et al. 2018).

Government procurement tools that aggregate demand can achieve better value for money and optimize resources. For example, many governments have developed mechanisms to procure large quantities of medical goods and services as part of a strategy to leverage greater purchasing and bargaining power to obtain better value for money and achieve economies of scale. Examples include pooled procurement, joint tenders, and centralized procurement schemes.[14]

Such mechanisms to aggregate demand in the health sector can be employed both within countries, such as in France and Sweden (OECD 2011), and among them—for example, in a joint initiative by Austria, Belgium, Ireland, Luxembourg, and the Netherlands to procure medicines for rare diseases as well as in an agreement by Estonia, Latvia, and Lithuania to jointly procure vaccines (Espín et al. 2016). Successful procurement schemes have reported substantial cost reductions for medical goods and services, confirming the efficiency of such tools to aggregate demand.[15] Despite their growing use, recent surveys suggest that they remain underused in the public health sector (WHO 2016).

Governments have liberalized access to their government procurement markets through unilateral action or through international trade negotiations under the 2012 WTO Government Procurement Agreement (further discussed in chapter 3) or other instruments (for example, regional trade agreements).

Competition policy

Competition policy can play important roles in ensuring access to medical goods and services and fostering innovation. In addition to addressing and preventing IPR abuses and other anticompetitive practices in the health sector, competition policy plays a broader role in two distinct ways: competition advocacy and law enforcement (Hawkins 2011). First, competition advocacy helps lawmakers and policy makers by informing legislative and regulatory processes in the health sector and encouraging the monitoring of health-related markets. It also helps private companies in the sector through provision of guidelines and advice on compliance with competition law and policy.[16]

Second, competition-law enforcement can address and correct anticompetitive behavior that can restrict R&D, limit the availability of resources needed to produce medical goods and services, create barriers to the market entry of medical goods and services, and restrict available distribution channels and consumer choices (WHO, WIPO, and WTO 2020c).

A variety of anticompetitive strategies to limit market entry of medical goods and services as well as potential competitors have attracted attention from competition authorities, such as the following:

- *Pay-for-delay (reverse payment) agreements:* Under this strategy, an incumbent holder of exclusive IPR pays its competitor to delay the entry of medical goods or services into a specific market.[17]
- *Misuse of patents and regulatory systems for medical goods and services:* Examples include (a) "sham litigation" (bringing baseless patent infringement suits to deter market entry of generic medical goods and services); (b) "patent thickets" (filing multiple patents on the same medical product); and (c) "product hopping" (unnecessarily forcing a switch from one version of a drug [with an expiring patent] to another version [with a new patent]).[18] Another anticompetitive patent strategy to delay the entry of generic products into health sector markets is referred to as "evergreening." This occurs when an incumbent files new patents to cover an already approved drug for which a new medical indication has been identified to extend the period of exclusivity after the original patents expire.[19]
- *Disparagement*: Under this strategy, an incumbent disseminates misleading information about its competitor's new medical products and services to prevent it from entering the market or expanding its presence in the market.[20]

Competition authorities are increasingly concerned about competition-law infringement that results in excessive pricing and other practices that inflate prices. For example, in 2022, the Competition Commission South Africa filed a referral with the South African Competition Tribunal for the prosecution of a health care provider for allegedly abusing its dominant position by charging excessively high prices (in both the private and public health care sectors) for a medicine used to treat breast and stomach cancer (CCSA 2022). In 2018, the Danish Competition Council ruled that a pharmaceutical distributor had abused its dominant position by charging excessive prices (OECD 2018).

Competition authorities also conduct merger control to ensure that mergers do not impede effective competition and suppress innovation. Competition laws usually provide remedies to block mergers or to require partial divestment as a condition for merger approval. For example, in 2015, the European Commission cleared Pfizer's acquisition of Hospira, which owned a medicine used to treat autoimmune diseases, subject to the condition that Pfizer's competing biosimilar development project be divested to another buyer (EC 2019).

In addition, competition authorities monitor anticompetitive behavior by market participants to ensure effective competition not only in private sector markets but, equally, in public sector markets for medical goods and services. Competition law and policy complement government procurement law and policy by helping to detect and combat anticompetitive behavior among suppliers of medical goods and services. For example, in a recent case in Japan, the court found that a group of large medical suppliers had been colluding for years (that is, they determined in advance who would bid, and they agreed on prices to be quoted) concerning procurement organized by the Japan Community Health Care Organization, which oversees more than 100 hospitals and medical facilities (EU-Japan Centre 2021).

POLICIES AFFECTING MEDICAL GOODS AND SERVICES TRADE DURING THE COVID-19 PANDEMIC

Medical goods trade

Import and export restricting and liberalizing policies

The uncertain scale, severity, and duration of the COVID-19 pandemic plus the imperative to overcome urgent domestic shortages of medical supplies shaped restrictions and reforms of the medical goods trade and allowed countries to apply discriminatory policies as an exception to WTO principles. This section provides evidence on the patterns of import and export policies—including tariffs, taxes, quotas, and licensing requirements—affecting COVID-19–related medical goods.[21]

Extent of restricting and liberalizing measures. Since the pandemic began, governments imposed both import liberalizing and export restricting measures on trade in medical goods. Import liberalization was most common, followed by curbs on exports and imports (figure 2.8, panel a).[22] Export liberalization was the least used among border-related trade policies.

Both import reforms and export curbs surged in the first two quarters of 2020, reaching a total of 200 and 134, respectively, in May 2020. From that moment onward, import liberalizing measures continued to grow, reaching a peak of 242 in December 2021. As of January 2022, the number of such measures decreased to 219, suggesting the temporary character of some liberalization efforts. Measures curbing exports slightly decreased during the first three months after their peak in April 2020 and then slowly increased over time, reaching a total of 138 in February 2022. Restrictive import measures also increased but at a slower pace and reached 88 in February 2022. Export liberalizing measures were seldomly used. Their maximum recorded number is 18.[23]

Figure 2.8 Patterns of trade policy intervention affecting medical goods during the COVID-19 pandemic

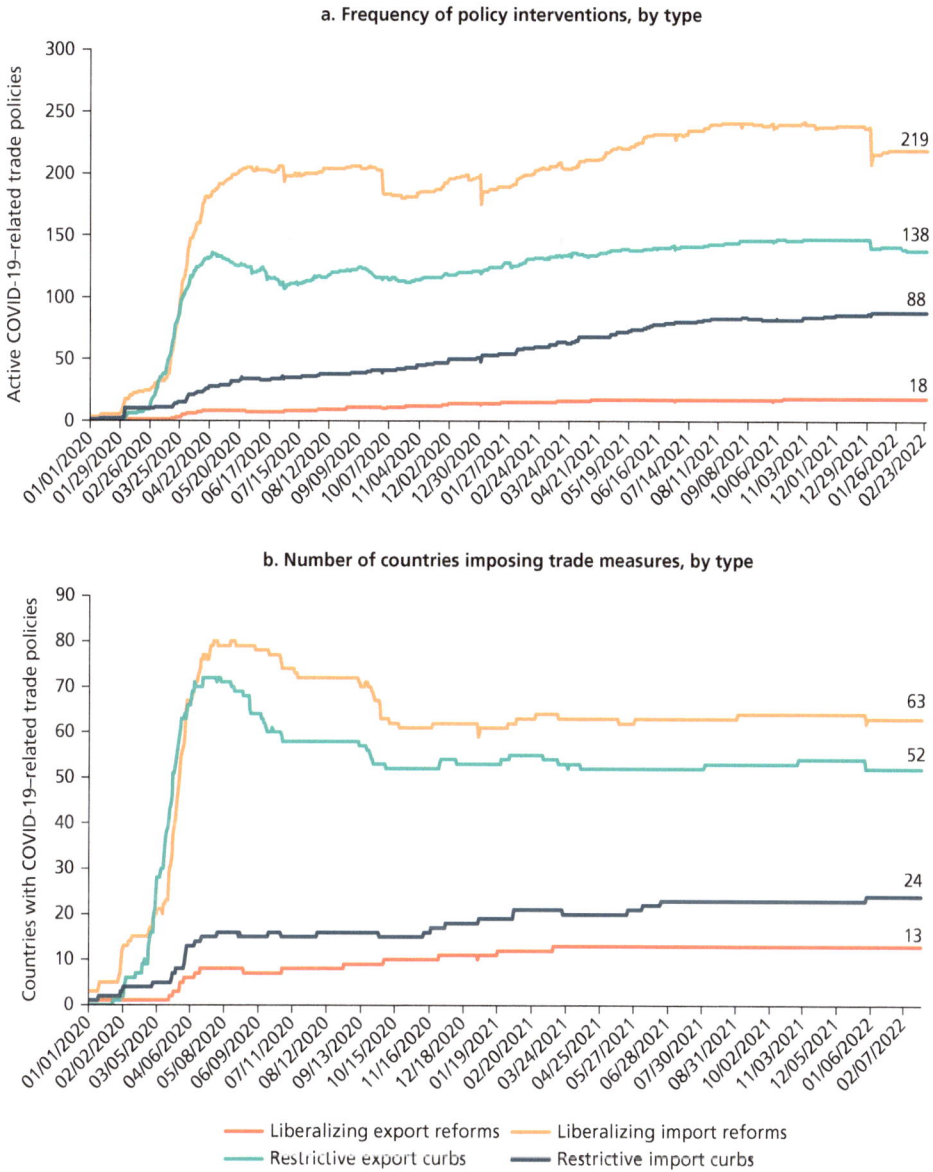

a. Frequency of policy interventions, by type

b. Number of countries imposing trade measures, by type

Legend:
— Liberalizing export reforms   — Liberalizing import reforms
— Restrictive export curbs   — Restrictive import curbs

Source: Calculations using the Essential Goods Initiative (EGI) database.

Note: The analysis covers 195 economies tracked by the EGI database, across all income groups. Numbers at the end of data lines indicate the total on the closing dates of February 23, 2022 (panel a) and February 7, 2022 (panel b). For more information about the analysis, the methodology, and the underlying data, see World Bank (2022).

More than two-thirds of the 195 countries tracked in the Essential Goods Initiative (EGI) database resorted to policy interventions to ensure domestic accessibility of medical goods during the pandemic. The number of countries implementing trade-policy changes affecting medical goods surged in the first wave of the pandemic (figure 2.8, panel b). By April 2020, a total of 82 countries eased import restrictions to improve accessibility of essential medical goods for dealing with the pandemic. Similarly, 72 countries increased their export restrictions to be able to respond to the increased domestic demand for medical goods. As of early 2022, 63 countries were implementing import reforms, and 52 were applying export restrictions.

Extent of medical goods trade affected. Trade reforms and trade restrictions covered up to 20 percent of trade in medical goods during the pandemic.[24] The trade covered by import liberalizing reforms affecting medical goods peaked in the fourth quarter of 2020 at US$137 billion and subsequently fell to US$105 billion by the end of 2021 (reflecting the lapse of some temporary import reforms on medical goods) (figure 2.9). In contrast, the trade covered by export curbs on medical goods peaked in the third quarter of 2021 (at US$103 billion) and fell only slightly (to US$98 billion) by the end of 2021. The trade covered by import curbs on medical goods has grown over time but has never exceeded US$30 billion. In February 2022, the total trade value of medical goods covered by trade restrictions likely exceeded that covered by trade liberalizing reforms.[25]

Figure 2.9   Medical goods trade covered by import and export policy measures, January 2020 to January 2022

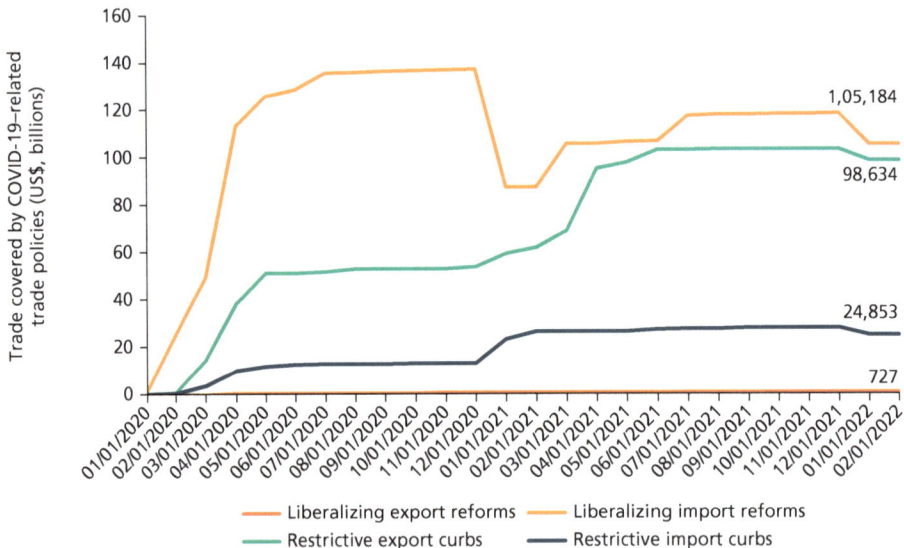

Source: Calculations using Essential Goods Initiative (EGI) database.

Note: The analysis covers 195 economies tracked by the EGI database, across all income groups. Numbers at the end of data lines indicate the respective totals on the closing date of January 1, 2022. For more information about the analysis, the methodology, and the underlying data, see World Bank (2022).

Pharmaceutical products and other medical supplies (such as syringes, needles, disinfectants, oxygen, and PPE) were the medical goods most heavily affected by prohibitions and restrictions before and during the pandemic. Import and export licensing procedures on medical goods were also notified to the WTO during the pandemic. The EU, for example, notified its export authorization scheme for COVID-19 vaccines, implemented by the European Commission in January 2021. This time-limited mechanism, initially meant to last until the end of March 2021, was renewed three times until it was removed on December 31, 2021.[26]

Duration of policy interventions. The duration of policy intervention during the pandemic casts doubt on their "temporary" natures. Few of the border-related trade policy interventions affecting medical goods in force as of February 2022 are less than 90 days old (table 2.1). In fact, 157 of the liberalizing import reforms enacted since the start of the pandemic have been in force for more than one year. A total of 109 export restrictions on medical goods have lasted longer than one year. Left unchanged, these findings presage a permanent change in the trade-policy treatment of medical goods.

Impacts of interventions on trade costs. Preliminary analysis suggests that trade policy measures significantly increased import trade costs for medical goods during the first months of the pandemic and then gradually decreased, reaching prepandemic levels by the end of 2021. This analysis studies the implications of this rising protectionism on trade costs and on flows of medical goods and vaccines, using information on policy measures adopted between January 2020 and December 2021 at the 6-digit Harmonized System code (HS6) traded-product level (Egger et al. 2022).[27]

Figure 2.10 illustrates the average percentage change in import trade costs across countries as a result of trade policies, both for medical products overall and for a set of cost-sensitive products. During the first four months of 2020, trade policies contributed to average trade cost increases of up to 60 percent for medical goods overall

Table 2.1   Duration of currently active COVID-19 policy measures affecting medical goods trade (as of February 2022)

Intervention type	Duration up to 30 days	Duration up to 90 days	Duration 90–365 days	Duration exceeding 1 year
Export curbs	0	1	27	109
Export reforms	0	0	4	14
Import curbs	0	6	26	56
Import reforms	1	12	49	157

Source: Global Trade Alert database, https://www.globaltradealert.org/data_extraction.

Note: Export and import "reforms" had trade-liberalizing rather than restrictive effects.

in April 2020 (figure 2.10, panel d). By the end of 2021, the impact of trade policies on trade costs gradually decreased to less than 10 percent over their pandemic
level. A similar pattern can be seen for selected products such as garments used to
produce masks and other PPE (figure 2.10, panel a) and for ventilators (figure 2.10,
panel c). The pattern of trade costs for vaccines confirms that efforts to facilitate
trade increased once these products became available in the first quarter of 2021
(figure 2.10, panel b).

Figure 2.10 Impact of COVID-19–related trade policies on trade costs of medical goods
imports, by type

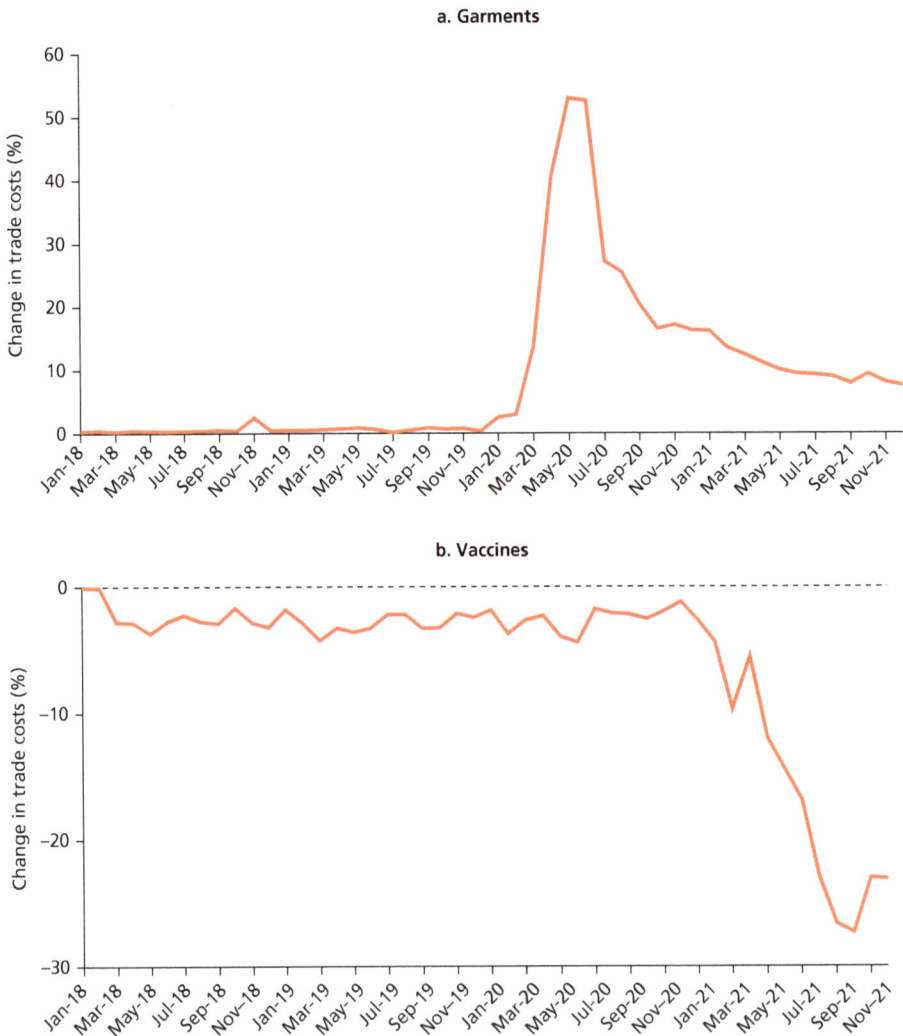

a. Garments

b. Vaccines

(Continued)

Figure 2.10   Impact of COVID-19–related trade policies on trade costs of medical goods imports, by type *(Continued)*

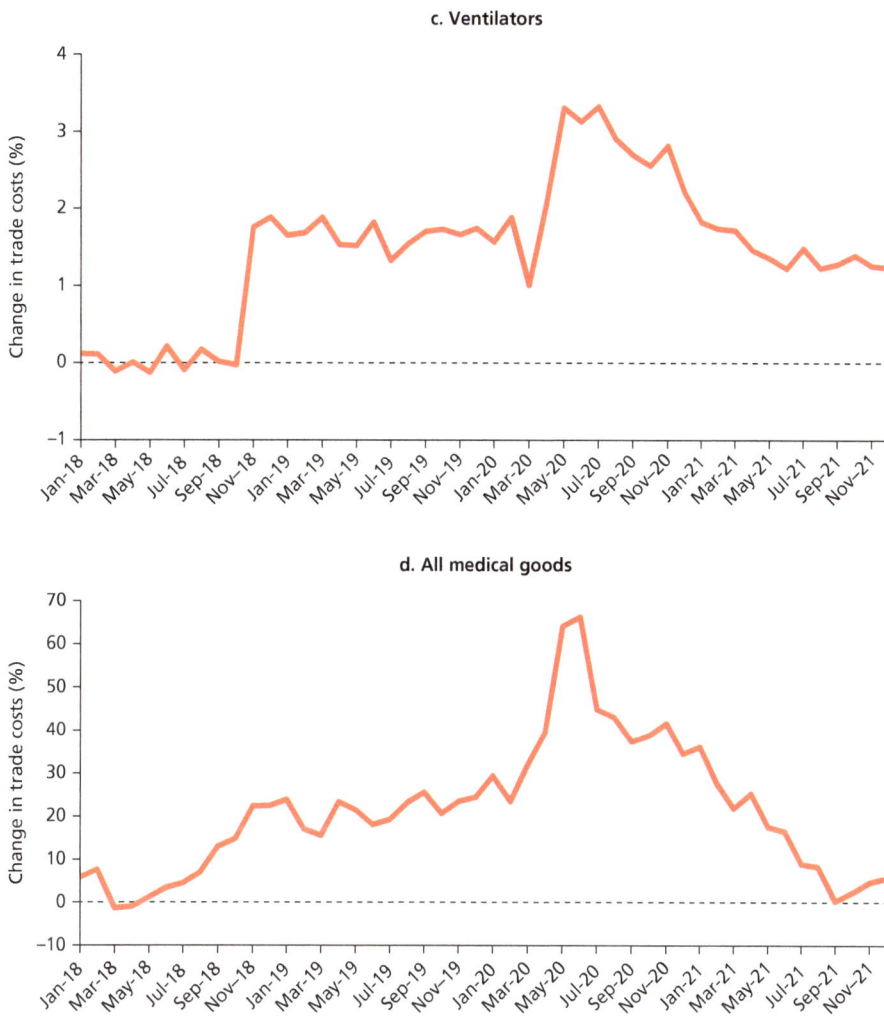

c. Ventilators

d. All medical goods

Source: Egger et al. 2022.

Policies affecting services trade that support medical goods trade

Border closures and travel restrictions at the start of the pandemic had a dramatic impact on trade in medical goods. Measures had to be taken to restore connectivity for medical goods, including the following actions affecting air transport:

- Airlines were asked to prioritize the international transportation of COVID-19–related medical goods and equipment over other types of cargo (see, for instance, Duncan 2020).

- Certain regulatory requirements were eased to provide flexibility to airlines and crews (WTO 2020),[28] and numerous governments granted support measures in favor of the sector.[29]
- To facilitate transport of medical goods during the crisis, several countries liberalized trade in air cargo transport services, such as by granting additional traffic rights for all-cargo services (see, for example, ICAO 2020b).
- Initiatives were also undertaken at the international level, including calls to ensure that air crews be designated as "key workers" (ICAO 2020a) and thus exempted from too-stringent travel restrictions, or guidance on appropriate health measures for air travel.

In addition, other modes of transport—although not dominant means of transport for medical goods—are particularly important for the movement of the raw materials and intermediary products needed for the medical manufacturing. Again, measures taken by governments slowed down transport and logistics operations and led to port congestions, shortages of empty containers, hinterland transport logjams, and severe delays in transit.

Trade facilitation policies

Many countries expedited a transition from paper-based to electronic documents in response to the pandemic. The use of electronic documents reduces the interaction between traders and border authorities in keeping with COVID-19 transmission controls, but such a change also increases trade efficiencies by reducing the time it takes to obtain and submit paper documents or to obtain corrections or replacements. Japan Customs, for example, relaxed several administrative procedures, such as to allow the acceptance of electronic versions of documents, hence reducing the need to submit documents including declarations and certificates of origin within a specified time frame. The country also relaxed authentication steps and simplified the declaration form for relief items to expedite clearance of these goods.

Transparency and access to information are key to compliance with requirements. In response to COVID-19, governments established websites or inquiry points to provide practical information on import, export, and transit procedures as well as access to required forms and documents. Other countries began conducting regular consultations with stakeholders to apprise them of changes and obtain feedback on bottlenecks to critical commodities. These issues were then raised to National Trade Facilitation Committees (NTFCs) or interagency consultations to develop resolutions. In many cases, these consultation forums allowed border agencies to better identify trade in critically required medicines, which could then be identified for expedited clearance.

In addition, traders were allowed to submit documentation before the arrival of a shipment, smoothing clearances. Early in the pandemic, for example, the EU established prioritized lanes at border crossings to facilitate the movement of PPE, medical goods, and perishable foods. Early documentation submission requirements expedited clearance of commodities. Minimal documentation requirements were established and the use of electronic submissions was increased, reducing interactions at the border as well as the risk of spreading the virus.

Effective implementation of risk-based border management is a key best practice for trade facilitation. Modern border management encourages administrations to focus on high risks. In response to COVID-19, administrations used risk management to prioritize the clearance of imports and exports of low-risk critical medical products. In responding to the pandemic, many countries adopted risk-based approaches to reduce interaction between officials and the trading community. For example, countries suspended border inspections of medical supplies, preferring to expedite goods to destination, then conducted postclearance audits to verify compliance with regulatory requirements. Since many imports may be subject to multiple agency requirements, the strategy had to be coordinated across relevant authorities.

Simplified trade procedures facilitated the flow of critical supplies. Chinese Taipei, for example, introduced measures to expedite customs clearance of critical medical goods, removed requirements for some documents (such as permits for mask exports), and established dedicated customs contact points to respond to trader inquiries.[30] India waived late fees for delayed filings of customs documentation.

Regulatory measures

To speed up trade in critical goods during the pandemic, economies took various trade-facilitating measures regarding the World Trade Organization's (WTO) Technical Barriers to Trade (TBT) and regulation. Countries streamlined regulatory and TBT measures, such as accelerating the approval processes for medical goods on an emergency basis, while maintaining safety, quality, and efficacy criteria. Several such measures were notified to the WTO. Since the start of the pandemic, 211 new or changed TBT regulations were notified, representing around 40 percent of all WTO notifications in response to COVID-19.[31] These notified TBT measures dealt with a range of extraordinary and temporary procedures for handling the public health emergency.[32] Such measures aimed in part to streamline or simplify certification and related procedures. To those ends, authorities

- Used information technology tools to conduct remote conformity assessment procedures;
- Relied on regulatory cooperation by, for instance, accepting test results from internationally accredited laboratories; and
- Suspended or relaxed authorization, registration, or certification procedures for certain medical goods and vaccines.[33]

In some cases, new requirements were added or existing ones strengthened. Several economies introduced new technical regulations or conformity assessment procedures for medical goods, including those on safety, quality, and efficacy criteria.[34] These new requirements aimed to ensure safety or quality of certain medical goods that were not previously

Figure 2.11   NRA decisions on WHO-EUL COVID-19 vaccines, December 2020 to February 2022

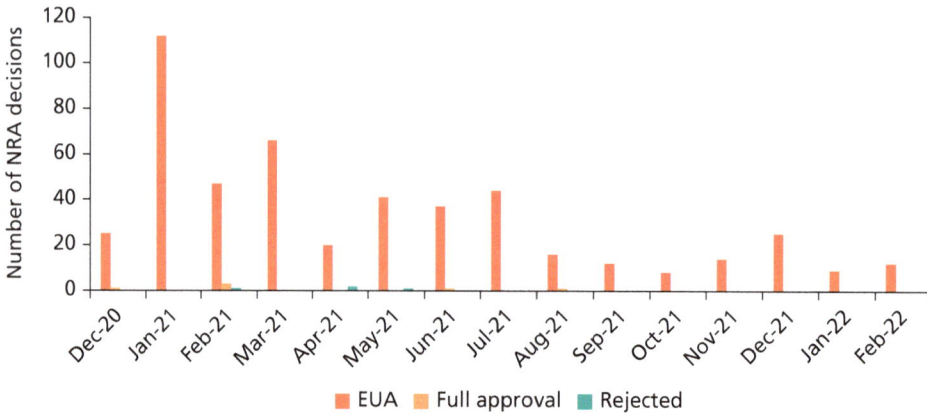

Source: Author's calculations, based on Airfinity 2022, https://science.airfinity.com/covid-19-vaccines.

Note: This figure includes decisions on only those COVID-19 vaccines that have received an Emergency Use Listing of the World Health Organization (WHO-EUL). EUA = emergency use authorization; NRA = national regulatory authority.

regulated (such as community face masks) or to enable domestic production that was initiated to avoid disruptions in supply. The majority (66 percent) of the COVID-19–related TBT notifications covered medical goods such as PPE, medicines, other medical devices and equipment (such as ventilators), and medical supplies (such as nasal swabs).

Many NRAs activated emergency use authorizations (EUAs) to fast-track vaccine approval.[35] Emergency authorization is temporary and is used to meet urgent health needs. A significant number of EUAs were granted to COVID-19 vaccines by national authorities in the first half of 2021 (figure 2.11). Some NRAs used expedited procedures to grant an EUA by relying on the work and data of other regulators and the Emergency Use Listing of the WHO (WHO-EUL). This was especially useful for NRAs in LMICs. For example, the Ghana Food and Drugs Authority approved some vaccines using its own EUA guidelines while it approved others relying on stringent regulatory authorities and the WHO-EUL (WTO 2021). NRAs have granted full approval to just six COVID-19 vaccines.

IPR policies during the pandemic

The COVID-19 experience suggests that biomedical innovation can be rapid even when patent protection is less dominant as an incentive (see, for example, Sampat and Shadlen 2021). Other factors—such as the support of research efforts by public entities and private sector actors with nonmonetary motivations and direct R&D subsidies—may have played more important roles. That said, the record time in which COVID-19 health technologies have been developed has also been attributed to R&D preceding the COVID-19 pandemic and the patenting of technologies building on earlier activities (WIPO 2022). This calls for a more subtle empirical analysis of the role of IPR as an incentive for R&D during pandemics (see also Conti 2022).

Rapid, equitable, and affordable access is crucial during a pandemic. Although prices for COVID-19 vaccines have been the subject of some controversy, some vaccine producers pledged at least initially not to profit from vaccine sales and thus not to exploit the full economic potential of exclusive IPR. Emerging research has shown that COVID-19 vaccines were sold at relatively low prices. Castillo et al. (2021) estimate the value of an immunization course at over US$5,800, with actual prices being two orders of magnitude lower. Indeed, there was clearly excess demand for COVID-19 vaccines, especially in the first half of 2021, with prices not adjusting to bring the market into equilibrium. In this sense, the lack of access to vaccines was attributable more to lack of supply than to high prices.

Governments responded to concerns about vaccine equity:

- *Some jurisdictions amended legislation governing the issuance of compulsory and government-use licenses.* Canada, Germany, Hungary, France, and Italy amended laws or enacted additional laws to streamline procedures for government use, compulsory licenses, or other measures.[36] In Canada, for example, Bill C-13 (An Act Respecting Certain Measures in Response to COVID-19) in April 2020 waived a requirement to show unsuccessful efforts to obtain authorization to use an invention from the patentee on reasonable commercial terms within a reasonable period.[37]
- *Some jurisdictions authorized the use of patented inventions under government-use or compulsory licenses.* For example, in March 2020, Israeli authorities authorized government use of lopinavir/ritonavir (an antiretroviral medication marketed under the brand name Kaletra), which is patented in Israel. The government-use authorization was based on the need to maintain essential supplies and services for the sole purpose of treating COVID-19 patients. Later in 2020, both Hungary and the Russian Federation used government-use or compulsory licenses to allow the use of another patented COVID-19 medication, remdesivir, to supply their domestic markets.[38]
- *Other measures introduced IP office procedures related to the grant of COVID-related patents.* One example is the COVID-19 Prioritized Patent Examination Pilot Program, launched by the US Patent and Trademark Office to allow accelerated examination for qualifying COVID-related applications.[39]

Several dedicated patent databases, search facilities, reports, and indexes have been established by national and regional intellectual property offices, intergovernmental organizations, nongovernmental organizations, as well as academics.[40] Patents on COVID-19 medical products and technologies increased exponentially following the identification of the virus (WIPO 2022), although the legal status of patents covering vaccine-related technologies remains highly divergent across jurisdictions (Chiang and Wu 2022). Because of the patent system's disclosure requirement, a vast amount of legal and technical information is in the public domain. This has major importance in response to public health emergencies because easy access to information supports policy makers, procuring entities, the pharmaceutical industry, and others in developing evidence-based policies or strategies to promote innovation, technology transfer, and licensing and to improve equitable access to medical products and services through collaborative efforts.

Many initiatives to improve access to COVID-19 medical products and technologies focus on sharing technology through pooling mechanisms and voluntary licensing (see, for example, Wu and Khazin 2020). For example, the first transparent, global, nonexclusive license for a COVID-19 serological antibody technology was granted to WHO's COVID-19 Technology Access Pool (C-TAP) by the Spanish National Research Council in November 2021 (WHO and MPP 2021). In early March 2022, the US National Institutes of Health (NIH) announced that it will offer several technologies related to therapeutics, vaccines, and diagnostic methods for COVID-19 to C-TAP (WHO and MPP 2022).

Several licenses were granted directly through a pooling mechanism such as the MPP. They include a Pfizer voluntary license for its oral antiviral Paxlovid,[41] which was announced shortly after Merck agreed to license its oral antiviral molnupiravir to the MPP (Taylor and Parker 2021). For Paxlovid, the MPP signed sublicense agreements in March 2022 with 35 generic manufacturers to produce low-cost, generic versions for supply in 95 LMICs (MPP 2022).[42] In addition, bilateral voluntary licensing agreements have been reached, such as the March 2022 agreement between Aspen and Johnson & Johnson to manufacture and make available an Aspen-branded COVID-19 vaccine (Aspenovax) throughout Africa (Beukes 2022). Furthermore, some rights holders have announced that, in light of the COVID-19 pandemic, they will not enforce their patent rights for related medical products.[43]

Medical services trade

Limitations on people's movement affected trade in services. The nature of the COVID-19 virus presented unique challenges for the services sector. Lockdowns and border closures limited the consumption of services abroad and the international movement of individuals supplying services (for example, crews for transportation services). These measures limited the movement of patients seeking treatment abroad and the mobility of health professionals, who were in greater demand in some countries because of the pandemic (Gillson and Muramatsu 2020). For the latter, some corrective measures were implemented, such as easing the entry of health personnel. However, limitations on the movement of people encouraged trade facilitation measures in areas such as telehealth services. Many of these measures were implemented temporarily, and some are now being made permanent.

Telehealth increased access to health care during the lockdown. At the peak of the pandemic's first wave, several countries suffered from severe shortages of hospital beds and health care workers. Regulators in some jurisdictions issued guidance to allow telehealth programs, while others accelerated existing plans to allow them. In many cases, only established health care suppliers were allowed to provide the services, with the potential for foreign suppliers to invest. But some other jurisdictions made it possible to develop platforms that connected health care providers and patients in different locations. For example, GrabHealth—a joint venture between the Singaporean ride-hailing company Grab and the Chinese telehealth company Ping An Good Doctor—built a telemedicine platform for Indonesia, which saw usage skyrocket during the first wave of the pandemic (Reuters 2020). Also, some policies were introduced to support the development of telehealth services and access by populations in remote areas (for example, using computer or telecommunication services).

Many countries lowered barriers to increase the pool of health workers, while others moved to retain essential workers to respond to their own national needs. To increase the pool of health care workers available to fight the pandemic, many countries sought to temporarily liberalize regimes for the mobility of health professionals. Australia and the United Kingdom streamlined the granting of visas and work permits. Chile, Italy, and New York State allowed foreign-trained doctors to practice within their systems without formally recognizing their qualifications. Belgium, Luxembourg, and Spain fast-tracked the recognition of qualifications. Other countries took steps to keep essential health workers from leaving. For example, the Philippines, a leading international supplier of nurses, temporarily banned health professionals from traveling overseas.

Investment screening measures were implemented to limit the economic impact of the pandemic, with consequences for the health care sector. Canada and the EU added health care to the list of sectors in which foreign investment is screened for national security purposes (WTO 2020). Others lowered the threshold that triggered investment reviews or prevented foreign investors from acquiring health care firms.

Policies affecting both medical goods and services trade

The use of policies such as subsidies, public procurement, and localization measures to favor local firms in the medical goods sector accelerated during the pandemic (as shown earlier in figure 2.7). Subsidies were the most common policy measure used by governments, representing 88 percent of the recorded instances (545 measures) in 2020. Government procurement and localization measures were used less frequently— representing 10 percent (59 measures) and 1 percent (16 measures), respectively, of the recorded instances in 2020.

Subsidies

Different forms of government support were provided to local producers of medical goods. A week-by-week breakdown of the total number of subsidies in effect since the start of 2020 is provided in figure 2.12.[44] This figure excludes 383 firm-specific subsidies awarded in China to publicly listed firms, because although the calendar year in which a financial grant was received is known, the exact date of the subsidy receipt is not. Excluding China, a total of 275 subsidies (300 if counting subsidies that have lapsed) to firms engaged commercially in the medical goods sectors have been documented, and state resources have been provided in the following ways, among others:[45] financial grants (99); state loans (78); tax or social insurance relief on imported medical goods (27); loan guarantees (25); and production subsidies (10).

State resources were made available along the entire production chain of COVID-19–related medical goods. Following is a breakdown of the types of medical goods firms receiving state support since January 1, 2020 (a subsidy may be given to a firm operating in more than one line of business): 45 percent of subsidy awards were received by medical equipment producers (such as manufacturers of ventilators); 62 percent were received by makers of medical supplies such as PPE; 45 percent were received by firms involved in discovering or producing medicines, including vaccines; and 71 percent of specific subsidy award decisions benefited firms involved in biologics production.

There are societal gains to be made by supporting the private medical sector both to accelerate manufacturing capacity investments at risk and to expand capacity beyond the profit maximizing level. Vaccine production can illustrate the point. A profit maximizing firm would wait until after resolution of uncertainty associated

Figure 2.12   Weekly breakdown of active subsidy policy interventions affecting medical goods since the onset of the COVID-19 pandemic (excluding China), January 2020 to March 2022

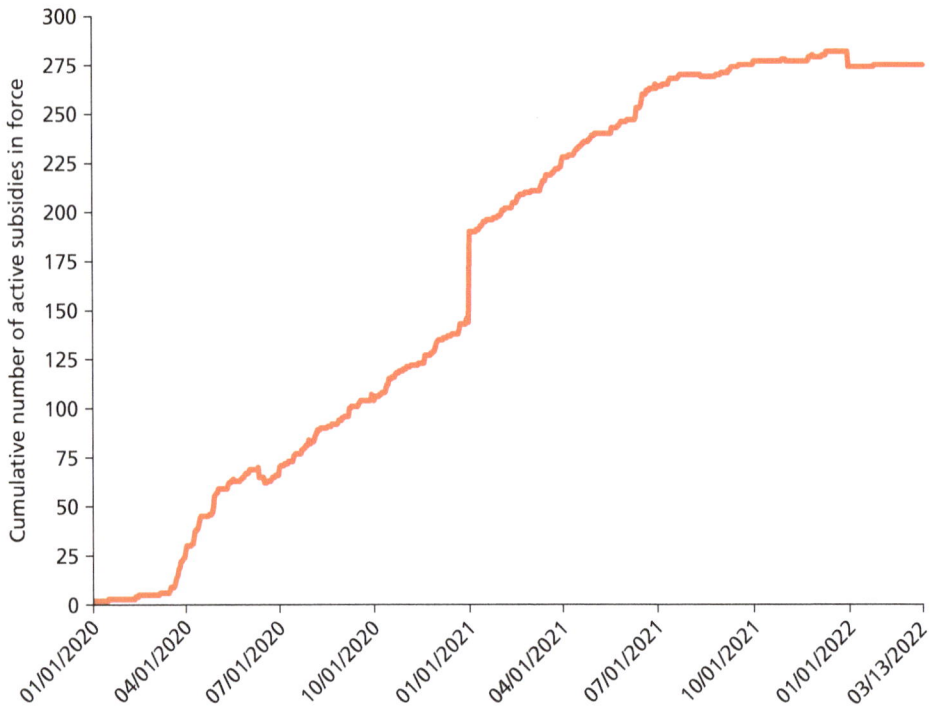

Source: Global Trade Alert database.

Note: The figure's data excludes subsidies in China.

with the lengthy phase 3 clinical trials. Furthermore, if prices for vaccines are relatively fixed, firms have little incentive to substantially increase production capacity to fill orders faster, especially because there is little risk of entry by competitors given the lack of options for consumers (Budish and Snyder 2021). (During COVID-19, prices were set in the range of US$6–US$40 per course of vaccination, well below their estimated social value of US$5,800 per course [Castillo et al. 2021]). Experts therefore recommend using "push contracts" for these types of subsidies. Thus, governments should not only provide subsidies to multiple vaccine sponsors to diversify scientific risk but also should do so *at their own risk* so that firms could begin building their manufacturing infrastructure in parallel with the phase 3 clinical trials.

Government procurement

The COVID-19 pandemic strained government procurement systems. One core responsibility of governments in the context of a pandemic is to procure medical goods such as PPE, vaccines, diagnostics, and therapeutics to respond to the crisis and support the provision of medical services to the population. It is thus not surprising that government procurement appeared at the forefront of the response to the COVID-19 pandemic in many jurisdictions. The resilience of government procurement systems was put to the test with the rapid and sustained increase in global demand for medical goods and services and the decrease in production capacity (see, for example, OECD 2020c).

Although some economies were prepared to respond quickly, others had to adjust existing government procurement rules and policy options to address challenges arising from the pandemic. These challenges included speeding up procedures to ensure timely availability of medical goods and services; addressing the potential lack of qualified domestic suppliers; engaging foreign suppliers; and encouraging or preserving competition among suppliers to keep prices down.

Framework agreements setting out the medical goods and services likely needed during the COVID-19 pandemic enhanced resilience and ensured a rapid response. These agreements helped governments avoid using limited tendering and emergency contracting. For example, early in the COVID-19 pandemic, the Italian Central Purchasing Body (Consip) acquired emergency medical goods through framework agreements with multiple suppliers (OECD 2020b).

Special emergency government procurement rules and flexibilities came into play. Some of these rules and flexibilities aim to accelerate the government procurement process—for example, by shortening applicable deadlines to be observed by suppliers. To some extent, this approach safeguards transparency and supplier competition. Economies such as the EU and Switzerland issued additional guidance and recommendations on the use of existing rules and flexibilities in their government procurement systems to ensure rapid and efficient procurement of medical goods and services (EC 2020b; Swiss Confederation 2020). Such existing flexibilities included reliance on electronic procurement and related e-tools and shorter time periods for competitive tendering.

Limited tendering was used for the timely procurement of medical goods and services. Under this method, the procuring entity contacts one or more suppliers of its choice and can waive most transparency and procedural requirements. For example, during the COVID-19 pandemic, the Slovak Republic purchased medical supplies amounting to €54.1 million through limited tendering (OECD 2020b).

Some countries aggregated demand through joint procurement or similar mechanisms to ensure the supply of essential medical goods and services. The urgency caused by the COVID-19 pandemic made the planning of demand very challenging, and governments quickly found themselves in competition with each other to procure essential medical goods and services from a limited number of global suppliers. This shifted bargaining power from the procuring entities to the suppliers, resulting in less value for money—an increase in prices and substandard goods (Kohler and Wright 2020). To address these challenges, countries including Canada, Colombia, and Italy used joint procurement or mechanisms such as pooled or centralized procurement. This has proved beneficial for increasing the bargaining power of procuring entities, achieving economies of scale, and avoiding excessive competition among buyers for a limited supply of essential medical goods and services. Such procurement tools have also been used at the regional level, as in the case of the EU (as further discussed in chapter 3).

Governments sought to preserve core principles of the government procurement systems—transparency, value for money, and accountability. Measures included (a) issuing standard technical specifications for different products, such as PPE and ventilators, to avoid substandard medical goods and ensure value for money; and (b) creating databases to ensure transparency of transactions related to the pandemic.[46]

Competition policy

Competition law and policy helped governments address health sector-related challenges. During a pandemic, competition law and policy play important roles, and competition authorities must be vigilant to ensure that competition remains effective. At the same time, the urgent need to ensure the availability of medical goods and services may call for additional flexibilities in the enforcement of competition laws and for allowing some forms of cooperation between competitors under certain conditions. Competition authorities can perform an important advocacy role by informing governments about the potential competitive impacts of proposed economic measures taken in response to a pandemic (ICN 2020; UNCTAD 2020).

Competitors cooperated to meet the increased demand for medical goods and services. To facilitate cooperation, several jurisdictions issued new rules (for example, block exemptions) or guidelines on the implementation of competition laws as well as information on how cooperation between private companies in the health sector would be assessed during the pandemic. The EU, for instance, issued a temporary framework for assessing competition issues related to business cooperation.[47] South Africa enacted a block exemption from the application of its competition law in the health care sector to enable firms to cooperate to prevent shortages during the pandemic (Naidu and Nxumalo 2020).

Competition authorities also stayed on the alert for other anticompetitive practices. For example, in Greece, the Hellenic Competition Commission initiated an ex officio investigation for suspected violations of the competition law in public procurement tenders of medical and other goods and services needed to respond to the pandemic (Greece, HCC 2020).

Competition authorities paid attention to the impact of the COVID-19 pandemic on merger control assessment. For example, on substance, several competition authorities issued guidance and clarified that the emergency would not affect their standards for merger review (for example, in the United Kingdom).[48] In terms of working arrangements, several competition authorities indicated that they would show some flexibility, such as by extending the periods for review and advising to notify only for "urgent and essential" deals (Latham & Watkins 2021).

NOTES

1. Tariff data are from *World Tariff Profiles* (2021 and earlier issues), a joint annual publication of the World Trade Organization (WTO), International Trade Centre (ITC), and United Nations Conference on Trade and Development (UNCTAD). For issues available to download, see the WTO's World Tariff Profiles web page: https://www.wto.org/english/res_e/reser_e/tariff_profiles_e.htm.

2. Data on quantitative restrictions are based on notifications submitted by WTO members. See the WTO Quantitative Restrictions Database: https://qr.wto.org/en#/home.

3. The air transport services sector is governed by a maze of bilateral, and a few plurilateral, air services agreements (ASAs), which provide for the reciprocal exchange of traffic rights. Most of these agreements are highly restrictive, dictating the prices charged, number of flights offered, types of aircrafts deployed, and cities served, and prohibiting any kind of third-party competition.

4. F. Hoffmann-La Roche Ltd. & Anr. v. Cipla Ltd. [RFA(OS) 92/2012]; and Cipla Ltd. v. F. Hoffmann-La Roche Ltd. & Anr. [RFA(OS) 103/2012], paras. 71–74.

5. For information on the research and regulatory review exceptions, see the World Intellectual Property Organization (WIPO) Database on Flexibilities in the Intellectual Property System: https://www.wipo.int/ip-development/en/agenda/flexibilities/database.html.

6. For example, some studies have shown that the effect of data exclusivity, as implemented pursuant to regional trade agreements, is to delay the entry of generic pharmaceuticals onto the market (Shaffer and Brenner 2009).

7. See also "Social Responsibility at the University of Manchester" (web page), University of Manchester website: https://www.manchester.ac.uk/discover/social-responsibility/.

8. See also the WTO Trade Monitoring Database (reporting period of October 16, 2020, to October 15, 2021): https://tmdb.wto.org/en.

9. The medical service delivery modes discussed in this section refer to the General Agreement on Trade in Services (GATS) modes: (1) cross-border supply, (2) consumption abroad, (3) commercial presence, and (4) presence of natural persons.

10. The data on restrictions to medical services trade are from the World Bank and WTO Survey on Impediments to Services Integration (Borchert et al. 2019). At the time of writing, the data covered 9 high-income economies, 44 middle-income economies, and 20 low-income economies.

11. Cross-border telehealth services primarily take place between practitioners or health businesses (for example, telediagnosis, teleradiology, laboratory testing, specialized services, second opinions, and remote surgery), but they increasingly involve practitioner-to-patient services where possible (for example, for surveillance or consultation).

12. This finding is based on data from the WTO Trade Monitoring Database for the period ending October 15, 2021, https://tmdb.wto.org/en.

13. Examples of economies with measures relating specifically to health data transfer include (a) Australia, which requires that no personal electronic health information be held or processed outside national borders; (b) the Canadian provinces of British Columbia and Nova Scotia, which mandate that personal information held by hospitals, among others, stay in Canada, with only a few limited exceptions; and (c) China, which prohibits population health information from being stored in servers outside of China and mandates local processing of health data (Ferracane 2017).

14. For a discussion of collective negotiation and pooled procurement in the public health context, see the joint study by WHO, WIPO, and WTO (2020a, 2020b).

15. For example, data from the World Health Organization's Global Drug Facility show that consolidating orders reduced costs by 26 percent for some tuberculosis treatments (Lunte, Cordier-Lassalle, and Keravec 2015). In another example, Denmark's use of centralized procurement contributed to health sector savings of €314 million in 2015 (WHO 2016). See also Bartels (2016).

16. For example, in 2015, the Italian Competition Authority (AGCM) conducted a sectoral investigation on vaccines for human use and recommended that the medical authorities adopt clear, transparent, and independent positions regarding national vaccination plans (EC 2019).

17. For example, in 2021, the UK Competition Appeal Tribunal found that GlaxoSmithKline (GSK) abused its dominant position by paying £50 million to generic suppliers of paroxetine in settlement of patent litigation to delay their potential market entry. See GSK et al. v. Competition and Markets Authority (CMA) [2021] CAT 9: https://www.catribunal.org.uk/sites/default/files/2021-05/1251-1255_Paroxetine_Judgment_CAT9_100521.pdf.

18. See Richards, Hickey, and Ward (2020); FTC v. AbbVie Inc., 976 F.3d 327 (3d Cir. 2020); and AbbVie Inc. v. Boehringer Ingelheim, Case No. 1:17-cv-1065 (D. Del. 2017).

19. See Novartis v. Union of India, AIR 2013 SC, App. No. 2706-2716 of 2013: https://perma.cc/53RA-2LDX.

20. For example, in 2016, the French Supreme Court upheld the French Competition Authority's finding that Sanofi abused its dominant position by misleading physicians and pharmacists about the quality and safety of competing generic medical goods. See Sanofi-Aventis v. ADLC, Court of Cassation (France), Civil, Commercial Chamber, 15-10.384, October 18, 2016: https://www.legifrance.gouv.fr/juri/id/JURITEXT000033297580/.

21. The analysis is based on data collected through the Essential Goods Initiative (EGI), which was launched in 2020 by the World Bank in cooperation with the St.Gallen Endowment for Prosperity through Trade and the European University Institute. For more details on the dataset, see Evenett et al. (2021).

22. Statistics including trade in biologics (medicines and downstream medical products) suggest that, by the start of 2022, the total number of import restrictions in force overtook the total number of export curbs in place.

23. The statistics provided in this section are based on data from the Essential Goods Initiative (EGI). Data from the International Trade Centre (ITC) and the WTO show similar patterns, although the number of implemented measures tends to be smaller, given that the ITC and WTO collect the data only from official sources. See Evenett (2022) for details.

24. To estimate the share of trade covered by policy measures, each of the recorded policies is assigned to a 6-digit Harmonized System (HS) code. The total amount of exports and imports of a certain code subject to a given measure represents the potential trade that could be covered by the measures. The trade coverage estimates reported here—which are based on recorded 2019 United Nations COMTRADE trade data—understate the total value of trade covered given the significant surge in trade in medical goods since early 2020.

25. When biologics are included in the trade coverage calculations, the estimates relating to import curbs double (now standing at US$202 billion) and exceed the trade covered by import reforms.

26. The European Commission indicated that it did not intend to propose a further extension of this mechanism after December 31, 2021 (EC 2021).

27. The analysis relies on information on policy measures that countries adopted affecting medical goods (and vaccines) between January 2020 and December 2021 at the 6-digit Harmonized System (HS6) traded-product level to measure their impact on trade costs. See Egger et al. (2022) for a description of the empirical methodology to assess the impact of trade policies on trade costs.

28. For example, several regulators have suspended "use it or lose it" slot requirements that oblige airlines to continue operating slots for a minimum share of the time to keep their entitlements for the following travel season. For examples of such measures, see WTO (2020).

29. Relevant measures included reductions in airport, air navigation, and other charges and broader financial support measures, including loan guarantees, long-term loans, and acquisition of equity stakes in airlines. For more information, see WTO (2020).

30. "Chinese Taipei"—defined by the WTO as the "Separate Customs Territory of Taiwan, Penghu, Kinmen and Matsu"—is used in this report to refer to a jurisdiction admitted to WTO membership since January 1, 2002. See the WTO member information page: https://www.wto.org/english/thewto_e/countries_e/chinese_taipei_e.htm.

31. Notifications data are as of April 26, 2022. The first of these notifications was received on March 16, 2020, and most of them in April 2020. See "WTO Members' Notifications on COVID-19" (last updated April 21, 2022), https://www.wto.org/english/tratop_e/covid19_e/notifications_e.htm.

32. A substantial number of the notified measures were reported as temporary (generally applying for a period of six months or one year or for the duration of the public health emergency).

33. Brazil also submitted several notifications related to the market authorization process for COVID-19 vaccines.

34. Some examples include mandatory laboratory verification specifically tailored for all COVID-19 test kits; new packaging and labeling technical specifications for hand-sanitizing solutions; or clearer information and additional marketing requirements for hygiene masks.

35. This is referred to variously as emergency use authorization (by the US Food and Drug Administration) or conditional marketing authorization (EMA), among other terms.

36. The WTO Secretariat compiled a list of some of these measures on the WTO web page, "COVID-19: Measures Regarding Trade-Related Intellectual Property Rights" (updated April 20, 2022), https://www.wto.org/english/tratop_e/covid19_e/trade_related_ip_measure_e.htm.

37. WTO, "Notification of Laws and Regulations under Article 63.2 of the TRIPS Agreement Document – Canada: Bill C-13 an Act Respecting Certain Measures in Response to COVID-19" (23 April 2020) IP/N/1/CAN/30. For the text of Bill C-13, see https://ip-documents.info/2020/IP/CAN/20_2850_00_e.pdf.

38. See WTO, "COVID-19: Measures Regarding Trade-Related Intellectual Property Rights" (updated April 20, 2022), https://www.wto.org/english/tratop_e/covid19_e/trade_related_ip_measure_e.htm.

39. For examples, see measures compiled by the WTO Secretariat on the web page, "COVID-19: Measures Regarding Trade-Related Intellectual Property Rights" (updated April 20, 2022), https://www.wto.org/english/tratop_e/covid19_e/trade_related_ip_measure_e.htm.

40. Examples of such databases include the World Intellectual Property Organization (WIPO) PATENTSCOPE COVID-19 Index, https://patentscope.wipo.int/search/en/covid19.jsf; the Korean Intellectual Property Office's COVID-19 Patents Information Navigation, https://www.kipo.go.kr/ncov/index_e.html; and the European Patent Office's "Fighting Coronavirus" platform, https://www.epo.org/news-events/in-focus/fighting-coronavirus.html.

41. Paxlovid is the brand name for the drug, which is made up of two generic medications: nirmatrelvir and ritonavir.

42. However, the licenses have also been criticized for their restricted geographical coverage and supply, noting that more measures are required to ensure adequate access by all patients in LMICs. See the letter, "Re: Equitable access nirmatrelvir + ritonavir," to Pfizer Chairman and Chief Executive Officer Albert Bourla, March 16, 2022: https://healthgap.org/pfizerletter.

43. In March 2022, Moderna announced an updated patent pledge that it would never enforce patent rights for COVID-19–related technologies in 92 LMICs, including South Africa (Moderna 2022).

44. The reference to subsidy measures in this subsection of the report is based on the GTA's characterization and without prejudice to whether any individual measure discussed is a "subsidy" within the meaning of the WTO Agreement on Subsidies and Countervailing Measures.

45. In 79 cases, nonstandard forms of government support were provided, often in conjunction with a government procurement contract.

46. For example, Chile and Ukraine have created interactive business intelligence (BI) tools and databases for government procurement related to the COVID-19 pandemic. See, Chile BI: Microsoft Power BI and Ukraine BI: https://ti-ukraine.org/en/news/ti-ukraine-presents-tool-for-covid-19-procurement-analysis/.

47. In addition, the European Commission, through its Directorate-General for Competition, indicated that it stood ready to issue "comfort" letters to private companies to increase the degree of legal certainty as regards compliance with competition laws (EC 2020a).

48. See, for example, the UK's guidance on merger assessment during the COVID-19 pandemic (United Kingdom, CMA 2020). For more about the possible effects of the pandemic on merger reviews, see OECD (2020a).

REFERENCES

Baiker, L., E. Bertola, and M. Jelitto. 2021. "Services Domestic Regulation – Locking in Good Regulatory Practices: Analyzing the Prevalence of Services Domestic Regulation Disciplines and Their Potential Linkages with Economic Performance." Staff Working Paper ERSD-2021-4, World Trade Organization, Geneva.

Ball, D., S. Roth, and J. Parry, 2016. "Better Regulation of Medicines Means Stronger Regional Health Security: Strengthening and Convergence of National Regulatory Agencies Has Benefits beyond Country Borders." ADB Briefs No. 54, Asian Development Bank, Manila.

Bartels, D. 2016. "Centralizing Procurement of Medicines to Save Costs for Denmark." *Eurohealth* 22 (2): 42–44.

Beierle, J., N. S. Cauchon, Y. Hedberg, M. Braathen Holm, J. V. Lepore, R. MacKenzie, K. Mistry, et al. 2022. "Toward a Single Global Control Strategy: Industry Study." *Pharmaceutical Engineering* January/February 2022.

Beukes, S. 2022. "Aspen Concludes Agreement to Manufacture and Make Available an Aspen-Branded COVID-19 Vaccine (Aspenovax) throughout Africa." Aspen Holdings News, March 8.

Borchert, I., B. Gootiiz, J. Magdeleine, J. A. Marchetti, A. Mattoo, E. Rubio, and E. Shannon. 2019. "Applied Services Trade Policy: A Guide to the Services Trade Policy Database and the Services Trade Restrictions Index." Staff Working Paper ERSD-2019-14, World Trade Organization, Geneva.

Branstetter, L., and K. E. Maskus. 2022. "Global Knowledge Flows, Absorptive Capacity and Capability Acquisition: Old Ideas, Recent Evidence and New Approaches." In *Trade in Knowledge: Intellectual Property, Trade and Development in a Transformed Global Economy*, edited by A. Taubman and J. Watal, 405–30. Cambridge: Cambridge University Press. doi:10.1017/9781108780919.017.

Budish, E., and C. Snyder. 2021. "Bigger Is Better when It Comes To Vaccine Production." *Wall Street Journal*, March 17.

Castillo, J. C., A. Ahuja, S. Athey, A. Baker, E. Budish, R. Glennerster, S. D. Kominers, et al. 2021. "Market Design to Accelerate COVID-19 Vaccine Supply." *Science* 371 (6534): 1107–09.

CCSA (Competition Commission South Africa). 2022. "Competition Commission Prosecutes a Multinational Healthcare Company, Roche, for Excessive Pricing of a Breast Cancer Treatment Drug." Press release, February 8.

Chanda, R. 2001. "Trade in Health Services." Working Paper No. 70, Indian Council for Research on International Economic Relations, New Delhi.

Chanda, R. 2017. "Trade in Health Services and Sustainable Development." In *Win-Win: How International Trade Can Help Meet the SDGs*, edited by M. Helble, B. Shepherd, and G. Wan, 400–36. Tokyo: Asian Development Bank Institute.

Chiang, T.-W., and X. Wu. 2022. "Innovation and Patenting Activities of COVID-19 Vaccines in WTO Members: Analytical Review of Medicines Patent Pool (MPP) COVID-19 Vaccines Patent Landscape (VaxPaL)." Staff Working Paper ERSD-2022-01, WTO, Geneva.

Cockburn, I. M., J. O. Lanjouw, and M. Schankerman. 2016. "Patents and the Global Diffusion of New Drugs." *American Economic Review* 106 (1): 136–64.

Conti, R. M. 2022. "The Determinants of COVID-19 Vaccine Development Success." Presentation at virtual workshop, World Intellectual Property Organization, Geneva, May 5.

Dai, R., and J. Watal. 2021. "Product Patents and Access to Innovative Medicines." *Social Science & Medicine* 291: 114479. doi:10.1016/j.socscimed.2021.11447.

Danzon, P. M., A. W. Mulcahy, and A. K. Towse. 2015. "Pharmaceutical Pricing in Emerging Markets: Effects of Income, Competition, and Procurement." *Health Economics* 24 (2): 238–52.

Duncan, I. 2020. "Drug Industry Warns that Cuts to Passenger Airline Service Have Put Medical Supplies at Risk." *Washington Post*, May 2.

EC (European Commission). 2019. "Market Monitoring and Advocacy Actions in the Pharmaceutical Sector Undertaken by the European Competition Authorities in the Period 2009–2017." Monitoring and action reports, by EU Member State, Directorate-General for Competition (DG-COMP) website: https://ec.europa.eu/competition/sectors/pharmaceuticals/report2019/list_monitoring_advocacy.pdf.

EC (European Commission). 2020a. "Communication from the Commission: Temporary Framework for Assessing Antitrust Issues Related to Business Cooperation in Response to Situations of Urgency Stemming from the Current COVID-19 Outbreak." (OJ C 116 I/02). EC, Brussels.

EC (European Commission). 2020b. "Guidance from the European Commission on Using the Public Procurement Framework in the Emergency Situation Related to the COVID-19 Crisis." (OJ C 108 I/01). EC, Brussels.

EC (European Commission). 2021. "Export Requirements for COVID-19 Vaccines: Frequently Asked Questions." Guidance document for COVID-19 vaccine exporters, November 5, EC, Brussels.

Egger, P., G. Masllorens, N. Rocha, and M. Ruta. 2022. "Estimating the Impact of Trade Policies on Trade Flows in Medical Goods." Unpublished manuscript, World Bank, Washington, DC.

Espín, J., J. Rovira, A. Calleja, N. Azzopardi-Muscat, E. Richardson, W. Palm, and D. Panteli. 2016. "How Can Voluntary Cross-Border Collaboration in Public Procurement Improve Access to Health Technologies in Europe?" Policy Brief No. 21, World Health Organization Regional Office for Europe, Copenhagen.

EU-Japan Centre (EU-Japan Centre for Industrial Cooperation). 2021. "Judgement on Collusion by Japan's Big Medical Suppliers Reveals Standing Practice of Many Years." Article, EU-Japan Centre, Tokyo and Brussels.

Evenett, S. J. 2022. "COVID-Era Trade Policy Interventions Affecting Medical Goods: Form, Frequency, Duration & Scale." Revised background paper for joint report, *Trade Therapy: Deepening*

Cooperation to Strengthen Pandemic Defenses. Washington, DC, World Bank; Geneva, World Trade Organization.

Evenett, S., M. Fiorini, J. Fritz, B. Hoekman, P. Lukaszuk, N. Rocha, M. Ruta, F. Santi, and A. Shingal. 2021. "Trade Policy Responses to the COVID-19 Pandemic Crisis: Evidence from a New Dataset." *The World Economy* 45 (2): 342–64.

Ferracane, M. F. 2017. "Restrictions on Cross-Border Data Flows: A Taxonomy." Working Paper No. 1/2017, European Centre for International Political Economy (ECIPE), Brussels.

Gaulé, P. 2018. "Patents and the Success of Venture-Capital Backed Startups: Using Examiner Assignment to Estimate Causal Effects." *Journal of Industrial Economics* 66 (2): 350–76.

Gillson, I., and K. Muramatsu. 2020. "Health Services Trade and the COVID-19 Pandemic." Trade and COVID-19 Guidance Note, World Bank, Washington, DC.

Global Data Alliance. 2020. "Cross-Border Data Transfers & Remote Health Services." Primer, Global Data Alliance, Washington, DC.

Greece, HCC (Hellenic Competition Authority). 2020. "The Interim Results of HCC's Investigations on Health and Hospital Equipment during COVID-19 Pandemic." Press Release, September 11.

Grosso, M., and E. Moïsé. 2003. "Transparency in Government Procurement: The Benefits of Efficient Governance and Orientations for Achieving It." Paper TD/TC/WP(2002)31/FINAL, Working Party of the Trade Committee, Organisation for Economic Co-operation and Development, Paris.

Hawkins, L. 2011. "Competition Policy." Working Paper No. 4, Review Series on Pharmaceutical Pricing Policies and Interventions, World Health Organization and Health Action International Project on Medicine Prices and Availability, Geneva.

ICAO (International Civil Aviation Organization). 2020a. "ICAO, ILO, and IMO Issue Joint Call to World Governments on Need for 'Key Worker' Designations for Essential Air and Sea Personnel." News release, May 26.

ICAO (International Civil Aviation Organization). 2020b. "New ICAO-LACAC Air Cargo Liberalization Agreement to Bolster Regional Vaccine Transport Long-Term Recovery." Press release, December 24.

ICN (International Competition Network). 2020. "Competition during and after the COVID-19 Pandemic." ICN Steering Group Statement, ICN, Quebec.

Kohler, J. C., and T. Wright. 2020. "The Urgent Need for Transparent and Accountable Procurement of Medicine and Medical Supplies in Times of COVID-19 Pandemic." *Journal of Pharmaceutical Policy and Practice* 13 (1): 58.

Kyle, M., and Y. Qian. 2014. "Intellectual Property Rights and Access to Innovation: Evidence from TRIPS." Working Paper No. 20799, National Bureau of Economic Research, Cambridge, MA.

Latham & Watkins. 2021. "Impact of COVID-19 on Global Merger Control Reviews." Summary country assessments, Latham & Watkins LLP, Los Angeles.

Lunte, K., T. Cordier-Lassalle, and J. Keravec. 2015. "Reducing the Price of Treatment for Multidrug-Resistant Tuberculosis through the Global Drug Facility." *Bulletin of the World Health Organization* 93 (4): 279–82.

Mimura, C. 2010. "Guidance and Sample Clauses for Use in Developing Strategies, Licenses, Research and Collaboration Agreements in IPIRA's Humanitarian/Socially Responsible Licensing Program (SRLP) at Berkeley." Memorandum (updated August 17), Office of Intellectual Property & Industry Research Alliances (IPIRA), University of California, Berkeley. https://ipira.berkeley.edu/sites /default/files/shared/docs/SRLP_Guidance_%26_Clauses_v100817.pdf.

Moderna. 2022. "Moderna's Updated Patent Pledge." Statement issued March 7, Moderna, Cambridge, MA.

MPP (Medicine Patents Pool). 2022. "35 Generic Manufacturers Sign Agreements with MPP to Produce Low-Cost, Generic Versions of Pfizer's Oral COVID-19 Treatment Nirmatrelvir in Combination with Ritonavir for Supply in 95 Low- And Middle-Income Countries." News release, March 17.

Naidu, L., and S. Nxumalo. 2020. "South Africa: Competition Law Exemptions and Regulations Applicable during COVID-19." InsightPlus article, May 11, Baker McKenzie, Chicago.

OECD (Organisation for Economic Co-operation and Development). 2011. "Centralised Purchasing Systems in the European Union." SIGMA Papers No. 47, OECD, Paris. doi:10.1787/5kgkgqv703xw-en.

OECD (Organisation for Economic Co-operation and Development). 2018. "Excessive Prices in Pharmaceutical Markets." Background Note by the Secretariat for the 130th Meeting of the Competition Committee, November 27–28, OECD, Paris.

OECD (Organisation for Economic Co-operation and Development). 2020a. "Merger Control in the Time of COVID-19." Policy note, Secretary-General of the OECD, Paris.

OECD (Organisation for Economic Co-operation and Development). 2020b. "Stocktaking Report on Immediate Public Procurement and Infrastructure Responses to COVID-19." Report and country factsheets, OECD Secretariat, Paris.

OECD (Organisation for Economic Co-operation and Development). 2020c. "The Face Mask Global Value Chain in the COVID-19 Outbreak: Evidence and Policy Lessons." Policy Note, OECD, Paris.

Qian, Y. 2007. "Do National Patent Laws Stimulate Domestic Innovation in a Global Patenting Environment? A Cross-Country Analysis of Pharmaceutical Patent Protection, 1978–2002." *Review of Economics and Statistics* 89 (3): 436–53.

Reuters. 2020. "Digital Doctors: Indonesia Uses 'Telehealth' to Fight Coronavirus." Al Jazeera, April 10.

Richards, K. T., K. J. Hickey, and E. H. Ward. 2020. "Drug Pricing and Pharmaceutical Patenting Practices." Report No. R46221, Congressional Research Service, Washington, DC.

Sampat, B. N., and K. C. Shadlen. 2017. "Secondary Pharmaceutical Patenting: A Global Perspective." *Research Policy* 46 (3): 693–707.

Sampat, B. N., and K. C. Shadlen. 2021. "The COVID-19 Innovation System." *Health Affairs* 40 (3): 400–09.

Sauvé, P., C. Blouin, A. Bhushan, and O. Cattaneo. 2015. "Trade in Health Services." In *Trade and Health: Towards Building a National Strategy*, edited by R. Smith, C. Blouin, Z. Mirza, P. Beyer, and N. Drager, 76–91. Geneva: World Health Organization.

Saxon, G. 2017. "Global Medical Device Regulatory Harmonization." Presentation, Third WHO Global Forum on Medical Devices, Geneva, May 10–12.

Shaffer, E. R., and J. E. Brenner. 2009. "A Trade Agreement's Impact on Access to Generic Drugs." *Health Affairs* 28 (5): w957–68.

Shrestha, M., R. Moles, E. Ranjit, and B. Chaar. 2018. "Medicine Procurement in Hospital Pharmacies of Nepal: A Qualitative Study Based on the Basel Statements." *PLOS One* 13 (2): e0191778.

Swiss Confederation. 2020. "Recommendations of the Confederation Purchasing Conference (CA) of March 27, 2020." [In French.] Federal Procurement Conference (BKB), Bern. https://www.bkb .admin.ch/bkb/fr/home/themen/coronavirus.html.

Taubman, A. 2010. "A Typology of Intellectual Property Management for Public Health Innovation and Access: Design Considerations for Policymakers." *The Open AIDS Journal* 4 (1): 4–24. doi:10.21 74/1874613601004020004.

Taylor, A., and C. Parker. 2021. "U.S. Drug Company Merck to Share License for Experimental COVID-19 Treatment with Non-Profit Organization." *Washington Post*, October 27.

UNCTAD (United Nations Conference for Trade and Development). 2020. "Defending Competition in the Markets during COVID-19." UNCTAD News, April 8.

United Kingdom, CMA (Competition and Markets Authority). 2020. "Merger Assessments during the Coronavirus (COVID-19) Pandemic." Guidance document, CMA, London.

University of Manchester. 2020. "Manchester 2020: The University of Manchester's Strategic Plan." University of Manchester, Oxford, UK.

WHO (World Health Organization). 2016. *Challenges and Opportunities in Improving Access to Medicines through Efficient Public Procurement in the WHO European Region.* Copenhagen: WHO.

WHO and MPP (World Health Organization and the Medicine Patents Pool). 2021. "WHO and MPP Announce the First Transparent, Global Non-Exclusive Licence for a COVID-19 Technology: CSIC Offers Serological Test to C-TAP." News release, November 23.

WHO and MPP (World Health Organization and the Medicine Patents Pool). 2022. "WHO and MPP Welcome NIH's Offer of COVID-19 Health Technologies to C-TAP." Joint statement, March 3.

WHO, WIPO, and WTO (World Health Organization, World Intellectual Property Organization, and World Trade Organization). 2020a. "Medical Technologies: The Access Dimension." In *Promoting Access to Medical Technologies and Innovation: Intersections between Public Health, Intellectual Property and Trade.* 2nd ed. Geneva: WHO, WIPO, and WTO.

WHO, WIPO, and WTO (World Health Organization, World Intellectual Property Organization, and World Trade Organization). 2020b. "Medical Technologies: The Innovation Dimension." In *Promoting Access to Medical Technologies and Innovation: Intersections between Public Health, Intellectual Property and Trade.* 2nd ed. Geneva: WHO, WIPO, and WTO.

WHO, WIPO, and WTO (World Health Organization, World Intellectual Property Organization, and World Trade Organization). 2020c. *Promoting Access to Medical Technologies and Innovation: Intersections between Public Health, Intellectual Property and Trade.* 2nd ed. Geneva: WHO, WIPO, and WTO.

WIPO (World Intellectual Property Organization). 2018. "Reference Document on Exception Regarding Acts for Obtaining Regulatory Approval from Authorities (Second Draft)." Document SCP/28/3, WIPO Secretariat, Geneva.

WIPO (World Intellectual Property Organization). 2022. *COVID-19 Related Vaccines and Therapeutics: Preliminary Insights on Related Patenting Activity during the Pandemic.* Geneva: WIPO.

World Bank. 2022. "COVID-19 Trade Policy Database: Food and Medical Products." Online brief, February 25. https://www.worldbank.org/en/topic/trade/brief/coronavirus-covid-19-trade-policy-database-food-and-medical-products.

WTO (World Trade Organization). 2019. *World Trade Report 2019: The Future of Services Trade.* Geneva: WTO.

WTO (World Trade Organization). 2020. "Overview of Developments in the International Trading Environment." Annual report by the Director-General covering mid-October 2019 to mid-October 2020, Document WT/TPR/OV/23, WTO, Geneva.

WTO (World Trade Organization). 2021. "Promoting Transparency and Convergence in the Regulatory Landscape." Session 4 of the COVID-19 Vaccine Supply Chain and Regulatory Transparency Technical Symposium, June 29, webcast and summary report produced by the WTO, Geneva.

Wu, X., and B. P. Khazin. 2020. "Patent-Related Actions Taken in WTO Members in Response to the COVID-19 Pandemic." WTO Staff Working Paper ERSD 2020-12, https://www.wto.org/english/res_e/reser_e/ersd202012_e.htm. World Trade Organization, Geneva.

3 Deepening Cooperation on Medical Goods and Services Trade

ABOUT THIS CHAPTER

This chapter examines how improved cooperation in trade and trade-related issues contributes to global health security. Starting from the gaps in cooperation that emerged during the COVID-19 pandemic, the chapter outlines what is needed to ensure that rules in trade agreements and mechanisms of cooperation beyond trade can support efforts to better respond to the next pandemic.

INTERNATIONAL COOPERATION ON TRADE IN MEDICAL GOODS

The role of trade agreements

The markets for medical goods and services have distinct features that make international trade and trade cooperation particularly important for global health security. The high concentration of medical goods production—reflecting economies of scale and high research and development (R&D) and skill intensity—combines with dispersed global demand to indicate an important role for trade. Given the high global demand for medical services as well, trade in medical services through all modes of supply could help address shortages in certain jurisdictions.[1] For instance, certain countries have created health care hubs that provide specialized services to foreign patients. Trade agreements support the exchange of medical goods and services by improving market access. The multilateral trading system contributes to freer, more stable, and more predictable trading conditions.

Box 3.1   RTA cooperation during the COVID-19 pandemic *(Continued)*

(NTMs) on Essential Goods" under its Hanoi Plan of Action on Strengthening ASEAN Economic Cooperation and Supply Chain Connectivity in Response to the COVID-19 Pandemic (ASEAN 2020a, 2020b). It commits members to refrain from imposing restrictive trade measures on more than 150 essential goods and supplies (mostly medical goods based on a list maintained by the World Customs Organization and World Health Organization) except in public health emergencies.

For several regional groups, the use of digital technologies has played a key role in both trade facilitation during the pandemic and as part of a longer-term strategy. The ASEAN Comprehensive Recovery Framework (ACRF), with its supportive ASEAN Digital Integration Framework (ADIF), identifies priority areas such as facilitating digital trade and enabling seamless digital transactions. The Pacific Alliance's Digital Agenda Group adopted a road map to accelerate the region's digital agenda (PA 2017). The EAEU's Strategy-2025 also includes digital initiatives in health care and the development of a common market for medicines and medical devices.

a. The SPS Agreement refers to the WTO Agreement on the Application of Sanitary and Phytosanitary Measures.

b. Steps taken include a common definition for medical devices, mutual recognition of the parties' sanitary registration of low-risk medical devices (procedure still to be agreed on), and good manufacturing practice requirements.

c. "Green lanes" are defined as lane border crossings open to all freight vehicles, whatever goods they are carrying. Under green lane or green channel provisions, crossing the border, including any checks and health screening, should take no longer than 15 minutes (EC 2020a).

d. For more information, see "REACT-EU" (web page), European Commission website: https://ec.europa.eu/regional_policy/en/newsroom/coronavirus-response/react-eu/.

Regional coordination and cooperation need not be limited to RTAs. The Asia-Pacific Economic Cooperation (APEC), for example, is a forum to share good practices, coordinate responses, and cooperate to ease trade in medical goods and the movement of essential personnel.[2]

Challenges to trade cooperation during global emergencies

The characteristics of the market for medical goods make it challenging to sustain trade cooperation during a global health emergency. Given that demand for certain medical goods can spike in response to global emergencies, geographic concentration in supply may disrupt regular trade patterns if products are allocated to satisfy national demand first. Governments are important players: They are large buyers and also regulate the production, distribution, and consumption of medical products, which often are subject to problems of asymmetric information and market failures.

In anticipation of possible emergencies, governments may seek to guarantee the availability of essential goods. Actions may include supporting domestic production, stockpiling, diversifying supply sources, and building capacity for flexible manufacturing. However, building up or extending production capacity in essential goods requires diverting resources from other sectors, which is costly. More generally, promoting domestic production would reduce the benefits of international specialization.

During a pandemic or other crisis, a government may also take direct policy measures to avoid critical shortages of essential goods or services in the short run. For example, it may impose export restrictions on domestic producers, creating a potential conflict between trade rules and unilateral government efforts to improve health security. As discussed in the following section, trade agreements provide for such situations.

Beyond trade, governments may subsidize the development of essential products and investment to expand production capacity. Also, governments could take measures to retain health personnel to respond to an internal shortage of staff in medical establishments.

Gaps revealed during the pandemic and need for cooperation beyond trade

The pandemic revealed the critical importance of trade as a way to source medical products from countries with a comparative advantage or the capacity to rapidly scale up production. It also revealed the challenge of meeting domestic needs for essential products when global demand far outstrips global stocks and supply capacity is expanded primarily to meet local needs rather than foreign demand.

In principle, international coordination to ensure the provision of essential goods under a regime of open trade comes with large economic benefits. It can address the time inconsistency problem that occurs when a net importer of essential goods, anticipating export restrictions during a crisis, supports domestic production of products for which it lacks a comparative advantage (Leibovici and Santacreu 2021). International cooperation can also help governments avoid costly and ineffective reshoring policies as a response to a crisis by increasing the robustness of global value chains and creating systems that support information exchange and policy transparency. Cooperation in the area of pricing policies is also key to ensure universal health coverage of medical goods (box 3.2).

Trade agreements, whether multilateral or regional, are mostly designed for "normal" times. They do not include robust frameworks to guide cooperation in times of crisis and do not address the time inconsistency problem. All trade agreements include provisions for emergencies, but these generally are limited to recognizing that governments may perceive a need to restrict trade to safeguard or enhance access to essential goods or services. They permit the use of trade measures on an exceptional basis that otherwise would be prohibited.

Box 3.2   Pricing policies for medical goods in the context of international trade

Universal health coverage ensures the right of everyone to access safe, quality-assured, effective, and affordable medicines.[a] Affordability depends on the price of medicines and one's income. The World Health Organization (WHO) works with countries to set pricing policies that reduce market prices so health systems don't have to spend resources subsidizing medicines for low-income patients. Pricing policies guide price negotiations within a specific country and can involve the publication of reference prices and regulation of tendering and procurement processes. Other pricing policies regulate prices directly by fixing prices, restricting markups in the distribution chain, or providing tax exemptions.

Third-degree price discrimination

Offering lower prices to more price-sensitive buyers is known in economics as third-degree price discrimination and can increase both sellers' profit and patients' access. For example, early in the COVID-19 pandemic, Moderna had one of the most expensive vaccines on the market, priced at US$30 per dose. At this price, the African Union declined to order doses of the Moderna vaccine and instead ordered doses of Johnson & Johnson's Janssen vaccine, which was priced at only US$7 per dose. Eventually, Moderna dropped its price to US$7 per dose, and the African Union placed orders for its vaccine. Since US$7 per dose was still above cost, Moderna would make a profit on these sales. Because the new price was affordable to African Union members, access to the vaccine also increased.

Reference prices

Despite the mutual benefit for developers and patients of offering lower prices to more price-sensitive buyers, these lower prices may not emerge naturally owing to the unique characteristics of the medical goods market—creating a role for pricing policy. Because of the home market effect, medical goods exporters are concentrated in a few large countries, and producers may not be able to recognize differences in demand across countries, leading them to offer a uniform price that is unaffordable to some. Even when multinationals do enter countries like India, a lack of information may keep them from building out marketing and distribution networks, leading to limited access within the country (Goldberg 2010). Reference prices provide guidance to exporters about how to price appropriately in a specific market to ensure access.

Another problem is that, even if manufacturers are willing (as was Moderna) to charge lower prices to more price-sensitive customers, intermediaries in the supply chain may nonetheless charge a markup over the manufacturer's preferred price—an economic problem called double marginalization. Pharmaceutical markets in low- and middle-income countries are dominated by a single or small number of intermediaries, and public procurers and consumers in these markets pay higher prices than buyers in high-income countries. Access to information on reference prices in external markets reduces the information asymmetry between buyers and sellers, providing buyers with more bargaining power.

(Continued)

Box 3.2 **Pricing policies for medical goods in the context of international trade**
(Continued)

Pooled procurement

Pooled procurement efforts, which involve formal agreements between sellers and groups of buyers within or between countries, can also increase countries' bargaining power and potentially reduce prices. In the Americas, the Pan American Health Organization's revolving fund (fondo rotario) pools resources from member countries to negotiate bulk purchases of vaccines at good prices (Agarwal and Reed, forthcoming).

Pooled procurement can also achieve economies of scale in negotiating indemnity for developers. Even if a medical product is approved by a stringent regulator, the producer may refuse to sell a good in a market unless it has indemnity—assurance that it will not be sued if a patient suffers a low-risk adverse event. During the pandemic, COVID-19 Vaccines Global Access (COVAX) established a program that offered no-fault, lump sum compensation to any individual who suffers a serious adverse event from any vaccine procured or distributed for free through the facility. This program made it easier for individuals to get fair compensation without having to go through a lengthy and expensive legal process, but also, crucially, provided developers with assurance they would not be sued, allowing them to provide access.

WHO efforts

Although trade improves access to medical goods, the free market does not currently provide affordable access to medicines for all. Despite existing pricing policies, countries remain concerned about "inequitable access to such products within and among Member States" and at the 2019 World Health Assembly made commitments to and requests of WHO to improve the transparency of markets for health products (WHA 2019).

WHO also has a strong recommendation encouraging the use of quality-assured generic and biosimilar medicines, which can increase competition and lower prices within and between countries (WHO 2021b). Low-income countries often rely more heavily than high-income countries on branded generics, which are more costly than unbranded generics (Silverman et al. 2019).

Work is in progress at WHO and other multilateral institutions to enable further information sharing and coordination among buyers so that prices achieve affordability, access, and health security.

a. See "Coverage of Essential Health Services (SDG 3.8.1)" (web page), World Health Organization Global Health Observatory: https://www.who.int/data/gho/data/themes/topics/service-coverage.

Thus, WTO prohibitions on quantitative restrictions do not apply to temporary restrictions imposed to prevent or relieve critical shortages of essential products (General Agreement on Tariffs and Trade [GATT] art. XI:2a).[3] Such exceptions are found even in deep integration arrangements such as the European Union (EU).[4] The exceptions constitute a recognition that sovereign governments will not accept binding constraints on measures to maximize the supply of essential products in emergencies. The aim of trade agreement provisions on exceptions is to limit their use to true emergencies and to induce governments to exercise restraint, with restrictions that are limited to the duration of the crisis, transparent, and proportional.

Early in the pandemic, provisions to guide the use of trade measures and ensure transparency were not always applied. As discussed in chapter 2, many WTO members imposed restrictive measures, many of which did not specify end dates (for example, export restrictions and controls of certain types of personal protective equipment [PPE]). Many did not quickly and comprehensively notify the WTO of new trade measures to respond to the pandemic. The unilateral and uncoordinated nature of initial trade policy responses paralleled the unilateral adoption of travel restrictions and bans in a manner inconsistent with the World Health Organization (WHO) International Health Regulations (Villarreal 2021). Dozens of borders remained closed to international travel of many non-nationals as of March 2020.[5]

Compliance with multilateral commitments and international law is distinct from the question of gaps in trade agreements or the need for cooperation beyond trade that was revealed by the pandemic. Three types of gaps emerged during the pandemic: information gaps, coordination gaps, and gaps in trade rules.

Information gaps

- Inadequate understanding of, and information on, the design and operation of global supply chains for essential products, giving rise to counterproductive export restrictions and inefficiencies in rapidly ramping up public procurement of essential goods
- Limited institutional mechanisms for communication and coordination between governments and industry to understand real-time production dynamics, demand-supply imbalances, and factors impeding the global production and international distribution of essential goods
- Absence of supply capacity monitoring and information-sharing systems for production of essential goods and cooperation in holding inventories to prevent excessive stockpiling
- Limited official statistics on trade in medical services to better grasp the trends in the sector (by detailed medical services subsector, partner, and mode of supply) and short-term statistics to better analyze the crisis response (in particular the use of telehealth and health worker mobility)

Coordination gaps

- Large differences across countries in the use and acceptance of digital technologies to document and certify essential goods, including for compliance with regulatory requirements pertaining to health and safety of critical products
- Inadequate market access framework and flexibilities to deal with health workforce shortages (international mobility and [practitioner-to-practitioner] telehealth)

- Lack of multilateral mechanisms to mobilize financing to develop vaccines and therapeutics and a joint procurement and distribution platform to provide essential medical products and vaccines to low- and middle-income countries (LMICs) that lack production capacity
- Absence of precrisis support for innovative international programs put in place following past global health threats to support vaccine development and production in LMICs

Gaps in trade rules

- Weaknesses in systems and procedures to facilitate the rapid cross-border movement of certified medical products
- Poor implementation of WTO provisions encouraging the use of international standards for products and production requirements
- Absence of mutual recognition arrangements between regulatory regimes for medical goods (including PPE) and for the qualifications of medical services providers
- Poor implementation of good regulatory practices, particularly in the area of medical services
- Lack or inadequate use of good practices for public procurement in times of global excess demand and limited mechanisms for international cooperation between public agencies procuring medical goods and services (for example, health care workers) through instruments such as joint purchasing across jurisdictions

Some of these gaps can be addressed within the framework of WTO agreements and RTAs. Others call for new forms of cooperation between states, nonstate actors, and the private sector, which is discussed in detail at the end of the chapter.

TRADE POLICY COOPERATION TO CONTRIBUTE TO GLOBAL HEALTH SECURITY

Policies affecting medical goods trade

Open trade in medical products would enable efficiency improvements in health care systems, thus increasing preparedness to address future pandemics. Restrictions of trade in medical goods reduce access, quality, and the choice and cost-effectiveness of medical goods. Similarly, trade restrictions on inputs needed to manufacture medical goods and on trade in services that support the functioning of medical value chains contribute to rising costs and reduced efficiency of health systems. As highlighted in chapter 2, open trade would lead to income gains equal to US$6.18 billion annually, in particular for LMICs.

Import and export interventions

Unilateral import and export responses. Export and import policy interventions during a pandemic—even when rational from the perspective of individual countries—can lead to collective losses and harm to the poorest countries. As the evidence in chapter 2 suggests, during a pandemic, governments face incentives to lower import barriers or increase export restrictions on critical medical goods to increase domestic supplies at a time of global scarcity. Exporters and importers face similar motives and act roughly at the same time (indeed, most measures were imposed in March and April 2020). As a result, world export supply decreases and import demand increases, worsening global scarcity and pushing up prices. This prompts governments to use additional trade policy measures to ensure adequate supplies and stabilize domestic prices. Thus, pandemic trade policies have been driven only in part by fundamentals; they are also a reaction to measures imposed by other governments, in a tit-for-tat commonly referred to as a "multiplier effect" (Giordani, Rocha, and Ruta 2016). All countries, and particularly vulnerable importers, stand to lose.

Unilateral export and import policies have longer-term consequences as well. If during a health crisis a country is subject to export restrictions by producing countries, it will see trade as an unreliable way to maintain access to essential products. It may therefore use import restrictions in normal times to achieve greater self-reliance as insurance against export restrictions during a health crisis. An escalation of pandemic measures—as seen during the first phase of the COVID-19 pandemic (chapter 2)—undermines trust in the system and jeopardizes global efficiency in production of medical goods.

Tariffs. Most medical goods tariffs are bound at relatively low levels at the WTO and in RTAs, but there are still important disparities between income groups. Over the years, different types of medical goods have been subject to different WTO sectoral tariff initiatives, such as the Agreement on Pharmaceuticals ("Pharma Agreement") and the Expansion of the Information Technology Agreement ("ITA Expansion").[6] This has resulted in an increased number of bound tariff lines (78 percent to date) and the progressive liberalization of trade in these products (average duty of 31 percent). But there are large disparities by income group, with lower-income countries having far fewer bindings, with higher tariffs (figure 3.1).

Significant tariff liberalization for medical products has also taken place under preferential trade agreements (PTAs). Whereas the applied most-favored-nation (MFN) tariff for all medical goods is 5 percent, the preferential tariff (as committed) under PTAs notified to the WTO and currently in force (2022) is approximately 1 percent. The preference margin (the difference between applied MFN and preferential tariffs) is greatest for PPE (11.5 percent MFN and 1.9 percent preferential) and lowest for pharmaceuticals (2.3 percent MFN, compared with 0.8 percent preferential).

Figure 3.1 Average MFN applied tariff, bound duties, and binding coverage of medical goods, by product category and income level

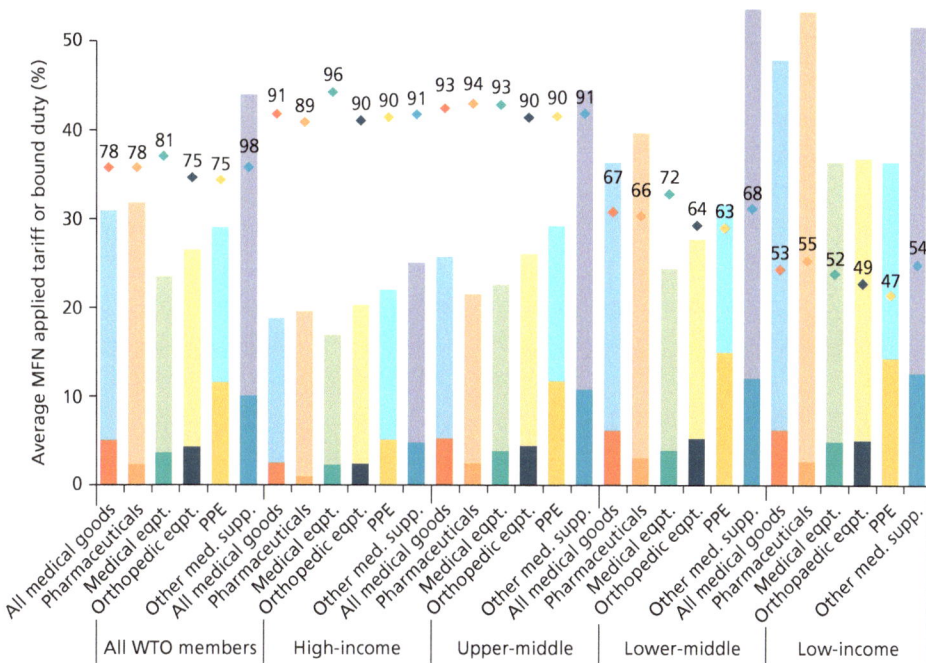

Source: World Trade Organization (WTO) Integrated Database and Consolidated Tariff Schedules Database.

Note: The data cover 136 WTO members: 32 high-income economies (counting the EU-27 as one and Liechtenstein and Switzerland as one); 41 upper-middle-income; 41 lower-middle-income; and 22 low-income, as defined in World Bank classifications. Applied most-favored-nation (MFN) data refer to 2021. In the bars, the solid portion represents MFN applied duty and the shaded portion, bound duty. The values shown as dots represent the binding coverage (percentage of tariff lines or products for which a WTO member has bound duty commitments). PPE = personal protective equipment.

While tariff commitments are not meant to discipline nondiscriminatory tariff reductions, the low applied tariffs established autonomously as a response to the pandemic could be used as a basis for new agreements. Even though high tariffs could induce foreign investment inflow in the sector or encourage domestic production (especially in low-technology products like PPE), the persistent lack of a bound duty for many medical goods, together with the wide gap between the legal maximum that can be applied and the relatively low MFN duties that are applied in practice, contributes to creating uncertainties and could lead to unpredictable price increases, leaving consumers worse off. This being said, during the pandemic, most economies resorted to eliminating or reducing import duties and other taxes and, instead, endeavored to ensure the smooth and prompt importation of these important goods.

The low applied tariffs resulting from national policies in response to the pandemic could be used as an opportunity for a tariff liberalization agreement for selected medical goods groups or a more overarching sectoral agreement on all medical goods (for example, by revisiting the WTO Pharma Agreement or ITA Expansion or by negotiating a new multilateral or plurilateral agreement).

Restrictions and licensing procedures. Disciplines on export restrictions did not provide a robust framework for cooperation during the crisis. As mentioned earlier, although WTO rules provide for the general elimination of quantitative restrictions (whether as quotas, import or export licensing procedures, or other measures), such restrictions are allowed in certain specific circumstances, as an exception.[7] The WTO framework and its notification requirements, however, were successful in ensuring transparency about these measures, both before and during the pandemic.[8] Also, depending on how they are designed and applied, import and export licensing procedures may add an important element of transparency to the measure they administer, but they could also have the opposite effect if they are arbitrary and opaque or add to the trade restrictiveness of the measure.

Applying the existing obligations and rules as set out in the WTO Agreement on Import Licensing Procedures and the general rules in the General Agreement on Tariffs and Trade (GATT) 1994 could facilitate trade in medical goods. In addition, negotiating new rules for exports analogous to the existing ones for imports would further support the liberalization of trade in medical goods.

Trade policy reforms to improve cooperation

Reforms to improve cooperation on trade policy in medical goods should aim to ensure the resilience of the health system during pandemics. Reforms could have three goals:

- Defuse the sudden escalation in export restrictions and tariff liberalizations created by the multiplier effect
- Increase predictability in export supplies and market access for medical goods
- Ensure that goods can flow smoothly across borders, whether in normal times or during a pandemic

These three goals complement and support each other. The essential element is to strike a balance between exporter and importer interests. Importers are hurt by export restrictions imposed by the producing countries of medical goods during a pandemic. Exporters are hurt by market access restrictions in importing countries during good times. Both sides lose from the policy escalation ignited by the multiplier effect. And both sides gain when markets are predictable and trade can smoothly flow across borders.

Striking a bargain. A bargain between exporters and importers can help avoid extreme market outcomes in future crises. Importers could agree to preserve the lower import restrictions implemented since the outbreak of the pandemic in exchange for assurances that their supplies of critical medical goods will not be arbitrarily cut off (Evenett and Winters 2020). Exporters could limit their rights to introduce temporary export controls in times of crisis in exchange for better market access in the importers' markets in normal times. This would not be a deal of reciprocal market opening (the standard practice in trade agreements) but a promise to limit supply disruptions during a health crisis in exchange for a promise to retain open markets in normal times. Box 3.3 summarizes specific policy commitments to support such a bargain.

Box 3.3   Potential commitments to bolster governance of trade policy in global crises

Suggested commitments on the use of trade policy instruments in public health emergencies can be grouped into five categories (Espitia, Rocha, and Ruta 2020):

1. *Commitments to limit trade policy discretion* on medical goods during a pandemic
   - By importers, to retain policy reforms on medical goods enacted during a pandemic for three years
   - By exporters, that any export restriction would not exceed a period of three months and would not lower exports to partners by more than 50 percent of the average of the past two years
   - By both exporters and importers, that proposed measures account for the impact on others—a requirement that exists for export controls on agricultural products

2. *Actions to ease flows of medical products across borders* could include commitments to abide by best trade facilitation practices for medical goods or to adopt international standards for critical medical goods for three years.

3. *A commitment to improve transparency* on policies and production of medical goods could include
   - A commitment to improve notifications (for example, by making information on new measures quickly available online), and
   - Strengthening of the World Trade Organization (WTO) monitoring function during a pandemic, including expanding its analysis of trade effects of policy actions and the Secretariat's capacity to collect and report on measures from sources other than government notifications.

4. *A commitment to basic principles for dispute resolution* could include, for instance, an agreement that partners' responses must be proportional and time-bound if a party walks away from its commitments to restrain export policy or retain import policy reforms.

5. *A commitment to create a consultation mechanism* could provide a forum to discuss common and country-specific problems, including the emergence of new critical areas such as shortages of medical goods or inputs not covered by the deal or the trade effects of policy changes by one party on other members. This mechanism could be informed by the analysis and enhanced monitoring of policies by the WTO Secretariat.

Such a bargain would have implications for multilateral trade rules, especially in times of systemic stress. First, multilateral rules should ensure that trade policy exceptions are truly temporary. WTO members invoking exceptions to raise trade barriers in emergencies should time-limit their interventions. WTO members could agree that such trade restrictions be allowed to lapse unless expressly and publicly extended. Strengthened monitoring by the WTO could contribute to ensure compliance with such commitments.

The second implication is deeper: The logic of providing for exceptions to multilateral trade rules is that trade-policy disciplines should not impede government efforts to protect human life from unanticipated threats. This logic must be challenged in light of developments over the past two years. As highlighted in the chapter 2 section on trade policies during the pandemic, several nations mounted an effective response to the health crisis without resorting to export curbs.

Improving monitoring and surveillance. Trade policy monitoring and surveillance should be improved to ensure transparency and provide timely information in periods of crisis. The International Trade Centre (ITC) and WTO should further improve mechanisms and tools to obtain information from governments on trade-related measures during crises. Such information can support the use of less-restrictive export controls—for example, a notification system instead of an outright prohibition.

In addition, the systems should be flexible in defining the set of products to be monitored. One potential oversight in recent trade policy surveillance, for instance, was the omission of biologics. The inclusion of these upstream products in the trade policy surveillance exercise highlights two important facts: (a) that the total number of recorded import restrictions rises considerably; and (b) the trade covered by import and export policy changes during the COVID-19 era multiplies (see chapter 2 subsection on import and export restricting and liberalizing policies). For over a decade, international organizations have recognized the importance of global value chains, yet trade policy surveillance has not fully accounted for such cross-border links.

Trade facilitation policies

Although the WTO's Trade Facilitation Agreement (TFA) goes a long way toward easing and expediting trade in medical goods, it is limited in scope, requires time for its full implementation (see the chapter 2 subsection on trade facilitation in normal times), and is subject to extensive implementation flexibilities. The TFA also does not fully cover several aspects of importance for medical goods trade. This has led to discussions on additional ways to facilitate trade—within Group of Twenty (G-20) working groups, in various WTO forums, and in the context of the discussions on the WTO response to the pandemic in the lead-up to the WTO's 12th Ministerial Conference.

Bolster TFA implementation and commitments. One suggestion is to enhance the TFA's impact by accelerating its implementation. This proposal, made in various WTO bodies and at forums such as G-20 summits and APEC Trade Ministers' meetings,[9] focused on advancing full implementation, which the TFA permits developing countries[10] and least developed countries (LDCs) to delay. Several aspects of the TFA were highlighted as priorities for expedited action, including measures relating to publication requirements; prearrival processing; separation of release from payments; expedited shipments; border agency cooperation; reduced formalities and documentation requirements; and single window implementation.[11] Suggestions were also made in the area of transit of goods.[12]

The impact of the TFA could be further enhanced by opting for high ambition when using flexibilities built into its disciplines, which often contain "best endeavor" or "best efforts" provisions and qualified commitments. For instance, the TFA merely calls on members to "endeavor to establish" the single window requirement and to use information technology (IT) "to the extent possible and practical." That means non-IT-based single windows can be compliant with the obligation.

Additional trade facilitation measures. Proposals beyond the scope of the TFA also emerged from the G-20 framework and discussions held under auspices of the Multilateral Leaders Task Force on COVID-19 Vaccines, Therapeutics, and Diagnostics.[13] In May 2020, the G-20's Trade and Investment Working Group complemented its call for accelerated TFA implementation with a statement encouraging the use of electronic documentation and processes, where possible and practical, including the use of smart applications (G-20 2020, annex section 1.2). Industry suggestions included calls for accelerated digitalization; establishing "green lanes"; and simplifying import, export, and transit procedures (especially in the form of paperless trade). Calls were also made for enhanced availability of customs authorities 24 hours a day, 7 days a week, to speed up clearance (WTO 2021b, 7).

Additional trade facilitation measures have been discussed in various WTO forums. They include strengthening prearrival procedures; providing postrelease verification and audits to control for compliance; reducing or eliminating procedures that require the physical presence of operators or the submission of physical documents; and, for countries sharing a common border, cooperation on additional working hours. Proposals were also made to reduce or eliminate penalties for bona fide mistakes in connection with importation of certain products (WTO 2020a, 6–7). Finally, based on the need to channel various efforts on the response to the pandemic, a process set up in June 2021 (in the lead-up to the WTO's 12th Ministerial Conference) also touches upon trade facilitation measures (see subsection on WTO response to the pandemic).

Liberalizing trade in services that support medical goods trade. Ideas outside the framework of the TFA propose the implementation of additional facilitative measures. Many LMICs lack the infrastructure and facilities needed for health logistics. For example, up to 70 percent of health facilities in these countries cannot store large volumes of COVID-19 vaccines at 2–8°C or –20°C (DHL 2021). Opening markets and cutting red tape to facilitate end-to-end health logistics services would bring much-needed foreign investment and expertise. This could be achieved through liberalization commitments in trade agreements.

Also, compliance with international standards would facilitate cross-border health logistics *because* they are subject to stringent regulations on storage and distribution of medical products. WHO has issued international standards for good manufacturing, storage, and distribution practices, and governments could transpose those into national regulations and guidelines. Furthermore, the pandemic highlighted the importance of transporting medical goods by air. Governments should therefore consider deregulating air cargo transport to increase competition and reduce costs.[14] The cargo infrastructure of airports could be improved by granting greater access to foreign airport operators and promoting foreign investments.

Distribution services are also key to international trade in medical goods and are subject to limited multilateral market access commitments. For instance, only 54 members of the WTO (counting the schedule of the EU-25 as 1) have undertaken specific commitments on wholesale trade services, and 53 have commitments on retailing services.[15] And of those members with binding commitments, a number have excluded, at least in part, medical goods from their wholesale trade commitments (14 of 54) or their retailing services commitments (15 of 53). These exclusions from commitments on distribution services often focus on pharmaceutical products.

Regulatory frameworks

The TBT Agreement. The WTO TBT Agreement offers guidance on achieving legitimate health and safety objectives while avoiding unnecessary or discriminatory barriers to trade in goods. The Agreement encourages regulatory harmonization by requiring economies, when possible, to base national regulations on international standards. It also encourages the use of other regulatory cooperation and coherence tools, such as recognition of conformity assessment (including mutual recognition agreements),[16] international and regional systems for conformity assessment,[17] and equivalence.[18] The Agreement establishes a transparency and notification system that opens avenues for cooperation on draft regulations (WTO 2021f, 38–42). These provisions contribute to more coherent and aligned regulatory systems, thereby reducing bottlenecks that can impede access to medical goods in both normal times and times of crisis.

International standards. Stronger alignment with international standards would improve the resilience of supply chains and enhance preparation for future pandemics. Greater convergence of national regulations with WHO standards and guidelines—or with International Council for Harmonisation of Technical Requirements for Pharmaceuticals for Human Use (ICH) standards on quality, safety, and efficacy of pharmaceuticals—would boost the potential of trade to contribute to global health security. For instance, harmonization with ICH standards would help overcome varying pharmacopeia requirements and allow pharmaceuticals to be developed and flow faster between countries (WTO 2021b). Aligning clinical trials and data sharing with common standards could increase the pace at which vaccines, therapeutics, and diagnostics are developed (PPP 2021). Broader use of internationally recognized Good Regulatory Practice (GRP) standards like transparency, public consultation, and internal coordination—including those discussed in the WTO TBT Committee (WTO 2021f, 46–48), the OECD (OECD RPC 2012), and WHO (WHO 2021a)—would facilitate trade and support global health security.

Developing countries may face challenges in effectively adopting international standards on medical goods, which are becoming increasingly complex. The TBT Agreement recognizes that such members should not be expected to use international standards that are not appropriate to their development, financial, and trade needs (TBT Agreement, art. 12.4).[19] To ensure that international standards are relevant and appropriate for developing countries, international standards bodies should seek to improve the countries' capacities to engage effectively and shape standards development, in line with the "six principles" decision of the WTO's TBT Committee.[20] Another part of the solution is to strengthen technical assistance between members, as emphasized under the TBT Agreement, and to enhance support for the development of national quality infrastructure (NQI).

Regulatory cooperation arrangements. Given that medical goods are produced in global supply chains and contain complex technologies, cooperation and reliance between regulators from different countries ensures the safety, quality, and efficacy of medical goods used domestically. Bolstering the breadth and depth of regulatory cooperation can help streamline regulatory frameworks and make them more coherent, as showcased in the WTO's TBT Committee. Regulatory cooperation takes a variety of forms and ambitions that depend on trust—ranging from information or work sharing to mutual or unilateral recognition of assessment and inspection results (WHO 2019). Regulatory cooperation arrangements (for example, the ICH, the International Medical Device Regulators Forum [IMDRF], the Pharmaceutical Inspection Co-operation Scheme (PIC/S), and the Global Harmonization Working Party) could be reinforced, and participation broadened, where appropriate. Additional guidance could be developed for future pandemic preparedness; for instance, the IMDRF could establish guidance for the regulatory flexibility needed during a pandemic (WTO 2021b).

Further work could also be advanced on recognition of marketing authorizations, GMP inspections could help avoid duplication, and inspections could be further harmonized through enhanced cooperation (building on PIC/S) to consider country-specific requirements (WTO 2021b). The work of the TBT Committee can help build awareness, share experiences, and promote the use of such arrangements, as in the case of medical devices (WTO 2021d [para. 2.2–2.3], 2022c).

RTA provisions. Provisions on regulatory cooperation and convergence in medical goods have increasingly featured in RTAs and can inspire the deepening of trade cooperation. The TBT Agreement encourages mutual recognition and use of international *and* regional systems of conformity assessment (in art. 6 and art. 9, respectively).

Medical-sector-specific provisions and annexes are found primarily in RTAs between WTO members in Asia, Canada, the EU, and Latin America, and the United States. They mainly focus on cooperation between regulatory authorities, transparency, and recognition of conformity assessment procedures (WTO 2020d). For instance, the Comprehensive and Progressive Agreement for Trans-Pacific Partnership (CPTPP) and United States–Mexico–Canada Agreement (USMCA) include provisions on aligning pharmaceuticals' marketing authorization processes with international and regional standards, such as those of ICH (Gleeson et al. 2019). Both agreements also include provisions on medical devices; the USMCA specifically encourages regulatory alignment based on the work of the IMDRF and requires that parties recognize audits conducted under the Medical Device Single Audit Program (MDSAP) (WTO 2020c).

The EU–Canada Comprehensive Economic and Trade Agreement (CETA) protocol on the mutual recognition of the compliance and enforcement program regarding GMP for pharmaceutical products promotes cooperation on inspections and mutual recognition of GMP certificates (Gleeson et al. 2019). The Colombia and Mexico RTA includes provisions for cooperation on registration of medicines and the application of good laboratory practices in line with international standards.[21] The Japan and India RTA and the India-Singapore Agreement[22] promote cooperation on regulation of generic medicine, the latter establishing a special scheme for registration of generic products from India that are already approved by a reference regulatory authority.[23]

Cooperation at a regional level can help back up the capacities of regulators in less-developed countries. Regional cooperation arrangements between regulators can help overcome capacity gaps and limitations. For instance, the African Medicines Regulatory Harmonization (AMRH) initiative has spawned harmonization activities in the East African Community (EAC) and between the national regulatory authorities (NRAs) of Zambia, Zimbabwe, Botswana, and Namibia (ZAZIBONA), among others. These arrangements employ a collaborative approach for registration of generic products to speed access to essential medicines and strengthen the capacities of the participating NRAs. WHO's support has been key in these efforts (Ball, Roth, and Parry 2016). The further development of the African Medicines Agency (created by a treaty that entered into force in November 2021) would further help to support NRAs in Africa and improve regional regulatory harmonization.

Reliance tools and work sharing. Experience from the COVID-19 pandemic has revealed a playbook of regulatory flexibilities for ready deployment in the event of a future pandemic for smoother and faster approval of medical goods, saving resources. A range of reliance tools and work sharing between regulators can build trust and strengthen health security and trade cooperation.[24] At the stage of development, clinical trials and data sharing could be improved to quickly determine safety and efficacy of new medical goods.

In a future pandemic, there could be automatic recognition of approvals (and associated recognition of manufacturing facilities) if already approved by one of the WHO-recognized stringent regulatory authorities (SRAs).[25] Similarly, NRAs could facilitate an emergency use authorization based on the WHO emergency use listing or collaborative work via regional networks such as the AMRH program[26] or in the context of Association of Southeast Asian Nations (ASEAN) cooperation (Ball, Roth, and Parry 2016; see also Saxon 2017). The NRA that received the first application for emergency authorization of a new product in the context of a pandemic could open the process for participation by other NRAs and WHO (Lumpkin and Lim 2020).

Confidential sharing of regulatory documentation and review outcomes from other NRAs as part of the country-specific application (concerning the same regional supply chain) can help the local NRA understand the scientific basis for the application to speed up its review, to the benefit of patients. Where appropriate, batch release testing from NRAs or national control laboratories of the releasing country (through the WHO-National Control Laboratory Network for Biologicals) could be used. Greater use of reliance and work sharing for quality, safety, and vigilance could also be encouraged.[27]

NQI capacity building. Addressing gaps in the national quality infrastructure (NQI) of LMICs would help make regulatory frameworks for medical goods more robust and trusted. By providing reliable measurement and trusted testing, the NQI is the invisible backbone that regulators lean on to deliver safe, effective, and high-quality medical goods. The NQI is also indispensable for postmarket surveillance and monitoring of medical goods, helping fight illicit trade in those goods. Building the capacity of the NQI institutions that is needed to complement the regulatory framework can boost regulatory cooperation and resilience in future pandemics. Robust NQIs build confidence between regulators from different countries and encourage cooperation. On the other hand, gaps in the NQI contribute to trade bottlenecks.

Technical assistance in this area is particularly important considering the growing complexity of medical goods, as related international standards create both opportunities and challenges for LMICs (TBT Agreement, art. 12.4.).[28] Regional cooperation networks such as the Africa Medical Devices Forum can help pool resources and bridge gaps.[29] The TBT Agreement puts particular emphasis on technical assistance, including with respect to the NQI (WTO 2021f, 36–37).

Digital solutions. Digital tools provide a further opportunity to improve trade cooperation but also create new challenges. Remote inspection and other use of emerging technologies to find digital solutions for conformity assessment, which became widely used during the pandemic, can help improve the resilience of supply chains in future health crises.

Sound digital regulatory approaches are needed for governments to create enabling environments for such approaches and for innovation to thrive. Moreover, as medical devices are increasingly connected (Internet of Things), regulatory frameworks for medical goods are also being shaped by information technology and digital standards (for example, those of International Organization for Standardization [ISO], International Electrotechnical Commission [IEC], International Telecommunication Union [ITU], and ASTM International),[30] creating new opportunities and challenges.

Effective international cooperation on these digital approaches is needed to manage traditional risks such as safety or quality and novel risks such as cybersecurity. The workplan of the WTO TBT Committee during 2022–24, which focuses on digital issues in the area of standards and regulations, is a key forum for cooperation.

Intellectual property rights, health technology, and knowledge

The global intellectual property (IP) system can facilitate equitable access to existing technologies and support R&D, manufacturing, and dissemination of new technologies, but much depends on its design and implementation. The WTO Agreement on Trade-Related Aspects of Intellectual Property Rights ("TRIPS Agreement") is the most comprehensive multilateral agreement on IP. It provides the framework for governments to accommodate a wide range of interests in a way that promotes public welfare.

IP rights. This search for a balance of rights and obligations is reflected by the objectives laid down in Article 7 of the TRIPS Agreement, which call for the protection and enforcement of IP rights in a way that contributes to "the promotion of technological innovation, and to the transfer and dissemination of technology to the mutual advantage of producers and users of technological knowledge," and in a manner conducive to "social and economic welfare, and to a balance of rights and obligations." Similarly, the TRIPS Agreement recognizes the right of members to adopt measures to protect public health and nutrition and promote the public interest in sectors of vital importance to their socioeconomic and technological development that are consistent with the provisions of the agreement (TRIPS Agreement, art. 8)—principles reaffirmed by the Doha Declaration on the TRIPS Agreement and Public Health in 2001.

Health technology. As seen during the COVID-19 pandemic, an integrated approach to health, IP, and trade is needed to achieve public health objectives. The pandemic highlighted the need for a strong and balanced link between support for innovative activities and partnerships (including by sharing technology, know-how, and clinical trial information) and ensuring swift and equitable access to new health technologies. The IP system can support collaboration among health technology developers, governments, and other stakeholders. Because technologies are usually owned by public and private sector actors who are located in a few innovative economies up to now, strengthening partnerships across borders is essential. Given the enormity of the COVID-19 challenge, all mechanisms—including voluntary licenses, technology pools, and flexibilities in WTO Agreements—should be considered in light of the countries' different needs and their ability to implement these mechanisms at the national level.

WTO members disagree as to whether voluntary initiatives and TRIPS flexibilities ensure the adequate and timely supply of health products and technologies for all to prevent, treat, or contain the COVID-19 pandemic and future health crises. The TRIPS Agreement gives governments scope to limit IP rights in the public interest. But India and South Africa (subsequently joined by many other WTO members) raised concerns that these voluntary initiatives and TRIPS flexibilities had proved insufficient during the COVID-19 pandemic—and in October 2020 called on the WTO General Council to waive members' obligations to protect and enforce certain IP rights in relation to the prevention, containment, or treatment of COVID-19.

Other WTO members believe, however, that the solution to any IP-related challenges can be found within the IP system, particularly by clarifying and facilitating the use of existing provisions to authorize the use of patent-protected inventions without the right holder's consent. On May 3, 2022, a communication from the TRIPS Council Chair containing the outcome of informal discussions between a group of Ministers was shared with WTO members for consideration by the TRIPS Council at the request of the WTO Director-General (WTO 2022a). It proposes practical ways of simplifying how governments can override patent rights, under certain conditions, to enable diversification of production of COVID-19 vaccines.

Establishing a solid basis for sharing technology and know-how will be a key component of the broader set of trade policies, which must be closely coordinated to jointly develop the capacity needed to respond to future health crises and to geographically diversify manufacturing capacities. Consistent with the objectives for the IP system laid down in TRIPS Article 7, a balanced IP system can help make this happen, but it must be accompanied by other factors that positively support the sharing of knowledge. The example of successful health-technology transfer programs provided by developed member countries[31] shows that the TRIPS Agreement can be instrumental in promoting technology transfer to LDCs (box 3.4).

It is therefore worth considering what else is needed to strengthen technology transfer, including through, but not limited to, the multilateral IP system as implemented in domestic law. Measures could include encouraging rights holders to adopt open and humanitarian licensing models for pandemic-related technologies, to contribute to international technology sharing platforms such as the COVID-19 Technology Access Pool (C-TAP), and to include equitable access considerations in their R&D planning.

Knowledge sharing. Enabling governments to implement and use the flexibilities included in the TRIPS Agreement is particularly important when voluntary licenses do not lead to the expected results. Following the WHO, World Intellectual Property Organization (WIPO) and the WTO Directors-General agreement in June 2021, the three organizations are organizing a series of capacity-building workshops[32] and have also launched a joint platform for technical assistance to address countries' needs for COVID-19 health technologies (WTO 2021e). These and other international organizations could also jointly develop an information platform that gives WTO members easily accessible and timely data on patents, regulatory status, and trade information. In turn, governments could use this platform to design policy responses to pandemics.

Countries must have access to technologies that are developed to tackle future pandemics. In this regard, there have been calls for making conditions in licensing and procurement agreements public to foster equitable access. Although this is not an issue covered by the global IP system or the TRIPS Agreement, transparency requirements

Box 3.4   Health technology transfer to least developed countries

The Agreement on Trade-Related Aspects of Intellectual Property Rights ("TRIPS Agreement"), Article 66.2, obligates "developed country" members to provide incentives to enterprises and institutions in their territories to promote and encourage technology transfer to least developed country (LDC) members, hence enabling them to create a sound and viable technological base.

In 2003, the TRIPS Council adopted a decision on the implementation of Article 66.2 (WTO 2003), requiring these developed country members to submit annual reports on their incentive programs. During the TRIPS Council's discussion, the LDC Group identified public health and pharmaceuticals as a priority needs area for technology transfer.

For the reporting period of 2018–20, developed country members[a] reported a total of 132 programs related to the transfer of health technologies, benefiting 42 LDC members and observers (figure B3.4.1). Collectively, the European Union and United

Figure B3.4.1   Health technology transfer programs reported by WTO developed country members under TRIPS Agreement, art. 66.2, and the LDC beneficiaries of those programs, 2018–20

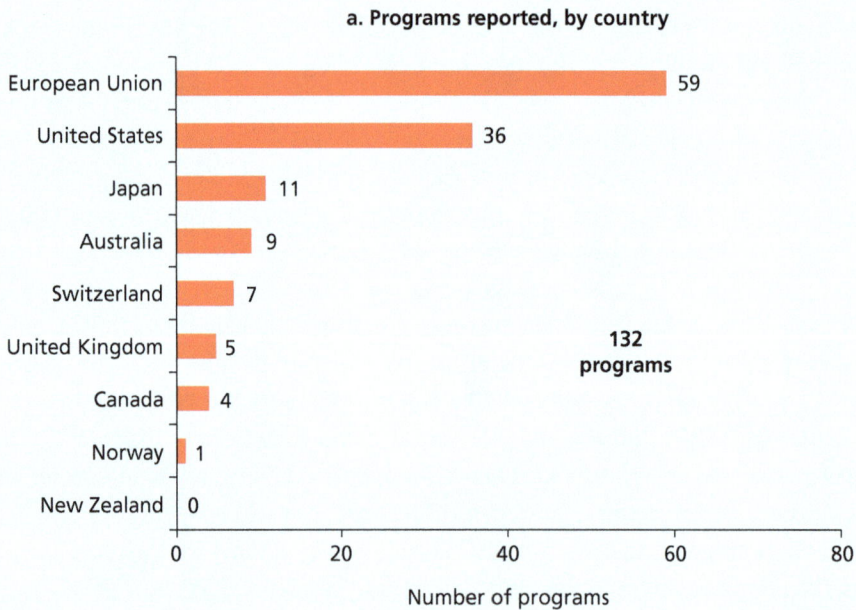

(Figure continued)

(Continued)

Box 3.4   Health technology transfer to least developed countries *(Continued)*

Figure B3.4.1   Health technology transfer programs reported by WTO developed country members under TRIPS Agreement, art. 66.2, and the LDC beneficiaries of those programs, 2018–20 *(Continued)*

b. LDCs' relative shares of benefits

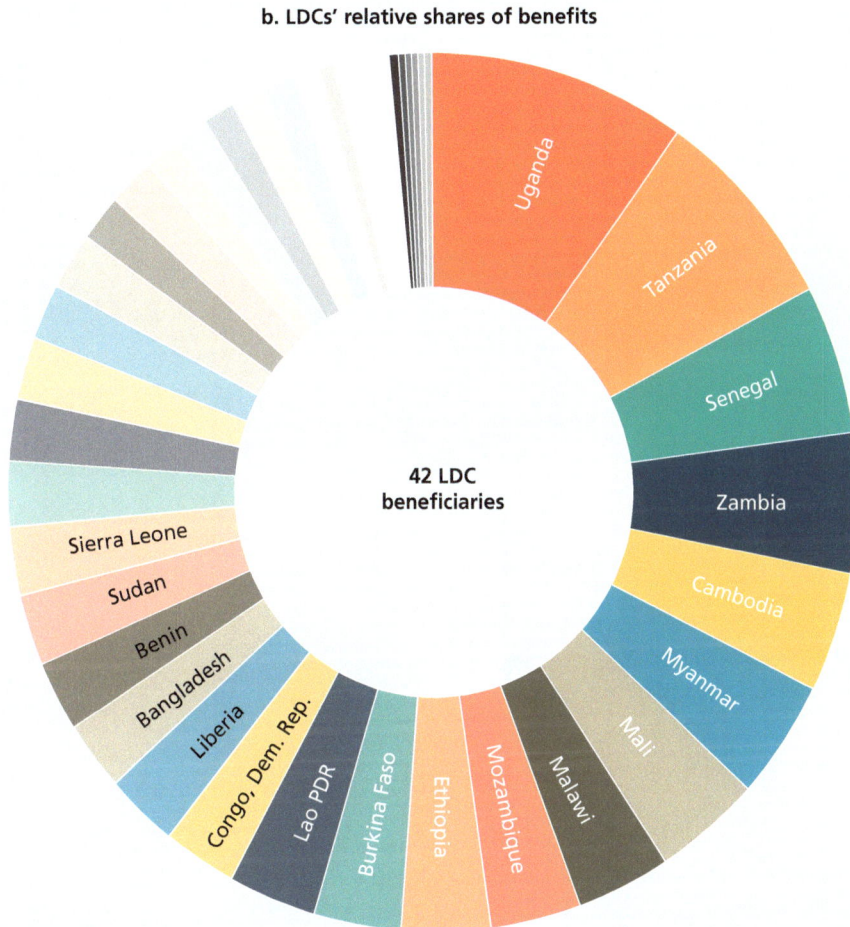

Sources: World Bank calculations based on the reports (required under WTO TRIPS Agreement, art. 66.2) submitted by the WTO developed country members.

Note: "Developed country members" include Australia, Canada, the European Union (and its member states), Japan, New Zealand, Norway, Switzerland, the United Kingdom, and the United States. LDC = least developed country; TRIPS = Trade-Related Aspects of Intellectual Property Rights; WTO = World Trade Organization.

(Continued)

Box 3.4   Health technology transfer to least developed countries *(Continued)*

Figure B3.4.2   Types of health technology transfer programs reported by WTO developed country members under TRIPS Agreement, art. 66.2, 2018–20

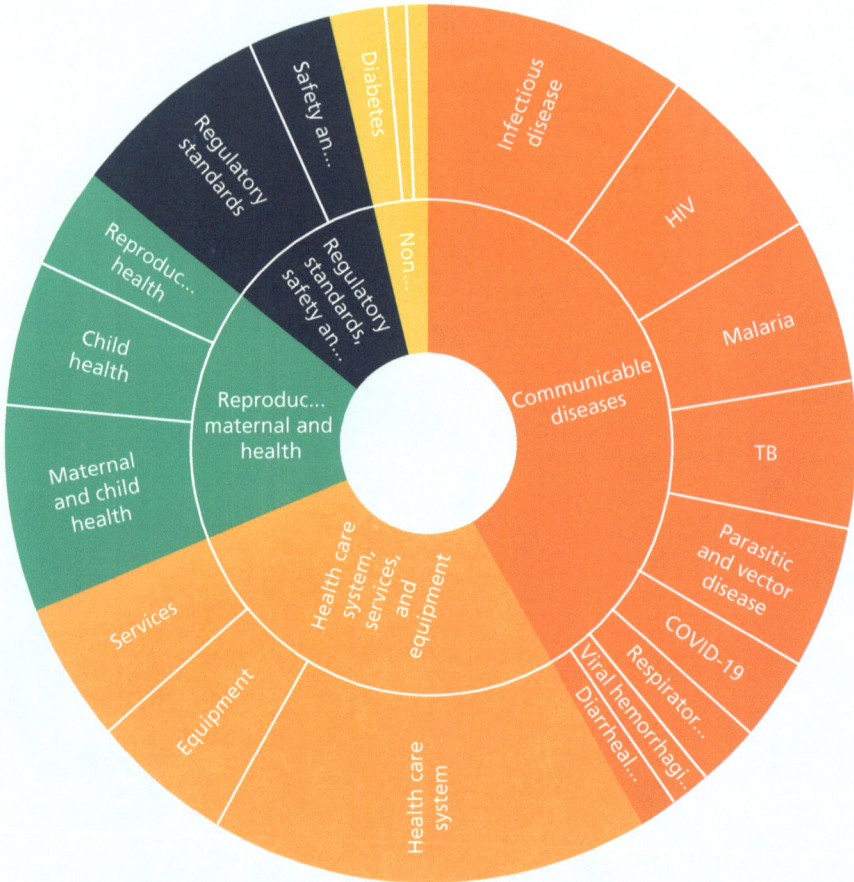

Source: World Trade Organization (WTO) calculations based on the reports (required under WTO TRIPS Agreement, art. 66.2) submitted by WTO developed country members.

Note: The figure indicates relative shares of the number of programs, by program focus. "Developed country members" of the WTO include Australia, Canada, the European Union (and its member states), Japan, New Zealand, Norway, Switzerland, the United Kingdom, and the United States. TB = tuberculosis; TRIPS = Trade-Related Aspects of Intellectual Property Rights.

States provided 72 percent of those programs. Uganda and Tanzania were among the top-ranking beneficiaries, each benefiting from at least 30 health technology transfer programs.

Around 42 percent of the reported health technology transfer programs have a particular focus on communicable diseases such as HIV, malaria, and tuberculosis (figure B3.4.2).

(Continued)

Box 3.4	Health technology transfer to least developed countries *(Continued)*

Four programs reported by the United States were related to COVID-19 training, testing, data collection, and analysis (WTO 2020b).

Research and technical assistance are the most prominent incentives used for delivering these health technology transfer programs.

a. The "developed country members" of the WTO are Australia, Canada, the European Union (and its member states), Japan, New Zealand, Norway, Switzerland, the United Kingdom, and the United States.

that would apply to IP licensing are closely related to the multilateral framework for IP rights. Making those conditions public merits close consideration in relevant international forums because they could affect, among other things, the pricing of licensed technologies and could influence trade in relevant technologies. Given significant government support for R&D and the extensive funding for product development initiatives provided by the governments of WTO developed member countries, reviewing the deployment of the results of publicly funded research has also been advanced as an area of work.

The severe global inequities in access to COVID-19 vaccines have motivated a debate on whether, and how, such funding programs should set conditions for sharing resulting IP rights. This could encompass engaging with multilateral technology-pooling initiatives, disseminating technologies, and leveraging access to COVID-19 vaccines and treatments. Contracts could, for example, cover conditions on how to manage IP rights in a manner that facilitates equitable access to transfer technology and manufacturing know-how, while improving transparency, in return for R&D funding.

Cooperation to address illicit trade

Illicit trade in medical goods can be addressed through improved regulatory coherence and international cooperation. Illicit trade in medical goods—and in particular the trafficking of substandard, unregistered, or falsified products—can have serious health, economic, and socioeconomic consequences (WHO 2017). There are a number of areas where the multilateral rules contained in WTO Agreements matter.

Customs controls. First, better customs procedures foster the sort of improvements in customs controls that can help in addressing illicit trade concerns. The TFA has several provisions that bolster the capacity of customs to maintain such controls, by requiring greater transparency of customs rules and procedures, the advent of risk management systems and pre- and postclearance processes, and a focus on increased domestic coordination and international customs cooperation. Greater transparency and customs functioning both enhances governments' ability to address the threat of illicit trade (including with respect to medical goods) and curbs discretionary practices that can give rise to malfeasance and corruption.

Regulatory coherence and coordination. Improving regulatory coherence and international coordination regarding medical product quality and safety can help address risks arising in national regulatory systems regarding illicit trade. To meet surging demand for medical goods during the pandemic, governments introduced a range of emergency measures to accelerate access, including by relaxing certain safety and quality approvals and other regulatory requirements. Although this approach was helpful in addressing acute shortages, it also has the potential to create opportunities for illicit trade.

The TBT Agreement helps regulators strike the appropriate balance between (a) adopting regulatory interventions for ensuring the safety, quality, and efficacy of medical goods, and (b) facilitating trade in these goods. The Agreement covers, in particular, conformity assessment procedures (CAPs) for ensuring that goods, including medical products, fully comply with safety and quality specifications. Well-designed and applied CAPs can be important tools for preventing and combating illicit trade, and the TBT Committee is currently preparing guidance in this regard.

TRIPS standards. Tackling illicit trade in medical goods also relies significantly on various disciplines in the TRIPS Agreement. TRIPS minimum standards provide a basis for action against the production, distribution, and sale of intellectual property rights (IPR)-infringing illicit goods and helps to protect consumers from their effects. In particular, the border measures spelled out in the Agreement provide effective tools to fight the importation and, where WTO members opt to do so, the exportation and transit of illicit IPR-infringing goods. The TRIPS Agreement also mandates international cooperation in that members are required to establish contact points and be ready to exchange information on trade in infringing goods. The TRIPS Council receives notifications and updates of these contact points from its members and serves as a forum for discussion in this regard.

Traceability programs. In addition, the safety of medical products crucially depends on supply chain integrity and transparency, and thus measures that ensure traceability along value chains are critical in addressing some of the harmful consequences of illicit trade. Traceability programs implemented in many high-income countries and in some LMICs, and adherence to global traceability standards, make it much harder for illicit products to enter legitimate supply chains. Theft, diversion, and parallel trade also become easier to spot. Initiatives such as those launched by the Global Steering Committee for Quality Assurance—hosted by the World Bank (box 3.5)—will improve LMICs' capacity to ensure health products' traceability.

Illicit health products plagued many low- and middle-income countries before the COVID-19 pandemic, and challenges with supply chain integrity and transparency during the crisis made matters worse. The simple fact that no single country in all of Sub-Saharan Africa has a functioning traceability system may have cost many non-COVID-19 deaths indirectly attributable to the pandemic (Heuschen et al. 2021).

The World Bank–hosted Global Steering Committee (GSC) for Quality Assurance launched broad-based public and private collaboration to help countries initiate global standards for medicines traceability. The onset of the pandemic heightened the focus and created new momentum around protecting the COVID-19 vaccines from theft and falsification through the rapid development of a verification system. Simple product barcoding and smartphone scanning apps offered a practical tool for the near term. This initial building block, while far short of the traceability goals embraced by some 25 African countries as part of the "Lagos Call to Action," raised critical awareness and galvanized support within the COVID-19 Vaccines Global Access (COVAX) Facility.[a]

For many African countries, the pandemic exposed weaknesses in the international trading system for health commodities. Without manufacturing capacity for essential medicines, let alone for COVID-19–related health products, poorer countries could only wait. Even as South Africa and others begin to fend for themselves with new vaccine manufacturing capacity, the basic structures that will ultimately determine the survivability of the infant pharmaceutical industry require parallel development efforts. Namely, medicines regulatory harmonization must advance across the dozens of small markets that make up Africa's regional economic communities. Harmonized regulations and processes will support an overall recognition that raising the regulatory standard, while difficult and incremental, will enhance trade competitiveness and help Africa better serve its own billion consumer market.

Shared national approaches to health product traceability are part and parcel of the access to safe and effective medicines imperative for lower-income regions like Africa. Already, every medicine manufactured in India bears a global standard–compliant two-dimensional barcode that contains critical data about the product. As those products cross borders and land in regions like Europe, that electronic data moves with the product and offers enhanced supply chain integrity and visibility. But when that product moves across borders and into a region like Africa, the lights go out—there is no attempt to follow the data. As a consequence, pharmaceutical manufacturers within Africa cannot hope to compete globally, nor can they provide quality assurance for their products to the potential customers in their neighboring country. Legitimate health products imported into the region suffer the same fate. They enter opaque and highly fractured supply chains that lack traceability and therefore cannot guarantee the integrity of the health care products.

Fortunately, African regulatory leaders are embracing the health product traceability challenge. Nigeria, Africa's largest consumer market, is not only helping to lead COVID-19 vaccine verification efforts but is also fully committed to the value of a national medicines traceability system through the National Agency for Food and Drug Administration and Control (NAFDAC).

When it comes to quality health product access, there are few more tangible or more practical steps that lower-income regions like Africa could take than to advance common regulatory policies, including medicines traceability. Predictable, transparent, and stringent regulatory oversight promotes efficient trade in health commodities. Knowing where a product was manufactured, which supply route it traveled, and how it came to the patient will save lives. The COVID-19 pandemic did not create this lesson but it certainly reinforced it.

a. The COVAX Facility is a global risk-sharing mechanism for pooled procurement and equitable distribution of COVID-19 vaccines, co-led by the Gavi, the Coalition for Epidemic Preparedness Innovations (CEPI), the World Health Organization (WHO), and the United Nations Children's Fund (UNICEF).

WTO response to the pandemic

Based on the demand from WTO members and the need to channel all various and useful efforts on the WTO response to the pandemic, on June 22, 2021, a facilitator-led, horizontal, and multilateral process was set up under the auspices of the WTO's General Council to streamline and organize work in this area and ensure transparency and inclusiveness.

At the time of writing, work on this outcome—possibly consisting of three parts—was being prepared in the lead-up to the 12th WTO Ministerial Conference:

1. The first part would be a factual reflection of WTO members' trade-related responses and the WTO Secretariat's contributions during the pandemic.
2. The second part would reaffirm relevant WTO obligations in various areas. In this regard, delegations noted the importance of having provisions on transparency, trade facilitation, and export restrictions as well as economic recovery, food security, services, regulatory coherence, and technology transfer, among others. Several noted the importance of ensuring resilience and pandemic preparedness and addressing supply-chain bottlenecks and transportation costs. Other suggestions include having a TRIPS and non-IP trigger mechanism, providing policy space, and preserving existing flexibilities. The precise elements and the various proposed paragraphs are currently being negotiated.
3. The third part would involve forward-looking provisions on what the WTO could do to take up matters related to pandemic preparedness and resilience—taking into account lessons learned from the current pandemic and the WTO response.

Policies affecting medical services trade

Trade in services and international trade agreements can ensure a response to health demand while also supporting public objectives such as health security. Given the specific nature of medical services, trade-related considerations have not taken center stage in national and international policy making. Health authorities are concerned with the quality of the services provided and equity in access to essential services domestically. Trade in medical services could support the fulfillment of public policy objectives (whether under the auspices of GATS, regionally, bilaterally, or unilaterally) while not constraining the right of governments to regulate.

In general, services trade rules, as in GATS, do not cover government services.[33] This would mean, for example, that health services provided for a nominal price by medical service suppliers that are not actively trying to attract customers (patients) are not disciplined by these agreements. Trade agreements also offer many flexibilities for governments to tailor what they are willing to open to foreign competition, and how, based on their public policy objectives—for example, by maintaining market access limitations or discriminatory practices deemed necessary to achieve public health policy objectives.

Commitments under GATS. GATS commitments for medical services are low compared with other sectors. Even where a sector is committed, there are many limitations. GATS offers flexibility to choose which service sectors to liberalize and how. As shown in figure 3.2, "medical and dental services" is the most committed medical services subsector (52 members, or 37 percent of total members, counting the EU-25 schedule as one); followed by "hospital services" (49 members, or 35 percent); "other human health services" (25 members, or 18 percent); and "nurses, midwives, and other paramedical personnel" (22 members, or 16 percent).

Mode 1 (cross-border supply) has the lowest level of commitments (averaging approximately 20 percent across the subsectors, with almost a third being partial commitments). Mode 2 (consumption abroad) and mode 3 (commercial presence) are committed by an average 25 percent of members, but mode 2 shows the fewest limitations. Mode 4 (movement of personnel) commitments are very limited in scope and linked to the horizontal commitments made for this mode (that is, indistinguishably for all sectors in the schedule of commitments, mainly referring to intracorporate transferees and business visitors).[34] The low levels of commitments for medical services trade has consequences in terms of transparency and predictability—especially important in times of crisis.

Bilateral or regional commitments. In the context of bilateral or regional trade agreements, many economies have made more commitments with favored partners, often reflecting the relative openness of current policies on medical service sectors.

Figure 3.2 Low levels of GATS commitments in medical services trade

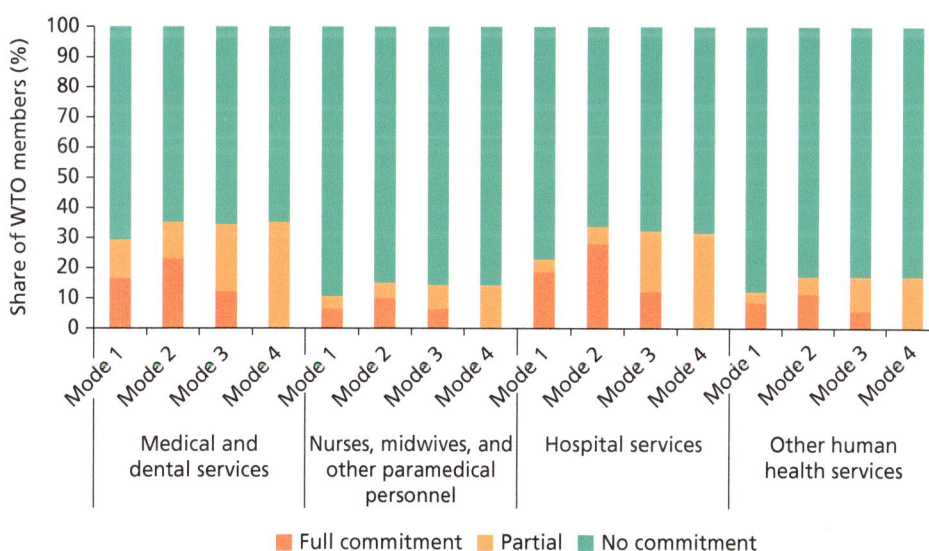

Source: World Trade Organization and World Bank I-TIP services database, GATS module (accessed in 2022), https://i-tip.wto.org/services.

Note: General Agreement on Trade in Services (GATS) modes of supply: (1) cross-border supply, (2) consumption abroad, (3) commercial presence, and (4) presence of natural persons. I-TIP = Integrated Trade Intelligence Portal.

Sixty-eight jurisdictions (counting EU-25 as one) have made commitments for medical services. Commitments made in the deepest agreements for the four subsectors identified previously are more numerous and often deeper than those in GATS (figure 3.3). There are commitments in at least three of the four medical subsectors for all modes of supply in high- and middle-income economies as well as in at least two low-income economies (limited to parties to the East African Community). The number of economies making RTA commitments for cross-border supply is 11 times higher than in GATS.

Benefits of binding policies in trade agreements. Reducing relevant trade barriers in medical services could enhance access to and quality of services, and it also has the potential for cost savings and efficiency gains. Policy makers need to find the right

Figure 3.3   The best bilateral or regional trade agreements include more medical services commitments than in GATS

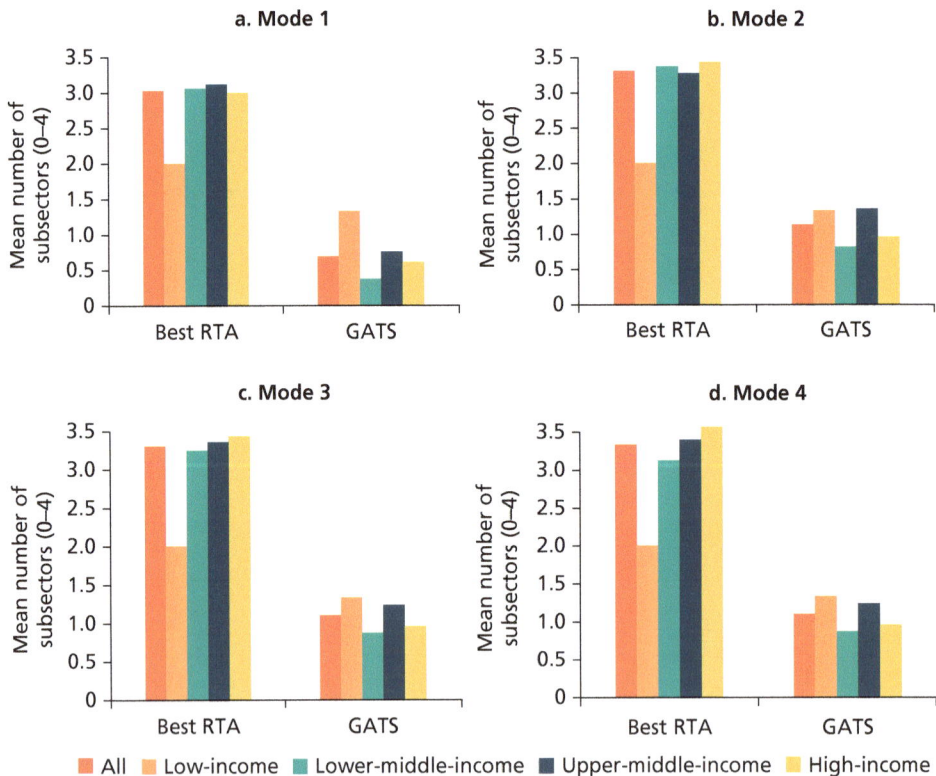

Source: World Trade Organization and World Bank, I-TIP services database, GATS and RTA modules (accessed in 2022), https://i-tip.wto.org/services.

Note: The charts show the average number of subsectors (out of four) with a modal commitment. The four medical services subsectors are (a) medical and dental services; (b) nurses, midwives, and other paramedical personnel; (c) hospital services; and (d) other human health services. General Agreement on Trade in Services (GATS) modes of supply: (1) cross-border supply, (2) consumption abroad, (3) commercial presence, and (4 presence of natural persons. RTA = regional trade agreement.

balance between introducing more competition and ensuring universal access to health care as well as quality and security for patients (Drager 1999). Keeping this in mind, governments could bind applied policies in their commitments as deemed relevant.

Trade agreements would enable governments to discuss liberalizing medical services and identify reciprocal market openings. Binding policies in trade agreements provide credibility and predictability of trading conditions. This could support the increase of trade in medical services, better serving demand and contributing to health security. Some further specific market openings could be committed in relation to cross-border supply for less sensitive practitioner-to-practitioner services, teleradiology, telediagnosis, or health-specific business process outsourcing. The activity of telehealth platforms could also be liberalized. Restrictions on the nonportability of health insurance coverage (pertinent for cross-border supply and consumption abroad) could be eased, and impediments to establishing foreign suppliers of services could be reduced.

In addition, barriers to the movement of health professionals could be eliminated or reduced, supporting health-worker mobility in response to demand. Health workers' mobility could also be improved through frameworks to deal with emergency shortages in national health systems. Recognition of qualifications is key to mobility and could be facilitated through recognition agreements. But when such tools do not exist, governments should strive for more transparent regulatory flexibilities ahead of an emergency (for example, planning ahead the procedures and requirements for fast-tracking the recognition of qualifications). Finally, consideration could be given to strengthening and advancing ethical mobility, as defined in the WHO Global Code of Practice on the International Recruitment of Health Personnel (discussed in chapter 1, box 1.2), using the trade-in-services frameworks and their flexibilities (Carzaniga et al. 2019).

Good-governance disciplines. Endorsing good-governance disciplines would promote transparent, predictable, and efficient practices to support expected gains from medical services trade liberalization while also meeting public policy objectives (WTO 2019b). GATS contains certain good-governance provisions and calls for the development of disciplines to promote good practices so that licensing and qualification requirements and procedures and technical standards do not create unnecessary barriers to trade.

Although WTO members have for many years worked toward developing generally applicable disciplines, there has been no outcome by the entire membership so far. However, progress was made in several bilateral and regional trade agreements that address regulatory obstacles and promote good governance (Baiker, Bertola, and Jelitto 2021). Moreover, based on the work done in the WTO, in 2017 a group of members decided to advance the work on generally applicable disciplines in the context of the Joint Initiative on Services Domestic Regulation, focusing on transparency and procedural aspects. In November 2021, 67 members concluded negotiations on an agreement that is expected to improve the business climate, lower trade costs, and cut red tape (WTO 2021c). For example, research suggests that implementing the new disciplines could reduce global trade costs by US$150 billion a year.

Once implemented, the agreed-upon disciplines will apply to medical services covered in schedules of commitments and will add transparency, predictability, and efficiency to administrative procedures. A significant number of these disciplines already exist in many countries, but codifying more of them in national legislation (as well as possible additional good practices) would further increase gains from liberalization without compromising universal access to health care and security for patients.

Mutual recognition agreements. International trade agreements could facilitate recognition of foreign qualifications of medical services suppliers. GATS as well as regional and bilateral agreements include provisions on the recognition of the supplier's education or experience, requirements met, or licenses or certifications granted in a particular country, on condition of transparency and nondiscrimination.[35]

GATS encourages recognition based on multilaterally agreed-upon criteria, wherever appropriate. It provides that WTO members cooperate with relevant international government and nongovernmental organizations (NGOs) to establish common international standards and criteria for recognition. In fact, in 1997 the WTO developed "Guidelines on Mutual Recognition Agreements (MRAs) in the Accountancy Sector" (WTO 1997), which are general enough to be potentially applied, mutatis mutandis, to the medical services sector. They are aimed at making it easier to negotiate recognition agreements and for third parties to join those agreements.

Although many bilateral or regional trade agreements include provisions on recognition, their breadth and content vary significantly. In many cases, they recognize that negotiating recognition agreements falls under the competence of professional associations. In this context, MRAs could focus on recognizing qualifications for medical professionals, as was done in the EU and ASEAN regions.[36]

Health education and training. Trade agreements can also strengthen the education and training of health personnel to meet domestic and international demand and address global crises. Trade agreements can support domestic reforms aimed at reducing barriers to entry and competition in higher education and hence to increase the number of providers of education and training for health personnel. Improving education opportunities by developing and updating curricula can address shortages of health professionals and workers in some regions, thereby enhancing access to medical services. The global shortage of nurses was estimated at 5.9 million in 2018. To address the shortage by 2030, the number of nurse graduates would need to increase by a projected 8 percent a year on average (WHO 2020c, 3–5).

Telehealth regulation. Clear regulation of telehealth services is essential to fully benefit from commitments, particularly when it comes to cross-border supply. The types of services that can be provided across borders and under which conditions should be clearly identified (for example, only through foreign-based suppliers authorized to provide their services in the jurisdiction, or where the professional's qualifications are recognized). Means to ensure that health services suppliers based abroad meet domestic regulatory requirements would have to be established, and issues like cross-border liability, especially in relation to patient safety, should be addressed.

For example, this could be established through international cooperation or agreements, or ensuring that all medical services suppliers, including foreign-based ones, are insured with a local or international insurance company in case of malpractice (Adlung and Carzaniga 2001). These steps would greatly improve the value of eventual bindings in this sector.

Greater remote trade of medical services requires adequate regulation and infrastructure. A regulatory framework that gives users confidence that their personal medical data are secure and remain private, while at the same time not unduly restricting trade, is a further critical component to the promotion of international telehealth services. Building the necessary information and communication technology infrastructure to enable fast, reliable, and affordable digital communications is an absolute prerequisite for this trade to flourish. International cooperation can contribute to these two outcomes. Some efforts are under way in the WTO. They include disciplines on personal data protection and cybersecurity as well as plurilateral negotiations to improve commitments covering telecommunications, develop rules to promote cross-border data flows, and forestall the application of customs duties to electronic transmissions.

Strengthened collaboration. Stronger national and international collaboration between health and trade-in-services stakeholders can increase health security. Enhancing the dialogue between health and trade policy makers at the national level helps ensure that trade in medical services supports health policy objectives.

International cooperation can also play a role in policy making—particularly regulatory coherence and coordination—to improve the quality and efficiency of regulations, exchange good regulatory practices, and enhance regulatory capacity in LMICs. This could be achieved by establishing standards and developing various guidance established by international agencies (as already done by WHO), in collaboration with other stakeholders, including from the trade community.

Other policies

Subsidies and investment incentives

The COVID-19 pandemic showed the need for subsidies to scale up capacity across medical supply chains, especially for vaccines. As discussed in chapter 2, vaccine production and consumption are affected by market failures: Absent government provision, individuals might not get vaccinated, generating negative health externalities, and producers may not have sufficient incentive to accelerate and commit to enhancing production capacity or providing vaccines at cost to low-income countries. Investors may be deterred by potential losses if governments limit payment to the marginal cost of production or decide not to buy vaccines if the disease outbreak is controlled before medicines are ready to be marketed.[37] It is therefore appropriate, from a public health perspective, for governments to make advance market commitments and purchase agreements with a range of companies and use subsidies to expand investment to levels that reflect the difference between the private and social returns of large-scale vaccinations (Castillo et al. 2021).

There is no indication that WTO rules on subsidies constrained government intervention during the pandemic. Governments made major investments and provided large amounts of financing to vaccine developers and guaranteed demand through advance purchase agreements with individual companies and by providing funds to COVID-19 Vaccines Global Access (COVAX) for the purchase and distribution of vaccines. These programs were not constrained by multilateral trade rules. WTO rules do not prohibit production subsidies and do not impose comprehensive disciplines on investment incentives. Its rules on subsidies are limited to trade in goods.[38] They aim to guide intervention by members to address the competitive distortions that subsidies may give rise to—which may be done through countervailing duties on subsidized imports that cause injury to domestic industries or by initiating dispute settlement procedures if foreign subsidies harm the trade interests of other members. As is the case for public procurement, discussed below, WTO disciplines are not designed to support coordination and subsidy cooperation at times of crisis, but they do not prevent governments from supporting an expansion in supply capacity.

Government procurement

Opening domestic public-health procurement markets to international competition can increase value for money for governments and citizens because it provides access to the best medical goods, services, and technologies and to the most efficient suppliers around the world. The WTO Agreement on Government Procurement (GPA), last amended in 2012, is the main binding instrument providing a framework for the conduct of international trade in government procurement markets. It can help make medical goods and services more accessible and affordable and help create more efficient and cost-effective health systems.[39]

The GPA 2012 rules can improve domestic health systems and help governments deliver better value for money for medical goods and services. The GPA 2012 is a plurilateral WTO agreement, meaning that only those WTO members that are signatories are bound by its rules. At present, 48 WTO members are bound by the GPA 2012.[40] In addition to its role as an Agreement that is an integral part of the WTO, the rules of the GPA 2012 commonly serves as a model in several bilateral and regional trade agreements. As a consequence, the basic disciplines of the GPA 2012 are relevant and extend their influence not just to its signatories but also to substantially more members.[41]

The GPA 2012 embodies legal guarantees of transparency and nondiscrimination intended to promote fair and competitive procedures in participating WTO members' government procurement markets. It also seeks to promote good governance and economic development, consistent with best practices in government procurement. In particular, a new provision (art. IV:4) requires GPA parties to avoid conflicts of interest and corrupt practices in GPA-covered government procurement. The Agreement is highly relevant to the public health sector, because it provides significant coverage of medical goods (for example, medicines, PPE, and vaccines) and, to a lesser extent, medical services. (For details, see WHO, WIPO, and WTO 2020a).

In emergencies such as a pandemic, the GPA 2012 permits a departure from some of its obligations to give governments and procuring entities several flexibilities to speed up procurement to obtain essential medical goods and services quickly:

- It permits parties to shorten time periods for tendering if a state of urgency substantiated by the procuring entities renders ordinary time periods impracticable.
- It allows for limited tendering, which is less transparent but can be critical to procuring medical goods and services quickly during a pandemic.
- It provides a general exception under which parties may impose measures necessary to protect human life or health, provided that such measures are applied in a manner that would not constitute (a) a means of arbitrary or unjustifiable discrimination between parties where the same conditions prevail, or (b) a disguised restriction on international trade.

International cooperation will likely become ever more important. The COVID-19 pandemic has demonstrated the potential usefulness of cooperative procurement tools, such as joint procurement or similar mechanisms (for example, pooled or centralized procurement), as discussed earlier. As a final point, it may also be noted that during the COVID-19 pandemic, temporary export restrictions and prohibitions have significantly affected the ability of governments and the private sector to procure essential medical products in a timely fashion. Further cooperation among WTO members on this question may positively contribute to the promotion and protection of global public health.

Competition policy

Competition law and policy have important international dimensions. This can be illustrated by the increasing number of competition-law enforcement cases in the health sector with cross-border dimensions. There are various examples of practices that trigger reviews or actions by competition authorities in multiple jurisdictions. First, in 2014, the proposed acquisition by Thermo Fisher of Life Technologies (two US health-related biotech companies with global presence) was reviewed by competition authorities in several jurisdictions, including Australia, Canada, China, the EU, Japan, the Republic of Korea, and the United States.[42] Second in 2016, the Italian Competition Authority (AGCM) asked the Irish authority to inspect the Irish premises of Aspen, a South African pharmaceutical company, for evidence of alleged excessive pricing of its anticancer drugs.[43]

Efforts to establish a multilateral agreement on competition policy within the international trading system have, to date, not been successful. Nonetheless, the interaction between trade and competition policy has been recognized by the incorporation of competition-related provisions in numerous free trade agreements and several WTO Agreements.[44] The importance of competition policy for international trade is also recognized and discussed in the Protocols of Accessions of new WTO members, in the context of WTO Trade Policy Reviews, and in different WTO bodies.[45]

The COVID-19 pandemic has underlined the usefulness of cooperation and communication among countries, competition authorities, and suppliers of medical goods and services. For example, cooperation and exchanges of information helped competition authorities in several jurisdictions to better respond to the pandemic, address anticompetitive cases in the health sector with cross-border dimensions, and reduce the potential for conflicting decisions or positions and unnecessary duplication of effort. Cooperation also helped international providers of medical goods and services comply with the competition laws and guidelines of different countries. Cooperation took place at the bilateral, regional, and multilateral levels.

Bilateral level. At the bilateral level, governments and competition authorities have engaged with each other through formal cooperation agreements (OECD 2021a), memoranda of understanding (OECD 2021b), or informal dialogue. For example, in 2021, the Japan Fair Trade Commission (JFTC) and the Competition Commission of India (CCI) signed a memorandum on cooperation that includes notifications and coordination of competition-enforcement activities, information exchange on competition laws and policies, and technical training and assistance (JFTC and CCI 2021).

Regional level. Cooperation and communication between competition authorities also took place at the regional level. A notable example is the European Competition Network (ECN), where competition authorities from all EU member states and the European Commission cooperate to address anticompetitive cross-border business practices.[46]

In addition, most RTAs with dedicated chapters on competition policy contain basic provisions to promote cooperation and coordination in competition law enforcement (Anderson et al. 2018). For example, Chapter 16 of the Comprehensive and Progressive Agreement for Trans-Pacific Partnership (CPTPP) recognizes the importance of cooperation and coordination between national authorities to foster effective competition law enforcement in the free trade area comprising 11 countries.[47]

Multilateral level. At the multilateral level, competition authorities have initiated ad hoc working groups to address sector-specific issues arising from the COVID-19 pandemic. One recent example is the Multilateral Pharmaceutical Merger Task Force initiated in March 2021 by the competition authorities of Canada, the EU, the United Kingdom, and the United States. The task force aims to review and update the analysis of mergers in the pharmaceutical sector (United States, FTC 2021).

In addition, international organizations and networks can also facilitate competition policy discussions, policy learning and exchange on best practices, as well as provide technical assistance to governments. For example, institutions including the World Bank, the Organisation for Economic Co-operation and Development, the United Nations Conference on Trade and Development, and the International Competition Network have published reports and recommendations on competition policy in the context of the COVID-19 pandemic (Goodwin and Barajas 2020; OECD 2020; UNCTAD 2020; ICN 2020).

COOPERATION BEYOND TRADE AGREEMENTS FOR GLOBAL HEALTH SECURITY

The Multilateral Leaders Task Force on COVID-19 Vaccines, Therapeutics, and Diagnostics ("Multilateral Leaders Task Force") has called on the international community to step up its response beyond trade by[48]

- Urgently closing financing gaps, including through up-front grant contributions to address the gap in the Access to COVID-19 Tools Accelerator (ACT-A), discussed further below;
- Accelerating vaccine deliveries and vaccine sharing;
- Ensuring that countries have the diagnostics, therapeutics, and other tools they need, including oxygen, to manage the health crisis;
- Addressing supply chain bottlenecks to scale up production and deployment of vaccines, testing, and therapeutics; and
- Working with countries to address readiness issues, such as cold chain storage and distribution, so countries are prepared to deploy vaccines as soon as they are available.

These efforts call for enhanced cooperation between states, between states and nonstate actors, and between international organizations.

Cooperation between states

International cooperation that contributes to global health security occurs in many domains beyond trade. WHO, the United Nations Children's Fund (UNICEF), the World Tourism Organization (UNWTO), and the International Civil Aviation Organization (ICAO), to name just a few international organizations, all pursue activities that have a direct bearing on global health security. Extensive cross-country collaboration among scientists and researchers in developing new vaccines and therapeutics, cooperation among regulators, and new multilateral initiatives such as ACT-A and COVAX are examples of cooperation to combat the global pandemic. COVAX established a 10-nation Regulatory Advisory Group to provide feedback and guidance on COVID-19 vaccine development and activities. Numerous groups of experts were created to resolve technical issues pertaining to COVID-19 vaccine development projects (McGoldrick et al. 2022). These examples of cooperation, both formal and informal, complement the work of the primary multilateral agency charged with safeguarding global health: WHO.

These initiatives confront major challenges in achieving their goals given the strong incentives for governments to prioritize the needs of their own citizens and the prepandemic deterioration in foreign relations between major economies. The United States did not join COVAX, instead withdrawing from WHO (a decision subsequently reversed by President Biden upon taking office in January 2021), while China—a major supplier to LMICs—has provided vaccines primarily through bilateral mechanisms.

Past global public health crises show that implementing multilateral commitments and sustaining cooperation is challenging, reflecting the revealed preferences of nation-states to exercise sovereignty (Benvinisti 2020). However, recognition of these realities and the associated challenges they pose to cooperation between states is an important tool to enhance resiliency and respond to a global emergency. Cooperation that is clearly in the self-interest of major economies will be easier to achieve. In many cases, such "self-interested" cooperation can expand global production capacity for critical medical products and keep markets open, thereby attenuating the economic costs of pandemics and pandemic policy responses.

What follows briefly discusses areas where cooperation beyond trade can contribute to global health security. A common feature of the examples is the creation of institutional frameworks during normal times that support the ability of both governments and industry to respond effectively to a global emergency.

Public procurement

The COVID-19 crisis called into question many pillars of public procurement law and practice. The pandemic greatly increased demand for essential goods, changing the procurement market from one where government agencies are local monopsonists to one where they competed for limited supplies with other public as well as private buyers across the globe. Time was of the essence, making standard procedures and controls difficult if not impossible to apply. (For example, instead of calls for tenders with competitive selection and payment on delivery, there was limited tendering with direct negotiations with suppliers and, at their request, up-front payments.)

Agencies actively sought to buy from foreign providers, breaking the standard pattern of sourcing primarily from domestic suppliers. The pandemic revealed the need for new policy frameworks to guide procurement in a global emergency and a lack of preparedness of the procuring entities. As discussed in the preceding subsection on government procurement, international procurement law—reflected in the GPA 2012 and international instruments such as the Model Law on Public Procurement developed by the United Nations Commission on International Trade Law (UNCITRAL 2014)—focuses primarily on national procurement procedures under normal conditions, on the principle that inducing competition between potential suppliers is a key means of ensuring value for money. During the COVID-19 crisis, public entities were forced to compete for products from suppliers that suddenly had temporary market power.

Joint reflection on the implications of the COVID-19 experience for the design of both national procurement processes (revisiting and defining good practice) and for international cooperation and coordination through trade agreements is an important area for future work. Folliot-Lallion and Yukins (2020) highlight four lessons:

- The importance of sustaining transparency and integrity during emergencies to assure accountability ex post, including liability for fraud and corruption
- The need for procuring entities to better understand the international supply chains of essential products and increase sourcing from certified foreign suppliers in normal times to facilitate international sourcing in crises
- The wisdom of establishing ex ante frameworks for coordination within and across countries, including for joint purchasing during a crisis[49]
- The usefulness of adapting procurement law and regulation to make procedures more flexible and enable adjustment to sudden changes in public procurement markets

Regulatory cooperation

Vaccines and therapeutics. As discussed in the earlier subsection on regulatory frameworks, action by NRAs to reduce regulatory heterogeneity by adopting international standards for the approval of vaccines, and acceptance of the WHO Emergency Use Listing procedure,[50] would help expand production of vaccines, diagnostics, and treatments globally. Efforts to ramp up vaccine production and supply were hampered by shortages of machinery and a range of inputs, revealing a need for sourcing alternatives to standard manufacturing inputs. Greater use of international standards and mutual recognition (reliance) would increase the potential for trade in inputs and thus the incentive to invest in production of inputs as well as vaccines and therapeutics.

Areas for action include using science- and risk-based approaches to regulation; developing and adopting international standards; increasing reliance on recognition and work sharing; and digitalizing regulation-related processes to reduce review times and support data exchange. Common approaches and reliance across agencies and regional authorities overseeing various facilities would facilitate the development and production of vaccines and therapeutics. In contrast, the current regulatory heterogeneity in production requirements, pharmacopoeias, and inspection processes limits industrial flexibility to ramp up supply. Such heterogeneity is especially costly in a crisis, given the opportunity cost of the time incurred for vaccine manufacturers to satisfy NRAs even when the initial dossier has been reviewed and approved by a WHO-recognized stringent regulatory authority (SRA).

Medical devices and other goods. WHO, together with SRAs, plays a lead role in shaping the global regulatory framework for medical goods in which national authorities operate. In addition, because medical devices are increasingly connected through the Internet of Things, regulatory frameworks are also being shaped by standards (for example, those of the ISO, IEC, and ITU) to ensure interoperability and address cybersecurity risks. Regulators have an opportunity to work together to improve resilience and functioning of supply chains and enhance pandemic preparedness.

Countries could make greater use of good regulatory and reliance practices, building on the work of WHO and the WTO TBT Committee. Existing regulatory cooperation arrangements could be strengthened, such as the IMDRF, PIC/S, or the International Coalition of Medicines Regulatory Authorities (ICMRA). Greater harmonization and alignment with international standards such as those of the ICH can strengthen supply chains. Sovereignty is not a compelling reason for opposing work toward global reliance regimes, since this has been achieved in other sectors such as civil aviation (McGoldrick et al. 2022; see also Hoekman and Sabel 2019).

Greater dialogue and information flow between regulators and manufacturers, in particular internationally, can help streamline and make regulatory frameworks more coherent. NQI gaps exacerbate or create trade bottlenecks. If regulators have a robust NQI system in place, they may be more assured when engaging in regulatory cooperation. Building the capacity of the NQI institutions that are needed to implement or complement the regulatory framework can boost cooperation and resilience to future pandemics.

Medical services. Greater coherence on the principles of health practitioner regulation would support trade in medical services. WHO is developing global guidance on health practitioner regulation to support countries in the design, strengthening, and implementation of health practitioner regulatory systems. Some of the topics covered and principles adopted in the guidance will affect trade in medical services, such as

- Establishing principles to define entry criteria for health professionals (transparency, objectivity, impartiality, fairness, and being no more burdensome than necessary);
- Recognizing qualifications across jurisdictions;
- Addressing malpractice and other complaints across jurisdictions (for example, in cases of short-term mobility of health practitioners or cross-border telehealth); and
- Enabling a regulatory environment and accountability mechanisms for safe provision of telemedicine.[51]

International travel policies

Travel restrictions and bans have direct and indirect effects on public health. Direct effects include the inability of patients to travel abroad to receive treatment or the restrictions on cross-border movement of health personnel. Indirect effects include, for example, the reduction of a household's income and its ability to pay for medical treatment. Such effects are reflected in the *WHO International Health Regulations (2005)* ("the *IHR*"), which establish criteria and procedures for states considering travel restrictions or bans (WHO 2006).

Many countries did not comply with the *IHR* and advisories issued by WHO during the COVID-19 pandemic, instead imposing restrictions that were unlikely to prevent circulation of the virus. For example, several countries responded to South Africa's notification of a new variant by banning travel from South Africa and neighboring countries (Villarreal 2021). The revealed preference of many countries has been to discount international law in this area (that is, the *IHR*) even though research suggests that imposing travel bans after the virus is already circulating is likely to be very costly economically without yielding a significant public health payoff (Docquier, Golenvaux, and Schaus 2021).

Future multilateral deliberations could reflect on the COVID-19 experience with a view to clarifying how and when travel restrictions are likely to result in significant health benefits, given their high economic cost, especially for tourism-dependent (or health-travel-dependent) states.

Cooperation between state and nonstate actors

Nonstate actors are critical in the production and distribution of essential products. Cooperation to bolster global health security must go beyond collaboration and coordination between states to include industry and NGOs as well. The pandemic response revealed the centrality of effective public-private cooperation. Future efforts should focus on instituting mechanisms in anticipation of shocks with global repercussions. Two areas stand out: (a) expanding supply and distribution capacity, and (b) bolstering mechanisms to share information on supply chain operation.

Cooperation to expand and diversify vaccine supply capacity

Many LMICs depend on imports of medical products needed to fight a pandemic. Most lack the capacity—including the technical skills and regulatory institutions—to establish and operate manufacturing facilities for vaccines that can supply effective products at scale while satisfying regulatory safety standards. Many are both small and poor and thus constrained in their ability to negotiate with pharmaceutical companies for supplies and obtain them on a timely basis. International cooperation and joint purchasing and delivery are needed, using mechanisms that pull together donors, manufacturers, NGOs, and international organizations.

The need for cooperation and coordination to ensure that vaccines are made available worldwide as rapidly as possible was recognized and acted upon during the COVID-19 pandemic. Aside from the fundamental moral and distributional equity considerations, cooperation is in all countries' self-interest. A global pandemic calls for a coordinated global response; no country is protected unless all countries are.

Multilateral initiatives. Much was done. The WHO-led Access to COVID-19 Tools Accelerator (ACT-A), established in 2020, is a major example of global collaboration to accelerate the development, production, and equitable access to COVID-19 tests, treatments, and vaccines. Myriad organizations came together to coordinate the financing and distribution of vaccines to countries. Their efforts include COVAX, the vaccines pillar of ACT-A, co-led by WHO, the Coalition for Epidemic Preparedness Innovations (CEPI), and Gavi, the Vaccine Alliance (which in turn includes UNICEF, the World Bank, and the Bill & Melinda Gates Foundation as copartners with WHO). In Africa, COVAX is complemented by the African Union's African Vaccine Acquisition Trust (AVAT).

Multilateral initiatives have played a vital role in mobilizing resources and distributing vaccines, but progress has been less rapid and comprehensive than desired. The effectiveness of the multilateral mechanisms (ACT-A and related initiatives) to coordinate action on enhancing supply and providing access to vaccines and other essential products has been hampered by a consistent gap between needs and funding. The approach pursued in practice had two steps: First, mobilize investment in new vaccines through advance market commitments and advance purchasing agreements by national governments and COVAX (through Gavi). Second, grant funding to COVAX to purchase and distribute vaccines and other essential medical products in low-income countries. Donations of doses to COVAX have dominated those obtained through Gavi advance market commitments, in part reflecting vaccine purchases at the national level that exceeded domestic needs.

Bilateral "vaccine diplomacy." Countries with a surplus also donate doses bilaterally, perhaps reflecting foreign policy incentives. Such "vaccine diplomacy" may come at the expense of national commitments to multilateral cooperation, with an associated erosion in support for multilateral mechanisms. Sirleaf and Clark (2021), reflecting on the implementation of the report by the Independent Panel for Pandemic Preparedness and Response (IPPPR 2021), place part of the blame on the patent system and associated attenuated incentives for the pharmaceutical industry to participate in voluntary licensing and technology transfer arrangements for COVID-19 vaccines.

Support for local production facilities. Several LMICs have responded to limited supplies of vaccines by encouraging local production. Ghana, Rwanda, and Senegal, for example, have negotiated agreements with vaccine manufacturers, supported by development finance institutions, to establish local production facilities (Walwyn 2021).[52]

In some cases, companies have agreed not to enforce patents for production in and for LMICs, with governments or nonstate actors supporting local production that is independent of contractual arrangements with major pharmaceutical companies. However, the process for producing vaccines is complex, requiring access to a vaccine technology as well as specialized skills and tacit knowledge. It has often been argued that this is a constraint, especially for new technologies such as mRNA vaccines. An implication is a need for greater attention to and support for collaboration and technology transfer to expand the distribution of vaccine production.

Ideally, new manufacturing facilities should be sought in countries with a latent comparative advantage whose relatively small population reduces the risk that the host-country government will intervene to meet domestic needs and reduces the impact of a potential intervention. WHO has supported initiatives to establish hubs to develop and produce vaccines in LMICs. A recent example is an mRNA vaccine technology transfer hub in South Africa, supported by WHO and cofunded by several EU countries and South Africa.[53] The hub aims to make mRNA technology accessible to LMICs and to train qualified staff to produce vaccines locally.[54] A member of the hub, South Africa's Afrigen Biologics and Vaccines, reverse engineered the Moderna COVID-19 vaccine in 2021, benefiting from Moderna's commitment not to enforce its patents for vaccines provided to LMICs (Mancini, Smyth, and Cotterill 2022). An important goal of the open-access hub concept is to enhance capacity to respond to future pandemics by supporting the capacity to develop vaccines as well as mastering the mRNA production process.

This type of cooperation between states and nonstate actors requires sustained engagement and support over time to ensure that capacity is available when needed. A key element is to retain and replenish the specialized skills needed to both develop and produce vaccines. This calls for covering the costs of maintenance and a minimum cadre of personnel. Although more general-purpose technologies may be used for other ends that are commercially viable, this is not assured. It is also important to set up systems that support rapid ramping up of activities when needed. Establishing training facilities that provide the skills—and certification—needed to operate facilities can help create a pool of expertise that can be drawn upon during emergencies. An example is a WHO center in Korea to help train workers needed to produce and manufacture vaccines. Finally, to help sustain the needed capacity in times of declining demand, support could be expanded to the capacity to develop more than one type of vaccine, or to health systems more broadly.

Enhancement of supply chain transparency and visibility

Access to a common pool of information can help governments work with industry, civil society groups, and international organizations to boost global production and distribution of essential products. Decisions to impose export restrictions and inefficient public procurement responses have resulted in part from a lack of real-time information on extant stocks and national and international production capacity for critical goods. Policy makers also had a limited understanding of how supply chains and international networks are used to combine inputs into final products.

In a pandemic, governments and the private sector need data to boost supply of vaccines. Examples include data on which inputs will be available, where, and when; which inputs or ancillary services are needed; where the shortages of inputs risk limiting production; and whether substitution possibilities exist. Intense competition among pharmaceutical and biotech companies in normal times may hamper the matching of vaccine creators to firms (some of whom may ordinarily be rivals) with production capacity. Better information on available vaccine production capacity worldwide can facilitate matches between vaccine developers, potential vaccine producers, and funding agencies.

Efforts to promote transparency. Promoting greater transparency along the relevant vaccine or other essential product value chains can help attenuate distrust between governments as well as between governments and the private sector. In a fast-moving situation such as a pandemic, holdups and other problems are inevitable as vaccine value chains respond to a massive increase in demand and as political decision-makers confront acute pressure to deliver essential products to safeguard public health.

Mechanisms are needed that enable firms to identify where national policies are a source of problems or, conversely, where governments can help to address production bottlenecks by limiting the potential for policy-induced disruption to the supply of ingredients. The same is true for policy-induced frictions that slow down delivery and distribution of essential products to public health providers. It is important, for example, to ensure availability of key qualified personnel (including through cross-border movement) as well as rapid border clearance and the ability of transport and logistics operators to move products between countries and across borders. Information in real time is needed to identify where policies or procedures could be relaxed with limited risks of adverse outcomes.

The Multilateral Leaders Task Force provided a forum for the exchange of information. It met with CEOs of leading vaccine manufacturers three times between mid-2021 and March 2022 to discuss ways to expand production of vaccines and therapeutics and improve access to vaccines in low- and lower-middle-income countries and in Africa. These meetings complemented technical meetings at the WTO with industry experts to explore new ways to address gaps in the global production and distribution of vaccines, PPE, and other needs. A technical working group was formed with industry representatives to exchange and coordinate information on vaccine production, donations, vaccine swaps, and delivery schedules and how best to tackle trade-related bottlenecks. Despite active industry participation, these meetings did not lead to a systematic compilation of information on the operation of supply chains.

Proposals for information sharing. As noted earlier, credible information sharing between governments, vaccine manufacturers, and suppliers can help avoid adverse policy responses and build confidence. Evenett et al. (2021) suggest creating a clearinghouse to enable public-private cooperation in support of vaccine production and serve as a platform for companies to report bottlenecks, improve visibility on production and capacity developments, and identify measures governments could take, such as addressing technology gaps through technology transfer and financing. Qualified parties with manufacturing capacity could register their potential willingness to supply vaccines or vaccine inputs for defined periods. Approved vaccine creators could specify their needs and the knowledge they are willing to transfer to potential contract manufacturers. The clearinghouse would help monitor bottlenecks reported by the private sector and identify measures governments could take to bolster the capabilities needed to manufacture and distribute vaccines at scale, including through aid programs and technical assistance to firms in LMICs.

Public-private information sharing platforms can also reduce the costs associated with regulatory heterogeneity, helping identify where greater standardization of supplies can facilitate matchmaking between manufacturers, including through use of substitutes that are equivalent in meeting regulatory requirements (Findlay and Hoekman 2021). More generally, a public-private platform approach can reduce the time and cost of compliance with regulatory requirements.[55] The design of such a mechanism can draw on lessons from the COVAX marketplace hosted by CEPI to improve availability of critical inputs[56] and the experience of participants in the Multilateral Leaders Task Force meetings.

Tensions between collaboration and competition. Whereas a time-bound approach would help defuse competitive and competition law concerns, the experience of 2020–21 suggests the need for an institutional structure. An important question is whether such a structure should operate only for the duration of a crisis or should be a standing mechanism. Compiling a repository of supply-chain data is a cost for businesses and also raises concerns about potentially revealing commercially sensitive or valuable information. In a crisis, pertinent information is a public good. In normal times, however, much of what may be relevant in a crisis is a private good.

Competition-law constraints are less binding during an emergency. Competition authorities in jurisdictions including the EU and the United States issued guidance in 2020 stressing that collaboration between firms is permitted if the aim is to expand output and not to increase prices (Jenny 2020). But in normal times, competition law restricts companies' ability to share information (as noted earlier). These factors affect the design of any mechanism to enhance visibility and share information during a crisis.

A two-track proposal. A two-track mechanism could be established to enhance medical supply-chain transparency. In normal times, companies face disincentives to share production data for both competitive and competition-law reasons. A solution to this issue would be to proceed on two tracks: First, encourage industry to implement internal processes and systems that provide a robust basis for rapid reporting on their supply chains' operational features when needed in a global emergency. Second, create an institutional framework to support public-private sector cooperation during global health or other emergencies.

The first element—action by firms to monitor their supply chains—can build on efforts by supply-chain managers to de-risk operations through diversification, greater redundancy in inventory management, and early warning systems such as stress tests to identify potential weak links. The second element—creating a platform and repository for compilation and analysis of pertinent data—calls for careful design to ensure the confidentiality of data that is commercially sensitive.

Cooperation between multilateral institutions

Combating the pandemic is a global public good that multilateral institutions can help provide. They did much in their areas of competence and expertise to work together to help member states fight the COVID-19 pandemic. International organizations play a critical role in supporting state-level responses and the activities of nonstate actors through coordination to address collective action problems. Cooperation between multilateral institutions, leveraging the different strengths of each organization, is paramount in doing so most effectively and efficiently. Some institutions have the capacity to mobilize finance to assist the activities of those that lack that capacity. Some have a country presence, which is critical for delivery and distribution of essential products and assistance more broadly. Others have the expertise needed to collect, analyze, monitor, and evaluate information and to establish a forum for discussion and negotiation.

Efforts to strengthen collaboration between international organizations should center on addressing the information and coordination gaps revealed by the pandemic. Many of the gaps discussed in this chapter call for collaboration between NRAs.

International organizations, consistent with their mandates to lead work in different areas of policy that are pertinent to dealing with a pandemic or other global emergencies, can do much by working together to help address the information and coordination gaps, as discussed in this chapter. Areas where cooperation between multilateral institutions is beneficial include supporting regulatory reliance; strengthening international standardization; bolstering the capacity of NRAs; supporting investments in trade facilitation; developing good-practice policy frameworks for public procurement during crises; and working with the private sector to encourage technology transfer to expand global emergency response capacity.

Cooperation between multilateral institutions to provide information and support for public-private cooperation across borders are two areas of particular salience for trade. One theme of this chapter is the importance of timely and comprehensive information on public and private sector activities that are of notable significance in addressing a crisis. Another theme is the need for international initiatives involving both state and nonstate actors to address coordination gaps. Both of these needs require support that national governments are unlikely to provide on their own.

Multilateral organizations should also continue cooperative efforts to provide transparency. Information asymmetries can undermine the trust needed to sustain international cooperation. This is not a new lesson. National governments might not fulfill commitments to notify changes in trade policies, and they are not required to make public the actions taken to contract supplies. As noted in previous chapters of this report, there was limited transparency early in the pandemic on both policy and on stocks and flows of essential products.

Matters improved with the creation of the Multilateral Leaders Task Force on COVID-19 Vaccines, Therapeutics, and Diagnostics, the ACT-Accelerator, the MLTF joint tracker, and the Global COVID-19 Access Tracker (GCAT). The task force aimed to help track, coordinate, and speed delivery of COVID-19 countermeasures. It improved the availability of data on vaccine supply and deliveries through an open-access website, helping document progress as well as the magnitude of gaps between commitments (plans) and what was provided to countries while also helping governments and citizens determine how total supply was evolving and being allocated. The data dashboard, building on the COVID-19 Vaccine Supply Tracker (developed by WHO and the International Monetary Fund), provides information on a country-by-country basis on vaccine supply, delivery delays, administration, donations of doses, and data on global production and trade, illustrating shortages of supply and delays in delivery to many LMICs.

The private sector and NGOs must also participate actively in filling information gaps. One example of a polylateral initiative (that is, an initiative involving state and nonstate actors) is the suggestion to ensure that information systems at the firm and supply chain levels be in place so data are available to governments in an emergency. A jointly managed platform that builds on the work of the Multilateral Leaders Task Force and ACT-Accelerator with industry could provide the institutional support for such a framework.

NOTES

1. The service delivery "modes of supply" referred to in this chapter and throughout the volume refer to the World Trade Organization (WTO) General Agreement on Trade in Services (GATS) modes: (1) cross-border supply, (2) consumption abroad, (3) commercial presence, and (4) presence of natural persons.

2. See, for example, the APEC resource page, "APEC COVID-19 Economic Response and Recovery Initiatives" (last updated February 2022), https://www.apec.org/covid-19/apec-covid-19 -economic-response-and-recovery-initiatives.

3. The general exceptions provision of the General Agreement on Tariffs and Trade (GATT), art. XX, permits restrictions if necessary to protect human, animal, or plant life or health (art. XX[b]) or that are "essential to the acquisition or distribution of products in general or local short supply [p]rovided that any such measures shall be consistent with the principle that all contracting parties are entitled to an equitable share of the international supply of such products, and that any such measures, which are inconsistent with the other provisions of the Agreement shall be discontinued as soon as the conditions giving rise to them have ceased to exist" (art. XX[j]). In all these cases, measures may not be applied in a manner that would constitute (a) a means of arbitrary or unjustifiable discrimination between countries where the same conditions prevail, or (b) a disguised restriction on international trade. (Although the WTO is the successor to the GATT, the original GATT text [GATT 1947] remains in effect under the WTO framework, subject to the modifications of GATT 1994.)

4. The EU treaties permit restrictions on intra-EU trade and other types of cross-border movement if member states deem these to be necessary to address emergencies and safeguard national public health and safety.

5. See, for example, "International Travel Restrictions by Country" (web page), Kayak.com (updated May 13, 2022): https://www.kayak.com/travel-restrictions?origin=CD.

6. During the Uruguay Round negotiations (1986–94), some major trading partners agreed to the so-called "Agreement on Pharmaceuticals" or "Pharma," through which participating countries agreed to eliminate tariffs on pharmaceutical products, including final products and chemical intermediates used for their production. The concessions were transcribed into WTO schedules and hence the tariff elimination applied on a most-favored-nation basis. In addition, participants also agreed to periodically review the Pharma to update and expand the list of items covered (last review in 2010). Also, in 2015, as part of the Expansion of the Information Technology Agreement (ITA Expansion), 53 WTO members, including several developing countries, agreed to eliminate tariffs on some high-technology products, including some medical equipment.

7. For more about quantitative restrictions, see the discussion of GATT 1994 (art. XI) on the WTO website: https://www.wto.org/english/tratop_e/markacc_e/qr_e.htm.

8. See "WTO Members' Notifications on COVID-19" on the WTO website: https://www.wto.org /english/tratop_e/covid19_e/notifications_e.htm.

9. See, for instance, G-20 (2020) and WTO (2021a).

10. "Developing countries," when referred to in the WTO context, are those that declare themselves as such. The WTO does not define "developing" or "developed" countries. However, other WTO members may challenge a member's decision to make use of WTO provisions available to developing countries. See "Who Are the Developing Countries in the WTO?" on the WTO website: https://www.wto.org/english/tratop_e/devel_e/d1who_e.htm.

11. See, for instance, a proposal made by a group of WTO Members to the Trade Facilitation Committee (WTO 2022b). A recommendation of the G-20's Trade and Investment Working Group, made in May 2020, focused on similar areas, highlighting prearrival processing, separation of release from payments, and expedited shipments (G-20 2020). It also called for speeding up and streamlining customs procedures in line with the TFA.

12. See, for instance, the Declaration on Facilitating the Movement of Essential Goods by the APEC Ministers Responsible for Trade (MRT): https://www.apec.org/Meeting-Papers/Sectoral -Ministerial-Meetings/Trade/2020_MRT/Annex-A.

13. The Task Force is a joint initiative of the leaders of the International Monetary Fund, the World Bank Group, WHO, and the WTO to accelerate access to COVID-19 vaccines, therapeutics, and diagnostics by leveraging multilateral finance and trade solutions, particularly for LMICs.

14. Note that trade policies for air transport services are highly restrictive and outside the WTO's purview (except for computer reservation system services, selling and marketing of air transport services, and aircraft repair and maintenance). Trade in air transport services is governed by a maze of bilateral, and a few plurilateral, air services agreements (ASAs), which provide for the reciprocal exchange of traffic rights.

15. The schedule of the EU-25 refers to the schedule that came into force in October 2019. It includes the United Kingdom, and it does not include Bulgaria, Croatia, and Romania, which have separate schedules of commitments.

16. "Members shall ensure, whenever possible, that results of conformity assessment procedures in other Members are accepted, even when those procedures differ from their own, provided they are satisfied that those procedures offer an assurance of conformity with applicable technical regulations or standards equivalent to their own procedures." (TBT Agreement, art. 6.1). For more details, see WTO (2021f) and (WTO and OECD 2019, 8, 10, 12, 45–47).

17. "Where a positive assurance of conformity with a technical regulation or standard is required, Members shall, wherever practicable, formulate and adopt international systems for conformity assessment and become members thereof or participate therein" (TBT Agreement, art. 9.1).

18. "Members shall give positive consideration to accepting as equivalent technical regulations of other Members, even if these regulations differ from their own, provided they are satisfied that these regulations adequately fulfil the objectives of their own regulations" (TBT Agreement, art. 2.7).

19. See also art. 12.8 ("It is recognized that developing country Members may face special problems, including institutional and infrastructural problems, in the field of preparation and application of technical regulations, standards and conformity assessment procedures. It is further recognized that the special development and trade needs of developing country Members, as well as their stage of technological development, may hinder their ability to discharge fully their obligations under this Agreement.") See also "6. Development Dimension" of the "Principles for the Development of International Standards, Guides and Recommendations" (web page), WTO website: https://www.wto.org/english/tratop_e/tbt_e/principles_standards_tbt_e.htm.

20. This requires taking into consideration the constraints on LMICs to effectively participate in standards development, finding tangible ways of facilitating their participation in international standards development, and making provision through international standardizing bodies for capacity building and technical assistance. See "Principles for the Development of International Standards, Guides and Recommendations" (web page), WTO website: https://www.wto.org/english/tratop_e/tbt_e/principles_standards_tbt_e.htm.

21. Free Trade Agreement between the United Mexican States, the Republic of Colombia and the Republic of Venezuela, art. 14-13 ("Health protection"): http://www.sice.oas.org/Trade/go3/text_s.asp#a14-13.

22. See the Japan-India Economic Partnership Agreement (https://www.mofa.go.jp/policy/economy/fta/india.html) and the Comprehensive Economic Cooperation Agreement between The Republic of India and the Republic of Singapore (https://commerce.gov.in/international-trade/trade-agreements/comprehensive-economic-cooperation-agreement-between-the-republic-of-india-and-the-republic-of-singapore/).

23. See "Special Scheme for Registration of Generic Medicinal Products from India" (https://www.enterprisesg.gov.sg/-/media/esg/files/non-financial-assistance/for-companies/free-trade-agreements/CECA_India/Legal_Text/Others/Side_letter_for_the_Special_Registration_Scheme_for_Generic_Medicinal_Products). The reference regulatory authorities are the US Food and Drug Administration (FDA), the UK Medicines and Healthcare Products Regulatory Agency (MHRA), the Australian Government's Therapeutic Goods Administration (TGA), the European Medicines Agency, and Health Canada.

24. WHO defines reliance as "the act whereby the NRA in one jurisdiction may take into account and give significant weight to assessments performed by another NRA or trusted institution, or to any other authoritative information in reaching its own decision. The relying authority remains independent, responsible and accountable regarding the decisions taken, even when it relies on the decisions and information of others" (WHO 2020b, 41).

25. The concept of a stringent regulatory authority was developed by the WHO Secretariat and the Global Fund to Fight AIDS, Tuberculosis and Malaria to guide medicine procurement decisions and is now widely recognized by the international regulatory and procurement community.

26. This African Union program works in collaboration with the AUC, Pan-African Parliament (PAP), World Health Organization (WHO), Bill and Melinda Gates Foundation, World Bank, UK Department for International Development (DFID) and US Government-PEPFAR and Global Alliance for Vaccines and Immunization (GAVI).

27. For example, the WHO *COVID-19 Vaccines: Safety Surveillance Manual* recommends regulatory reliance (WHO 2020a).

28. See also TBT Agreement, art. 12.8: "It is recognized that developing country Members may face special problems, including institutional and infrastructural problems, in the field of preparation and application of technical regulations, standards and conformity assessment procedures. It is further recognized that the special development and trade needs of developing country Members, as well as their stage of technological development, may hinder their ability to discharge fully their obligations under this Agreement." In addition, see "6. Development Dimension" of the "Principles for the Development of International Standards, Guides and Recommendations," agreed upon by the WTO TBT Committee in 2000 to guide Members in the development of international standards: https://www.wto.org/english/tratop_e/tbt_e/principles_standards_tbt_e.htm.

29. Other examples include the African Medicines Regulatory Harmonization (AMRH) initiative, or the African Vaccine Regulatory Forum (AVAREF). See WHO (2019).

30. For these resources and others, see "Standards Development Organizations, Committees and Standards for Medical Technology" (web page), Inter-American Coalition for Regulatory Convergence for the Medical Technology Sector website: https://www.interamericancoalition-medtech.org/regulatory-convergence/policy/international-standardization/standards-development-organizations-committees-and-standards-for-medical-technology/.

31. "Developed country members" of the WTO include Australia, Canada, the European Union (and its member states), Japan, New Zealand, Norway, Switzerland, the United Kingdom, and the United States.

32. For information on the COVID-19 pandemic-related capacity-building workshops, see "Trilateral Cooperation on Public Health, Trade and Intellectual Property" (web page), WTO website: https://www.wto.org/english/tratop_e/trips_e/who_wipo_wto_e.htm.

33. GATS (art. 1.3) excludes from its coverage measures taken in the context of services supplied in the exercise of governmental authority. These are defined as services that are supplied neither on a commercial basis nor in competition with one or more service suppliers (Adlung 2010).

34. Some WTO members have accorded preferences to LDC services suppliers in the context of the LDCs services waiver.

35. Note that few recognition agreements covering health professionals have been notified to the WTO so far. There are 86 notifications to the WTO on recognition measures and agreements, involving 45 members and covering more than 210 bilateral agreements.

36. That many recognition agreements are negotiated only after the conclusion of the RTA, however, means that there is little or no information about the actual agreements being concluded.

37. Moreover, insofar as pandemic vaccines are one-offs, not requiring a follow-up treatment, the recovery on production costs and investment in capacity expansion must occur during a relatively short period because the potential for future revenues is limited. This disincentive is attenuated if there is an expectation of demand for repeated doses to be administered, given that this offers the prospect of a multiyear revenue stream, supporting higher production capacity (Evenett et al. 2021).

38. Besides the application of national treatment to subsidies, GATS only suggests that sympathetic consideration be given to a request for consultation raised by a member considering that it is affected by subsidies, and it calls for negotiations to develop multilateral disciplines.

39. This section draws upon and updates materials published in the trilateral study by WHO, WIPO, and WTO (2020b).

40. The following WTO members are covered by the GPA 2012: Armenia; Australia; Canada; the EU (including its 27 member states); Hong Kong SAR, China; Iceland; Israel; Japan; the Republic of Korea; Liechtenstein; Moldova; Montenegro; the Kingdom of the Netherlands with respect to Aruba; New Zealand; Norway; Singapore; Switzerland; Ukraine; the United Kingdom; and the United States, as well as the Separate Customs Territory Chinese Taipei. Another 35 WTO members/observers participate in the Committee on Government Procurement as observers. Eleven of these members with observer status are in the process of acceding to the Agreement. For more details, see "Parties, Observers and Accessions" (web page), WTO website: https://www.wto.org/english/tratop_e/gproc_e/memobs_e.htm.

41. The GPA 2012 is also consistent with the United Nations Commission on International Trade Law (UNCITRAL) Model Law on Procurement of Goods, Construction and Services, including the 2011 revision, which has inspired the national legislation of many countries. In addition, it reinforces other international instruments such as World Bank guidelines and the work of the Organisation for Economic Co-operation and Development on prevention of corruption as well as procurement provisions in RTAs. See Anderson, Müller, and Pelletier (2017).

42. The European Commission informally took the lead to collect and notify each other's time frames to ensure compatibility of remedies (OECD and ICN 2021).

43. The documents gathered by the Competition and Consumer Protection Commission were subsequently given to the AGCM (OECD and ICN 2021).

44. See, for example, GATT 1994 (art. II.4); GATS (arts. VIII and IX); the TRIPS Agreement (arts. 8, 31, and 40); the Agreement on Trade-Related Investment Measures ("TRIMS Agreement") (art. 9); and the GATS Annex on Telecommunications and Reference Paper on regulatory principles. Furthermore, the WTO Working Group on the Interaction between Trade and Competition Policy (WGTCP) was active from 1997 to 2002 (Anderson et al. 2018).

45. For example, in 2018–19, discussions took place in the WTO Council for TRIPS on the promotion of public health through competition law and policy. These discussions took place in the framework of a broader discussion on IP and the public interest. See WTO (2018a, agenda item 13); WTO (2018b, agenda item 13); WTO (2019a, agenda item 12); and their addenda and corrigenda.

46. The ECN serves as a platform for notifications of new cases and envisaged enforcement decisions, exchange of confidential information, investigative assistance and relocation, and cooperation in merger control among EU member states. For more information, see "European Competition Network (ECN)" (web page), European Commission website: https://ec.europa.eu/competition-policy/european-competition-network_en.

47. See Chapter 16 (Competition Policy), Comprehensive and Progressive Agreement for Trans-Pacific Partnership (CPTPP): https://www.mfat.govt.nz/assets/Trade-agreements/TPP/Text-ENGLISH/16.-Competition-Policy-Chapter.pdf.

48. See the Multilateral Leaders Task Force web page: https://www.covid19taskforce.com/en/programs/task-force-on-covid-19-vaccines/data.

49. The EU concluded several voluntary joint procurement calls for specific products based on framework agreements with suppliers. COVAX is an important example of multilateral joint procurement of vaccines.

50. See "Emergency Use Listing" (web page), Regulation and Prequalification, WHO website: https://www.who.int/teams/regulation-prequalification/eul.

51. WHO is also developing guidance on how to develop bilateral agreements involving international health worker mobility.

52. Other examples include the Bill & Melinda Gates Foundation's cofunding of the production of the AstraZeneca and Novavax vaccines by the Serum Institute of India and the production of the Johnson & Johnson vaccine by Biological E. Limited, another producer in India (Evenett et al. 2021).

53. "The mRNA Vaccine Technology Transfer Hub," WHO website: https://www.who.int/initiatives/the-mrna-vaccine-technology-transfer-hub#. See also Mancini, Smyth, and Cotterill (2022).

54. The hub concept draws inspiration from a 2007 WHO program to provide seed grants to manufacturers in LMICs to establish or improve pandemic influenza vaccine production capacity (Hendriks et al. 2011). The companies involved were supported by an influenza vaccine technology platform ("hub") at the Netherlands Vaccine Institute for training and technology transfer. During its first two years of operation, a robust and transferable monovalent pilot process for egg-based inactivated whole virus influenza A vaccine production was established under international GMP standards as well as in-process and release assays. The hub developed training tools, including a practical handbook on production and quality control, and provided hands-on training courses to employees from manufacturers in LMICs.

55. A possible model is provided by Accumulus Synergy, a nonprofit company providing a cloud-based platform to support interactions between the biopharmaceutical industry and health authorities worldwide, leveraging advanced technology and tools for data exchange to support global regulatory reliance mechanisms by giving all agencies access to information and data provided by vaccine manufacturers, run regulatory work-sharing activities, provide parallel review of dossiers, and produce reliance- or recognition-based assessments, under a single and global management system. For more information, see https://www.accumulus.org/.

56. "The COVAX Marketplace," Coalition for Epidemic Preparedness Innovations (CEPI) website: https://cepi.net/the-covax-marketplace/.

REFERENCES

Adlung, R. 2010. "Trade in Healthcare and Health Insurance Services: WTO/GATS as a Supporting Actor(?)" *Intereconomics* 45 (4): 227–38.

Adlung R., and A. Carzaniga. 2001. "Health Services under the General Agreement on Trade Services." *Bulletin of the World Health Organization* 79 (4): 352–64.

Agarwal, R., and T. Reed. Forthcoming. "Financing Vaccine Equity: Funding for Day Zero of the Next Pandemic." *Oxford Review of Economic Policy* 38 (4).

Anderson, R. D., W. E. Kovacic, A. C. Müller, and N. Sporysheva. 2018. "Competition Policy, Trade and the Global Economy: Existing WTO Elements, Commitments in Regional Trade Agreements, Current Challenges and Issues for Reflection." Staff Working Paper ERSD-2018-12, World Trade Organization, Geneva.

Anderson, R. D., A. C. Müller, and P. Pelletier. 2017. "Regional Trade Agreements and Procurement Rules: Facilitators or Hindrances?" In *The Internationalization of Government Procurement Regulation*, edited by A. Georgopoulos, B. Hoekman, and P. C. Mavroidis, 56–85. Oxford: Oxford University Press.

ASEAN (Association of Southeast Asian Nations). 2020a. "AEM Signing of the MOU on the Implementation of Non-Tariff Measures on Essential Goods under the Hanoi POA in Response to the COVID-19 Pandemic." News release, November 24, ASEAN Secretariat, Jakarta.

ASEAN (Association of Southeast Asian Nations). 2020b. "Hanoi Plan of Action on Strengthening ASEAN Economic Cooperation and Supply Chain Connectivity in Response to the COVID-19 Pandemic." Plan implementing the April 14 "Declaration of the Special ASEAN Summit on the Coronavirus Disease 2019 (COVID-19)." Adopted June 4 at the ASEAN Economic Ministers Meeting, Jakarta.

Baiker, L., E. Bertola, and M. Jelitto. 2021. "Services Domestic Regulation – Locking in Good Regulatory Practices: Analyzing the Prevalence of Services Domestic Regulation Disciplines and Their Potential Linkages with Economic Performance." Staff Working Paper ERSD-2021-4, World Trade Organization, Geneva.

Ball, D., S. Roth, and J. Parry. 2016. "Better Regulation of Medicines Means Stronger Regional Health Security: Strengthening and Convergence of National Regulatory Agencies Has Benefits beyond Country Borders." ADB Briefs No. 54, Asian Development Bank, Manila.

Benvinisti, E. 2020. "The WHO—Destined to Fail? Political Cooperation and the Covid-19 Pandemic." *American Journal of International Law* 1114 (4): 588–97.

Carzaniga, A., I. Dhillon, J. Magdeleine, and L. Xu. 2019. "International Health Worker Mobility & Trade in Services." World Health Organization and World Trade Organization Joint Staff Working Paper No. ERSD-2019-13, WTO, Geneva.

Castillo, J. C., A. Ahuja, S. Athey, A. Baker, E. Budish, R. Glennerster, S. D. Kominers, et al. 2021. "Market Design to Accelerate COVID-19 Vaccine Supply." *Science* 371 (6534): 1107–09. doi:10.1126/science.abg0889.

DHL. 2021. "Revisiting Pandemic Resilience: The Race against the Virus: What We've Learned One Year into COVID-19 and How the World's Healthcare Supply Chains Will Be Ready for the Next Public Health Emergency." White paper, DHL Research and Innovation, Bonn.

Docquier, F., N. Golenvaux, and P. Schaus. 2021. "Are Travel Bans the Answer to Stopping the Spread of COVID-19 Variants? Lessons from a Multi-Country SIR Model." arXiv:2112.09929 [q-bio.PE]. doi:10.21203/rs.3.rs-1254291/v1.

Drager, N. 1999. "Making Trade Work for Public Health." *BMJ* 319 (7219): 1214.

EC (European Commission). 2020a. "Coronavirus: Commission Presents Practical Guidance to Ensure Continuous Flow of Goods across EU via Green Lanes." Press release, March 23.

EC (European Commission). 2020b. "Guidance on Free Movement of Health Professionals and Minimum Harmonisation of Training in Relation to COVID-19 Emergency Measures – Recommendations Regarding Directive 2005/36/EC." Communication from the Commission C(2020) 3072 final, EC, Brussels.

Espitia, A., N. Rocha, and M. Ruta. 2020. "A Pandemic Trade Deal: Trade and Policy Cooperation on Medical Goods." In *Revitalizing Multilateralism: Programmatic Ideas for the New WTO Director-General*, edited by S. Evenett and R. Baldwin, 189–201. London: CEPR Press.

Evenett, S. J., B. Hoekman, N. Rocha, and M. Ruta. 2021. "The Covid-19 Vaccine Production Club: Will Value Chains Temper Nationalism?" Policy Research Working Paper 9565, World Bank, Washington, DC.

Evenett, S., and L. A. Winters. 2020. "Preparing for a Second Wave of COVID-19: A Trade Bargain to Secure Supplies of Medical Goods." Briefing Paper No. 40, UK Trade Policy Observatory, University of Sussex, UK.

Findlay, C., and B. Hoekman. 2021. "Value Chain Approaches to Reducing Policy Spillovers on International Business." *Journal of International Business Policy* 4 (3): 390–409.

Folliot-Lallion, L., and C. R. Yukins. 2020. "COVID-19: Lessons Learned in Public Procurement. Time for a New Normal?" *Concurrences* 1 (3): 46–58.

Giordani, P. E., N. Rocha, and M. Ruta. 2016. "Food Prices and the Multiplier Effect of Trade Policy." *Journal of International Economics* 101: 102–22.

Gleeson, D., J. Lexchin, R. Labonté, B. Townsend, M.-A. Gagnon, J. Kohler, L. Forman, and K. C. Shadlen. 2019. "Analyzing the Impact of Trade and Investment Agreements on Pharmaceutical Policy: Provisions, Pathways and Potential Impacts." *Globalization and Health* 15 (Suppl. 1): 78.

Goldberg, P. K. 2010. "Intellectual Property Rights Protection in Developing Countries: The Case of Pharmaceuticals." *Journal of the European Economic Association* 8 (2–3): 326–53.

Goodwin, T., and R. Barajas. 2020. "Safeguarding Healthy Competition during COVID-19: Competition Policy Options for Emergency Situations." Policy note, World Bank, Washington, DC.

G-20 (Group of Twenty). 2020. "G20 Trade and Investment Ministerial Meeting: Ministerial Statement." Adopted at virtual meeting, May 14.

Hendriks, J., M. Holleman, O. de Boer, P. de Jong, and W. Luytjes. 2011. "An International Technology Platform for Influenza Vaccines." *Vaccine* 29 (Suppl 1): A8–11.

Heuschen, A.-K., G. Lu, O. Razum, A. Abdul-Mumin, O. Sankoh, L. von Seidlein, U. D'Alessandro, and O. Müller. 2021. "Public Health-Relevant Consequences of the COVID-19 Pandemic on Malaria in Sub-Saharan Africa: A Scoping Review." *Malaria Journal* 20 (339): 1–16.

Hoekman, B., and C. Sabel. 2019. "Open Plurilateral Agreements, International Regulatory Cooperation and the WTO." *Global Policy* 10 (3): 297–312.

ICN (International Competition Network). 2020. "Competition during and after the COVID-19 Pandemic." Steering Group Statement, ICN, Quebec.

IPPPR (Independent Panel for Pandemic Preparedness and Response). 2021. "COVID-19: Make It the Last Pandemic." Report, IPPPR, Geneva.

Jenny, F. 2020. "Competition Law Enforcement and the COVID-19 Crisis: Business As (Un)usual." Scholarly Paper ID 3606214, Social Science Research Network. https://papers.ssrn.com/sol3/papers .cfm?abstract_id=3606214.

JFTC and CCI (Japan Fair Trade Commission and Competition Commission of India). 2021. "Memorandum on Cooperation between Japan Fair Trade Commission and the Competition Commission of India." Signed August 6 by JFTC, Tokyo; and CCI, New Delhi.

Leibovici, F., and A. M. Santacreu. 2021. "International Trade Policy during a Pandemic." Working paper, Federal Reserve Bank of St. Louis.

Lumpkin, M. M., and J. C. W. Lim. 2020. "Pandemic Best Regulatory Practices: An Urgent Need in the COVID-19 Pandemic." *Clinical Pharmacology & Therapeutics* 108 (4): 703–05.

Mancini, D. P., J. Smyth, and J. Cotterill. 2022. "Will 'open-source' Vaccines Narrow the Inequality Gap Exposed by Covid?" *Financial Times*, March 15.

McGoldrick, M., T. Gastineau, D. Wilkinson, C. Campa, N. De Clercq, A. Mallia-Milanes, O. Germay, et al. 2022. "How to Accelerate the Supply of Vaccines to All Populations Worldwide? Initial Industry Lessons Learned and Practical Overarching Proposals Leveraging the COVID-19 Situation." *Vaccine* 40 (9): 1215–30.

OECD (Organisation for Economic Co-operation and Development). 2020. "Competition Policy Responses to COVID-19." Policy brief, April 27, OECD, Paris.

OECD (Organisation for Economic Co-operation and Development). 2021a. "OECD Inventory of International Co-Operation Agreements on Competition." Data resource, OECD, Paris (last updated July 2021), https://www.oecd.org/competition/inventory-competition-agreements.htm.

OECD (Organisation for Economic Co-operation and Development). 2021b. "OECD Inventory of International Co-Operation Agreements between Competition Agencies (MoUs)." Data resource, OECD, Paris (last updated July 2021), https://www.oecd.org/daf/competition/inventory-competition -agency-mous.htm.

OECD RPC (Organisation for Economic Co-operation and Development Regulatory Policy Committee). 2012. "Recommendation of the Council on Regulatory Policy and Governance." Policy statement adopted by the Council of the OECD, Paris, March 22.

OECD and ICN (Organisation for Economic Co-operation and Development and International Competition Network). 2021. "OECD/ICN Report on International Co-operation in Competition Enforcement." Report, OECD, Paris; and ICN, Quebec.

PA (Pacific Alliance). 2017. "Roadmap, Digital Agenda Subgroup." [In Spanish.] https://alianzapacifico .net/wp-content/uploads/Hoja-de-Ruta-SGAD2016-2017.pdf.

PA (Pacific Alliance). 2020. "Plan of Action against COVID-19." [In Spanish.] https://alianzapacifico .net/wp-content/uploads/PLAN_TRABAJO_COVID_19.pdf.

PPP (Pandemic Preparedness Partnership). 2021. "100 Days Mission to Respond to Future Pandemic Threats: Reducing the Impact of Future Pandemics by Making Diagnostics, Therapeutics and Vaccines Available within 100 Days." Report to the Group of Seven (G-7), PPP, UK Government, London.

Saxon, G. 2017. "Global Medical Device Regulatory Harmonization." Presentation, Third WHO Global Forum on Medical Devices, Geneva, May 10–12.

Silverman, R., J. M. Keller, A. Glassman, and K. Chalkidou. 2019. "Tackling the Triple Transition in Global Health Procurement: Promoting Access to Essential Health Products through Aid Eligibility Changes, Epidemiological Transformation, and the Progressive Realization of Universal Health Coverage." Final report of the Working Group on the Future of Global Health Procurement, Center for Global Development, Washington, DC.

Sirleaf, H. E. E. J., and H. Clark. 2021. "Losing Time: End This Pandemic and Secure the Future. Progress Six Months after the Report of the Independent Panel for Pandemic Preparedness and Response." Progress report of the cochairs, Independent Panel for Pandemic Preparedness and Response (IPPPR), Geneva.

UNCITRAL (United Nations Commission on International Trade Law). 2014. *UNCITRAL Model Law on Public Procurement.* Vienna: United Nations.

UNCTAD (United Nations Conference for Trade and Development). 2020. "Defending Competition in the Markets during COVID-19." UNCTAD News, April 8.

United States, FTC (Federal Trade Commission). 2021. "Multilateral Pharmaceutical Merger Task Force Seeks Public Input." Press release, May 11.

Villarreal, P. A. 2021. "Punishing Compliance with International Law: The Omicron Variant and the International Health Regulations (2005)." *EJIL Talk!* (blog), December 2. https://www.ejiltalk.org /punishing-compliance-with-international-law-the-omicron-variant-and-the-international-health -regulations-2005/.

Walwyn, D. R. 2021. "Rwanda and Senegal Will Host Africa's First COVID-19 Vaccine Plants: What's Known So Far." *WIPO Magazine* 4/2021: 6–9.

WHA (World Health Assembly). 2019. "Improving the Transparency of Markets for Medicines, Vaccines, and Other Health Products." Resolution adopted at the 72nd World Health Assembly (WHA72.8), World Health Organization, Geneva, May 28.

WHO (World Health Organization). 2006. *International Health Regulations (2005).* Geneva: WHO.

WHO (World Health Organization). 2017. *A Study on the Public Health and Socioeconomic Impact of Substandard and Falsified Medical Products.* Geneva: WHO.

WHO (World Health Organization). 2019. "Delivering Quality-Assured Medical Products for All 2019–2023: WHO's Five-Year Plan to Help Build Effective and Efficient Regulatory Systems." Document WHO/MVP/RHT/2019.01, WHO, Geneva.

WHO (World Health Organization). 2020a. *COVID-19 Vaccines: Safety Surveillance Manual.* Geneva: WHO.

WHO (World Health Organization). 2020b. "Good Regulatory Practices for Regulatory Oversight of Medical Products." Draft working document QAS/16.686/Rev.3, WHO, Geneva.

WHO (World Health Organization). 2020c. *State of the World's Nursing 2020: Investing in Education, Jobs and Leadership.* Geneva: WHO.

WHO (World Health Organization). 2021a. "Annex 11: Good Regulatory Practices in the Regulation of Medical Products." In *WHO Expert Committee on Specifications for Pharmaceutical Preparations. Fifty-Fifth Report*, 269–304. Geneva: WHO

WHO (World Health Organization). 2021b. *Promoting the Use of Quality-Assured Generic and Biosimilar Medicines: WHO Guideline on Country Pharmaceutical Pricing Policies. A Plain Language Summary.* Geneva: WHO.

WHO, WIPO, and WTO (World Health Organization, World Intellectual Property Organization, and World Trade Organization). 2020a. "Medical Technologies: The Innovation Dimension." In *Promoting Access to Medical Technologies and Innovation: Intersections between Public Health, Intellectual Property and Trade*. 2nd ed. Geneva: WHO, WIPO, and WTO.

WHO, WIPO, and WTO (World Health Organization, World Intellectual Property Organization, and World Trade Organization). 2020b. *Promoting Access to Medical Technologies and Innovation: Intersections between Public Health, Intellectual Property and Trade*. 2nd ed. Geneva: WHO, WIPO, and WTO.

WTO (World Trade Organization). 1997. "Guidelines for Mutual Recognition Agreements or Arrangements in the Accountancy Sector." Document S/L/38, Council for Trade in Services, WTO, Geneva.

WTO (World Trade Organization). 2003. "Implementation of Article 66.2 of the TRIPS Agreement." Decision of the Council for TRIPS, February 19. Document IP/C/28, Council for Trade-Related Aspects of Intellectual Property Rights, WTO, Geneva.

WTO (World Trade Organization). 2018a. "Minutes of Meeting Held in the Centre William Rappard on 5–6 June 2018." Document IP/C/M/89, Council for Trade-Related Aspects of Intellectual Property Rights, WTO, Geneva.

WTO (World Trade Organization). 2018b. "Minutes of Meeting Held in the Centre William Rappard on 8–9 November 2018." Document IP/C/M/90, Council for Trade-Related Aspects of Intellectual Property Rights, WTO, Geneva.

WTO (World Trade Organization). 2019a. "Minutes of Meeting Held in the Centre William Rappard on 13 February 2019." Document IP/C/M/91, Council for Trade-Related Aspects of Intellectual Property Rights, WTO, Geneva.

WTO (World Trade Organization). 2019b. *World Trade Report 2019: The Future of Services Trade*. Geneva: WTO.

WTO (World Trade Organization). 2020a. "How WTO Members Have Used Trade Measures to Expedite Access to COVID-19 Critical Medical Goods and Services." Information note, September 18, WTO Secretariat, Geneva.

WTO (World Trade Organization). 2020b. "Report on the Implementation of Article 66.2 of the TRIPS Agreement—United States of America." Communication IP/C/TTI/USA/1, Council for Trade-Related Aspects of Intellectual Property Rights, WTO, Geneva.

WTO (World Trade Organization). 2020c. "Thematic Session on Good Regulatory Practice: Encouraging Regulatory Compatibility and Cooperation." Moderator's report, Committee on Technical Barriers to Trade, Document G/TBT/GEN/287, WTO, Geneva.

WTO (World Trade Organization). 2020d. "The Treatment of Medical Products in Regional Trade Agreements." Information note, April 27, WTO Secretariat, Geneva.

WTO (World Trade Organization). 2021a. "APEC Ministers Responsible for Trade Virtual Meeting, Joint Statement 2021, 4–5 June 2021." Communication of the General Council WT/GC/232, WTO, Geneva.

WTO (World Trade Organization). 2021b. "Indicative List of Trade-Related Bottlenecks and Trade-Facilitating Measures on Critical Products to Combat COVID-19." Information note, October 8, WTO Secretariat, Geneva.

WTO (World Trade Organization). 2021c. "Negotiations on Services Domestic Regulation Conclude Successfully in Geneva." News release, December 2.

WTO (World Trade Organization). 2021d. "Ninth Triennial Review of the Operation and Implementation of the Agreement on Technical Barriers to Trade under Article 15.4." Document G/TBT/46, Committee on Barriers to Trade, WTO, Geneva.

WTO (World Trade Organization). 2021e. "WHO, WIPO, and WTO Map Out Further Collaboration to Tackle the COVID-19 Pandemic." News release, June 24.

WTO (World Trade Organization). 2021f. *The WTO Agreements Series: Technical Barriers to Trade.* 3rd ed. Geneva: WTO.

WTO (World Trade Organization). 2022a. "Communication from the Chairperson." Document IP/C/W/688, Council for Trade Related Aspects of Intellectual Property Rights, WTO, Geneva.

WTO (World Trade Organization). 2022b. "COVID-19 and Beyond: Trade and Health." Communication from 60 WTO Members to the WTO General Council, Document WT/GC/W/823/Rev.8, February 18, WTO, Geneva.

WTO (World Trade Organization). 2022c. "Thematic Session on Conformity Assessment Procedures (Accreditation)." Moderator's report, Committee on Technical Barriers to Trade, Document G/TBT/GEN/323, WTO, Geneva.

WTO and OECD (World Trade Organization and Organisation for Economic Co-operation and Development). 2019. *Facilitating Trade through Regulatory Cooperation: The Case of the WTO's TBT/SPS Agreements and Committees.* Geneva: WTO; Paris: OECD Publishing.

4 Leveraging Medical Goods and Services Trade for Future Pandemics: An Action Plan

THE NEED FOR ACTION AND REFORM NOW

Previous chapters have shown the upsides and downsides of trade during a pandemic and have discussed the economic rationale for trade reforms and actions that can improve global health security. Based on this analysis, this concluding chapter offers a concrete action plan of policy priorities.

Policy action and reform are needed now to leverage trade for future crises. The cost of action is likely to be dwarfed by the potential cost of another pandemic. Yet historically, inaction has been the norm. One reason is short-termism; another is a poor track record for collective action. Governments tend to prioritize pressing short-term needs over reforms with long-term payoffs. Moreover, they fail to appreciate the positive effects that measures to strengthen the world trading system, such as enhanced regulatory transparency or tighter disciplines on export restrictions, have on other countries.

Furthermore, the catastrophic consequences of the coronavirus (COVID-19) pandemic have generated a consensus that policy action and reform are needed at the country, regional, and global levels to manage future crises. This time of consensus presents a historic opportunity that should not be missed.

PROPOSALS AND PRIORITIES

This report puts forward an action plan for trade and trade-related policies to improve pandemic prevention, preparedness, and response. *Prevention* and *preparedness* refer to ex ante policy actions and reforms that would help determine, assess, avoid, mitigate, and reduce public health threats and risks when a disease outbreak occurs. *Response* refers to ex post policy actions and reforms to reduce the disease outbreak's economic, social, and health consequences.

Clearly, prevention, preparedness, and response require actions well beyond trade that are outside the scope of this report (see, for example, World Bank 2022). The action plan in table 4.1 offers a menu of options for trade and trade-related policies that governments can enact nationally and in regional and multilateral contexts.

Policy priorities depend on country conditions and the evolution of the current crisis. As the COVID-19 pandemic lingers, the focus of policy action is on the response—including actions to remove bottlenecks to, and provide government support for, equitable access to vaccines. As the emergency subsides, the focus should shift to prevention and preparedness. These priorities should be (a) steps to close information gaps, building on the work of the Multilateral Leaders Task Force on COVID-19 Vaccines, Therapeutics, and Diagnostics and the ACT-Accelerator; and (b) policy reforms to open markets, such as negotiating tariff reductions on medical goods and greater market access for services.

Also important are measures to improve the efficiency of markets, which include harmonizing regulation through mutual recognition or equivalence of standards and creating international standards for essential medical goods, inputs, and production processes. Agreeing on a crisis rule book to deploy during an emergency—including clear and agreed-upon limits on export policy for critical goods as well as shared rules on intellectual property flexibilities—would provide a more solid policy foundation to address future challenges.

Table 4.1 Trade and trade-related policy actions to improve prevention, preparedness, and response for future pandemics

Measures affecting medical goods

Instrument	National	Regional	Multilateral
Tariffs	• Reduce or eliminate tariffs and internal taxes imposed on essential medical goods. • Establish, publish, and maintain a national list of essential medical goods (generating specific tariff lines for these products in the national tariff schedule), and create an interagency coordination mechanism to update and modify the list when needed. *Crisis response: Cease imposing import tariffs on critical medical products in short supply. If not permanent, tariff reductions should be for a minimum period to preserve market stability (for example, three years).*	• Ensure that all medical goods are fully liberalized in the context of regional trade agreements (RTAs). • Review and simplify the relevant rules of origin on medical goods to ensure preference utilization.	• Develop an international list of essential medical goods in consultation with the relevant international organizations (such as the WCO, WHO, and WTO). • At the WCO, negotiate the creation of new HS subheadings (6-digit codes) to facilitate the national classification and improve the collection of trade statistics in medical goods. • Bind currently unbound products (tariff lines) on medical goods in the WTO goods schedules. • Revisit the WTO's Agreement on Pharmaceuticals and Expansion of the Information Technology Agreement to liberalize trade in additional medical goods or negotiate a new agreement to this effect.
Prohibitions and restrictions on imports and exports	• Eliminate export restrictions in essential medical goods. • Review and improve interagency coordination for the introduction of prohibitions and restrictions on imports and exports, including licensing requirements. *Crisis response: Refrain from imposing export prohibitions or restrictions during a global health emergency, and ensure that any such measures are implemented as a last resort and only when necessary to prevent or relieve critical shortages of medical goods. If an export prohibition or restriction is introduced, then* • *Ensure the measure is targeted, transparent, proportionate, temporary, and consistent with WTO obligations;* • *Establish a short duration of the measure (for example, three months) and a review mechanism to extend or modify it subsequently if necessary;*	None	• Share experiences in the relevant forums on the way these measures are introduced, administered, and removed, with a view to drawing lessons and identifying best practices that may assist during a crisis. *Crisis response: Limit the duration of export restrictions on essential goods, and establish a consultation mechanism to assess the adverse impact on partners of the emergency measures that have been imposed.*

(Continued)

Table 4.1 Trade and trade-related policy actions to improve prevention, preparedness, and response for future pandemics *(Continued)*

Instrument	National	Regional	Multilateral
Import and export licensing procedures	• *Periodically review the measure to assess its relevance;* • *Ensure publication of the measure at the national level and, to the extent possible, before it takes effect; and* • *Implement the prohibition or restriction in a manner that limits, to the greatest extent possible, disruptions of global supply chains of essential medical products. (For example, no prohibitions should be used, and restrictions should not reduce exports to partners by more than 50 percent of the average of the past two years.)* • Streamline existing import and export licensing procedures at the border to ensure they do not become an obstacle to trade. • Review and eliminate unnecessary import and export licensing requirements (for example, temporary licenses that were introduced to respond to an emergency as soon as market conditions stabilize) and simplify procedures (for example, reduce time required to obtain a license). • Coordinate licensing requirement procedures to remove duplication of information submission. • Implement national single window to digitalize import and export licensing procedures and provide access for traders to use digitalized services. • Enhance communication between the relevant ministries and agencies administering export and import licensing regimes, periodically consulting with stakeholders. *Crisis response: Eliminate unnecessary import and export licensing requirements and procedures, and ensure that customs and border authorities are rapidly informed on any changes in import and export licensing procedures.*	• Align regional policies on import and export licensing. • Ensure systematic coordination between border and customs authorities on import and export licensing rules and procedures.	• Fully apply the transparency and notification obligations of the WTO's Import Licensing Agreement and the Decision on Notification Procedures for Quantitative Restrictions. • Respond to specific trade concerns and questions raised by other WTO members relating to import licensing. • Fully apply GATT 1994 rules regarding transparency and formalities relating to export licensing (art. VIII and X). • Negotiate specific multilateral rules on export licensing procedures analogous to the existing disciplines of the WTO's Import Licensing Agreement.

(Continued)

Table 4.1 Trade and trade-related policy actions to improve prevention, preparedness, and response for future pandemics *(Continued)*

Instrument	National	Regional	Multilateral
Trade facilitation	• Accelerate implementation of the WTO's Trade Facilitation Agreement (TFA) where relevant for essential medical goods (for example, prearrival processing of certain custom procedures) to ensure timely access. *Crisis responses:* • *Extend use of digital or digitalized trade documents.* • *Review the need for prescriptive border measures (such as postentry audits and recognition of equivalent prearrival measures) related to critical consignments.* • *Review procedures associated with critical consignments, and implement expanded risk management measures where appropriate.* • *Cooperate with trading partners and other border agencies to improve coordinated border management and to identify and target potentially high-risk imports (such as illegitimate goods being traded in response to the crisis).* • *Establish specific expedited channels (for example, green lanes) to facilitate key imports.* • *Establish joint private-public sector working groups (particularly building from existing NTFCs) to identify and prioritize the access issues to address.*	• Encourage regional approaches to TFA implementation. • Share implementation experiences. • Advance regional cooperation on the use of prearrival and postentry measures to reduce border bottlenecks.	• Expand guidance on best practices for TFA implementation, and enhance cooperation and coordination in the delivery of related technical assistance and capacity building.
Services supporting medical goods GVCs	• Reduce or eliminate barriers to transport, logistics, insurance, and distribution services trade relevant to medical goods GVCs.		• Negotiate trade opening of transport, logistics, insurance, and distribution services sectors supporting medical goods GVCs.

(Continued)

Table 4.1   Trade and trade-related policy actions to improve prevention, preparedness, and response for future pandemics *(Continued)*

Instrument	National	Regional	Multilateral
Intellectual property rights (IPR)	• Implement flexibilities of the WTO Agreement on Trade-Related Aspects of Intellectual Property Rights (TRIPS) to facilitate timely access to needed pharmaceuticals into domestic law and to use those flexibilities, as appropriate. • Streamline existing legislation and adapt administrative processes (for example, provide for fast-track examination of patents). • Include conditions in publicly funded research projects to manage IPR in a manner that facilitates equitable access to medical technology and know-how. • Require public research institutes to adopt socially responsible licensing policies to ensure access to needed health technologies. • Make full use of the TRIPS Article 66.2 mechanism for the transfer of technologies to least developed countries (LDCs), and ensure its effective implementation so that incentive programs to transfer technology respond to the needs identified by LDCs. • Facilitate access to information about technologies protected by patents.	• Implement TRIPS Agreement flexibilities in regional frameworks.	• Develop a set of model provisions that could be used by governments in publicly funded R&D contracts. • Promote measures to strengthen technology transfer to geographically diversify manufacturing capacities to effectively respond to health crises. • Encourage rights holders to adopt open and humanitarian licensing models for pandemic-related technologies, to contribute to international technology-sharing platforms such as WHO's COVID-19 Technology Access Pool (C-TAP), and to include equitable access considerations in their R&D planning. • Develop a platform to facilitate governments' access to information on patents, regulatory status, and trade. • Facilitate the effective implementation of TRIPS Article 66.2 for the transfer of technologies to LDCs. • Coordinate national needs assessment projects for LDCs for health-related technology transfers. • Reinforce cooperation among relevant multilateral organizations and other relevant stakeholders to make available tailored, evidence-based technical assistance. • Bolster and raise awareness of the WHO-WIPO-WTO COVID-19 Technical Assistance Platform.

(Continued)

Table 4.1 Trade and trade-related policy actions to improve prevention, preparedness, and response for future pandemics *(Continued)*

Instrument	National	Regional	Multilateral
Regulatory measures	• Promote greater alignment with international standards for medical goods, or develop relevant international standards when they do not exist. • Assist low- and middle-income countries and LDCs in using international standards. • Based on best practices, prepare an "emergency model" for national regulatory frameworks or "checklists" that can be quickly triggered when pandemics arise or threaten to arise. *Crisis responses:* • *Implement an emergency model for national regulatory frameworks, and use regulatory flexibilities to accelerate access to medical goods.* • *Rely on the WHO Emergency Use Listing (EUL) or the work of WHO-recognized stringent regulatory authorities to facilitate emergency authorization.* • *Temporarily streamline regulatory requirements and processes while respecting safety, quality, and efficacy criteria.*	• Promote regulatory cooperation (such as mutual recognition or harmonization) in medical goods through RTAs. • Strengthen the capacity of national regulatory authorities (NRAs), including through regional networks. • Support capacity building to address gaps in the national quality infrastructure (NQI) of low- and middle-income countries. *Crisis response: Deepen regional cooperation for work sharing or joint conformity assessment.*	• Promote regulatory cooperation and coherence (broadening existing arrangements such as through the IMDRF, ICH, and PIC/S) to improve the quality and efficiency of regulations, and increase regulatory capacity in low- and middle-income countries, with collaboration between health and other stakeholders (including trade). • Strengthen coordination between international organizations in provision of technical assistance to (a) bolster the capacity of NRAs to respond to crises, and (b) facilitate the use of recognition and equivalence of regulatory regimes and certification. • Support capacity building to address gaps in the NQI of low- and middle-income countries and LDCs. • Cooperate on the use of digital tools for conformity assessment, including by low- and middle-income countries and LDCs. • Strengthen processes and support for international standardization. *Crisis response: Promote transparency and exchange experiences about regulatory responses, including at the WTO TBT Committee.*

(Continued)

Table 4.1 Trade and trade-related policy actions to improve prevention, preparedness, and response for future pandemics *(Continued)*

Instrument	National	Regional	Multilateral
Measures affecting medical services			
Market access	• Reduce or eliminate relevant market access limitations and discriminatory measures to close gaps in national health systems including in the following areas (ensuring that public health policy objectives are met): ○ Allow or encourage the development and liberalization of the telehealth sector (domestically and across borders). ○ Attract relevant foreign investment in the medical services sector (such as in health establishments and telehealth-related activities). ○ Establish a temporary market access framework and necessary flexibilities to address health workforce shortages through international mobility and practitioner-to-practitioner telehealth). ○ Remove nationality or prior residency requirements for professionals to be allowed to supply their services. ○ Ensure that quantitative limits for foreign health professionals are clearly defined according to identified needs (also taking into account, through dialogue, the needs of the countries of origin). ○ Increase the supply of health education, such as through liberalization, to develop the health workforce to respond to demand (international and domestic). ○ Liberalize trade in telecommunication and computer services as enablers of telehealth, among others, particularly for the benefit of remote areas or low-income communities. *Crisis response: Ease temporary market access restrictions on telehealth and foreign health professionals, where deemed necessary.*	• Use regional trade agreements to advance and innovate on medical services trade liberalization initiatives. • Develop regional initiatives to facilitate the movement of health professionals at the regional level in times of crisis. • Develop frameworks in the context of RTAs to facilitate cross-border provision of (tele) health services in times of crisis.	• Reduce relevant barriers to medical services trade (for example, by binding existing policies relating to medical services); to education and training services for health professionals; and to relevant infrastructure services (see national policy column), and consider their liberalization, including ○ Making specific market commitments regarding cross-border supply of less-sensitive practitioner-to-practitioner services, teleradiology, telediagnosis, and activity of telemedicine platforms; ○ Easing the portability of health insurance coverage; ○ Reducing foreign investment barriers; and ○ Reducing barriers to the movement of health professionals. • Establish frameworks to address global health worker mobility emergency needs and the necessary flexibilities for cross-border practitioner-to-practitioner telehealth in emergency cases.

(Continued)

Table 4.1   Trade and trade-related policy actions to improve prevention, preparedness, and response for future pandemics *(Continued)*

Instrument	National	Regional	Multilateral
Domestic regulation	• Adopt good regulatory practices to improve transparency (for example, publicly available licensing information), and facilitate administrative procedures (such as single window). • Facilitate assessment of foreign qualifications to ensure that procedures to verify the competence of foreign health professionals are not disguised restrictions to trade. • Address cross-border liability issues related to insurance policies of foreign-based medical suppliers by ensuring that they are insured with a local or international insurance company. • Establish a framework for cross-border data flows to protect personal health data and privacy and support the supply of telehealth services while not unduly restricting trade. • Establish transparent procedures for regulatory flexibilities (for example, fast-track recognition of foreign qualifications for health professionals) to address emergency needs. • Adopt domestic reforms that can limit the risk of a dual health services system and promote its inclusiveness. *Crisis response: Temporarily ease regimes for the mobility of health professionals, and implement fast-track recognition to address emergency needs.*	• Promote good-governance principles and disciplines beyond what may be achieved in the WTO context. • Promote work on recognition of foreign qualifications. • Establish regional mutual recognition agreements. • Develop regional frameworks to address issues like cross-border liability, especially in relation to patient safety. *Crisis response: Support use of regional recognition of qualifications and mobility mechanisms.*	• Cooperate to identify and adopt good regulatory practices and governance principles to improve the quality and efficiency of regulations, with collaboration between health and other stakeholders (including trade). • Promote work on recognition of foreign qualifications. • Foster cooperation to ensure cross-border liability of foreign-based medical services suppliers. • Strengthen processes and support for international standardization. *Crisis response: Coordinate international efforts to help national and regional regulatory agencies to implement fast-track recognition of qualifications to address emergency needs.*

(Continued)

Table 4.1   Trade and trade-related policy actions to improve prevention, preparedness, and response for future pandemics *(Continued)*

Instrument	National	Regional	Multilateral
Measures affecting both medical goods and services			
Government procurement	• Introduce competitive and transparent government procurement procedures that use digital technologies (e-procurement) to enable firms to respond rapidly to emergency needs. • Revisit processes to procure products in emergencies to ensure transparency and ex post accountability. • Put in place procurement tools to aggregate demand across national bodies (such as joint, pooled, or centralized procurement and framework agreements). *Crisis response: Use emergency government procurement rules and flexibilities (including limited tendering) to accelerate procurement of medical goods and services.*	• Develop procurement tools that can be triggered to aggregate demand at the regional level in crisis situations (such as joint procurement). *Crisis response: Implement joint procurement initiatives to source common needs.*	• Strengthen international competition in public health procurement markets via international trade negotiations under the WTO Government Procurement Agreement 2012. • Develop procurement tools that can be triggered to aggregate demand between countries in crisis situations (such as joint procurement). *Crisis response: Implement joint procurement initiatives to source common needs.*
Competition policy	• Adopt legislation to revisit the ability of firms to exchange information on supply trends, prices, and market developments during public health emergencies. • Use competition law and policy to address, correct, and prevent IPR abuses and other anticompetitive practices in the health sector. • Use competition advocacy to inform legislative and regulatory processes in the health sector. *Crisis response: Consider the need for targeted, time-limited exceptions and flexibilities in the enforcement of competition laws and for some cooperation between competitors (for example, to allow firms to share information) only during crisis situations.*		• Identify good practice for competition law and policy communications and enforcement in a global health emergency. *Crisis response: Coordinate on initiatives to allow additional flexibilities in the enforcement of competition laws and for some cooperation between competitors (under certain conditions).*

(Continued)

Table 4.1 Trade and trade-related policy actions to improve prevention, preparedness, and response for future pandemics *(Continued)*

Instrument	National	Regional	Multilateral
Transparency and statistics	• Develop systems to identify, collect, and publish timely information on measures affecting trade in medical goods and services, and report in the context of the WTO monitoring exercise and notifications. • Put in place mechanisms and processes that bring together the relevant regulatory and government agencies to identify data needs and mechanisms to compile and share information on demand for and availability of medical products. • Develop more detailed statistics on trade in medical services (by type of service, partner, and mode). • Monitor, analyze, and publish import and export statistics on trade in essential medical goods and services to draw lessons from previous crises. • Develop supply chain traceability harmonized to global standards to reduce illicit trade. *Crisis responses:* • *Publish promptly in a central repository all information and analysis on trade in medical goods and services related to measures taken in the context of an emergency.* • *Notify measures taken in response to the crisis to the relevant WTO bodies, and report in the context of the WTO monitoring exercise.* • *Establish public-private dialogue mechanisms to best anticipate needs and potential trade bottlenecks.*	• Support development of more detailed statistics on trade in medical services. • Promote interoperability of global traceability standards regionally to reduce illicit trade.	• Reinforce the independent monitoring of trade and trade-related measures by international organizations. • Compile, analyze, and publish world trade statistics on medical goods and services based on detailed national data. • Provide support and technical assistance for the development of trade in medical services statistics. • Ensure traceability of health products through global supply chains to reduce illicit trade. • Build on the Multilateral Leaders Task Force to maintain a jointly managed platform that can provide real-time firm-level and industry- or supply-chain-level information to identify frictions and actions by governments to enhance emergency responses. *Crisis responses:* • *Monitor, compile, and report information on measures taken by governments in response to the emergency, including trade restrictions, trade-facilitating actions, and information on industry- and firm-specific subsidy programs put in place by governments.* • *Evaluate or analyze the effects of measures imposed during the emergency, and monitor and report on their removal over time.* • *Publish short-term statistics on medical goods and services in an international database.* • *Consult with other WTO members to monitor and assess the adverse impact of national emergency measures on partners.*

(Continued)

Table 4.1 Trade and trade-related policy actions to improve prevention, preparedness, and response for future pandemics *(Continued)*

Instrument	National	Regional	Multilateral
Subsidies	• Design incentive measures to improve the resilience and diversification of critical medical supply chains by supporting emerging medical goods and services producers, especially in smaller countries. • Establish mechanisms for governments to provide funding and coordinate production and supply of critical goods. • Design incentive policies in accordance with the provisions of the WTO Agreement on Subsidies and Countervailing Measures, particularly on prohibited subsidies, by avoiding contingency on export performance and use of local content. *Crisis response: Boost cooperation between government and private stakeholders to support R&D and expand manufacturing facilities.*	• Mobilize and coordinate financing at the regional level to increase capacity to develop and supply critical products in a global crisis. • Develop guidelines for regional cooperation in times of crisis for coordinating financial support to medical goods and services providers. *Crisis response: Increase regional cooperation to support provision of public health–related goods and services.*	• Task international organizations with mobilizing and coordinating financing to increase the capacity of low- and middle-income countries to develop and supply critical products in a global crisis. • Develop guidelines for international cooperation in times of crisis for coordinating subsidy actions regarding crisis-related medical goods and for mobilizing financing to develop, produce, and distribute vaccines and therapeutics. • Identify and address information gaps on subsidies for crisis-related medical goods. *Crisis response: Increase multilateral cooperation, including through international organizations, to support provision of public-health-related goods and services.*

(Continued)

Table 4.1 Trade and trade-related policy actions to improve prevention, preparedness, and response for future pandemics *(Continued)*

Instrument	National	Regional	Multilateral

Institutional frameworks	• Create institutional frameworks that can be mobilized to support the ability of both governments and industry to respond effectively to a global emergency.
	• Establish or enhance dialogue between health and trade policy makers, as well as other stakeholders, to ensure that the potential for trade to support health policy objectives is maximized.
	• Coordinate across the multiple areas of government relevant to intellectual property to promote coherent policy choices and national strategies as well as coherent policy positions in regional or international forums.
	• Develop cooperation between state and nonstate actors to support expanded production of medical products and critical supplies and the capacity to distribute these where needed during a crisis.
		• Develop regional frameworks for cooperation between state and nonstate actors to support expanded production of medical products and critical supplies and the capacity to distribute these where needed during a crisis.	• Building on the ACT-Accelerator and the Multilateral Leaders Task Force on COVID-19 Vaccines, Therapeutics, and Diagnostics under a future end-to-end pandemic preparedness and response medical countermeasure mechanism tasked with developing an international framework to
			  ○ Compile and share information on the operation of critical supply chains;
			  ○ Act as a clearinghouse to support the ramping-up of production;
			  ○ Serve as a platform for companies to report bottlenecks and improve visibility on production capacity, stocks, and distribution performance; and
			  ○ Support technology transfer to expand global emergency response capacity.

Note: "Prevention" and "preparedness" refer to ex ante actions to determine, assess, avoid, mitigate, and reduce public health threats and risks when a disease outbreak occurs. "Response" refers to ex post actions to reduce a disease outbreak's economic, social, and health impacts. GATT = General Agreement on Tariffs and Trade; GVC = global value chain; HS = Harmonized System; ICH = International Council for Harmonisation of Technical Requirements for Pharmaceuticals for Human Use; IMDRF = International Medical Device Regulators Forum; IPR = intellectual property rights; LDCs = least developed countries; NTFC = National Trade Facilitation Committee; PIC/S = Pharmaceutical Inspection Co-operation Scheme; R&D = research and development; RTA = regional trade agreement; TBT = Technical Barriers to Trade; WCO = World Customs Organization; WHO = World Health Organization; WIPO = World Intellectual Property Organization; WTO = World Trade Organization.

REFERENCE

World Bank. 2022. "Disease Outbreak and Pandemic Prevention, Preparedness and Response (PPR)." Unpublished position paper, World Bank, Washington, DC.

www.ingramcontent.com/pod-product-compliance
Lightning Source LLC
Chambersburg PA
CBHW041420290326
41932CB00042B/26